THE GOLDEN AGE
OF BLACK NATIONALISM
1850-1925

The
Golden Age
of
BLACK NATIONALISM
1850-1925

by

Wilson Jeremiah Moses

Archon
Books
1978

Library of Congress Cataloging in Publication Data

Moses, Wilson Jeremiah, 1942-
The golden age of Black nationalism, 1850-1925.

Bibliography: p.
Includes index.
1. Black nationalism—United States—History. 2. Pan-
Africanism—History. 3. Afro-Americans—History. I. Title.
History. I. Title.

E185.61.M886   320.9'73   77-14566
ISBN 0-208-01690-2

For my parents

Contents

7

Preface

The Golden Age of Black Nationalism extends from the Compromise of 1850 to the imprisonment of Marcus Garvey in 1925. Such dismal occurrences as the Compromise of 1850, with its Fugitive Slave Act, or the imprisonment of Garvey, one of Black America's most popular leaders, would hardly seem to be bench marks of a golden age. But as John Hope Franklin has observed, 1850 was a crucial point in the development of American black nationalism; it was a point at which many black Americans despaired of ever finding a place within American society and culture and turned to various emigration schemes. The anxieties of the fifties stimulated a burst of literary output, and nurtured the growth of a tradition that would survive till the end of the century, and undergo a powerful revitalization with the rise of Marcus Garvey and the ideological Pan-Africanism of W.E.B. Du Bois.

I have divided the work into four sections. Part one is an introduction to backgrounds that provides working definitions of black nationalism and the practically indistinguishable ideology of Pan-Africanism. It is also an introduction to the patterns of black nationalism and assimilationism on the eve of the Civil War, when the traditions with which we are concerned were being shaped. Part two treats some specific manifestations of the tradition in the intellectual and institutional history of black Americans. The focus has been on elements of traditional black nationalism as expressed by Alexander Crummell and W.E.B. Du Bois. There is also a new treatment of Frederick Douglass and Booker T. Washington which emphasizes the elements of continuity in their thought and departs from the usual interpretation that views Washington as the betrayer of Douglass's vision. The chapter on the National Association of Colored Women emphasizes the strain of black national and separatist thought in the unlikely setting of middle class women's clubs. Part three is a treatment of genteel black nationalism in literature, emphasizing the novels of Martin Delany and Sutton Griggs, and the early poetry of W.E.B. Du Bois. The methodology employed in these chapters is not literary criticism, but literary history. An attempt has been made to identify those qualities that are particularly Anglo-African in the works under discussion. Part four provides a description of those trends that led to the decline of classical black nationalism at the time of the Harlem Renaissance, and the "New Negro Movement," which attempted to redefine the cultural and spiritual goals of Afro-Americans.

The purpose of this book is to offer a critical, though largely sympathetic, treatment of the black nationalist movement in the United States. The main focus is on the assimilationist or acculturating tendencies dominating black nationalist ideology in the Golden Age. A number of points are argued in the course of these chapters:

1. Ideological black nationalism has been chained to the concept of "civilization" and has embraced an evolutionary conception of history. Most black nationalists have believed that European cultures are more advanced than African cultures—an idea that has barely begun to erode with the emergence of "social relativity" theory in the twentieth century.
2. The black nationalist view of history is mystical, based on the prophecy that "Ethiopia shall soon stretch forth her hands unto God," that Africa's redemption will be accompanied by a decline of the West; that God will make a new covenant with black people.
3. Black nationalism assumes the shape of its container and undergoes transformations in accordance with changing intellectual fashions in the white world.

4. Black nationalism is a genteel tradition in English letters.
5. Black nationalism therefore becomes a prime vehicle for acculturation processes, because black nationalism in the nineteenth century was much concerned with preserving Anglo-American values and transmitting them, in modified form, to the black community.

The book is intended to provoke controversy and to provide a new thesis concerning the Golden Age of Black Nationalism—that during these years the ideology was conservative rather than radical. The principal document of black nationalist conservatism is Du Bois's American Negro Academy Paper, *The Conservation of Races*, which is discussed in chapter six. A recurrent theme in conservative black nationalism is African civilizationism, which embodied a sense of obligation to aid in the uplifiting, not only of the continent itself, but of black people everywhere, and argued that if the internal life of the continent could be improved, black folk in England and America would experience a corresponding elevation of status. Another common trend was a messianic self-conception, or Ethiopian mysticism, that has already been mentioned. This was accompanied by an authoritarian collectivism, a belief that all black people could and should act unanimously under the leadership of one powerful man or group of men, who would guide the race by virtue of superior knowledge or divine authority. The fourth of these attitudes was black separatism, which in its extreme form advocated the perpetual physical separation of the races, but usually referred only to a simple desire to see black people making independent efforts to sustain themselves among hostile peoples.

While my major concern has been with the Golden Age of Black Nationalism, 1850-1925, I have made some generalizations about eighteenth-century protonationalism and twentieth-century trends. This book is not a definitive study of black nationalism and makes no such pretensions, but it is a challenge to those who have viewed black nationalism as if it were invariably a leftist movement.

A number of persons have provided constructive criticism and encouragement to make this work possible. Rhett S. Jones was willing on numerous occasions to debate, from sundown to sunup, many of the issues raised here. William G. McLoughlin first encouraged me to treat on the subject of Afro-American conservatism in the dissertation upon which the present work is based. Charles H. Nichols provided a steadying influence and some helpful assurances, as well as substantive suggestions for revisions. John L. Thomas asked many disquieting questions and was never patronizing. Several graduate students at Brown University and the University of Iowa have been especially helpful because of their willingness to debate the issues. Among them are Virgil Gooding, James Hill, Vashti Lewis, Debbie Long, Felix Miamo, Gerald Patton, Wilfred Samuels, Vernon Williams. Economic and or moral support was provided at critical stages by Robert Allen, Charles Davis, Ralph Giesey; Donald Gibson, David Herreshoff, David Hirsch, Daniel Hughes, Sidney James, Barry Karl, Jay McCormick, Okechukwu Mezu, Hermann Rebel, Otey Scruggs, Geneva Smitherman, Bart St Armaud, Ely Stock, and Raymond Wells. The editors of *American Literature, Journal of Negro History,* and *The Review of Black Political Economy* kindly granted permission to utilize material originally printed in their journals. Special thanks are due to the late Ada Stofflet of the University of Iowa Library and to my wife Maureen for their invaluable technical assistance.

WILSON J. MOSES

Dallas, Texas
1977

PART ONE

Backgrounds

The moment one city, one single city of free civilized Christian blacks, is placed near the equator, on the western coast of Africa, then the mighty prize is won! From that instant, the whole problem in all its complexity and vastness as to the black race, is solved. The slavetrade dies, the civilization and conversion of Africa is fixed; the destiny of the race of Ham is redeemed; the equatorial region of the earth reclaimed; and the human race itself launched into a new and glorious career, of which all the triumphs of the past afford no parallel.

Speech of ROBERT J. BRECKINRIDGE
before the Maryland State
Colonization Society, 2 February
1838
(*African Repository*, XIV 141)

Chapter One

Introduction
Political Nationalism
and
Cultural Assimilation

The handful of black people who were literate in English at the end of the eighteenth century were painfully and furiously aware of the debasement of Africa in the eyes of the civilized world. Everywhere, they witnessed symbols of Anglo-Saxon dominance and power. Nowhere on the face of the earth was there a race of colored people who could seriously think to challenge the English-speaking nations on their own turf. Africa was technologically "backward." Its contacts with Europe were based on the unbalanced trade of valuable raw materials and human labor for European firearms and other artifacts of technology. The Europeans, cruel and arrogant, could afford to be profligate with the functionally inexhaustible supply of agricultural laborers exported by the equally fierce African kings.[1] The status of Africans whether in England or the Americas was seldom anything other than slavery. True, the Sommersett case of 1772 had nominally emancipated the minority of Africans who dwelt on English soil. Several of the United States were in the process of emancipating their slaves, as well. But the personal freedom of individuals from the economic status of slavery did not necessarily mean that the group status of slavery was less shared by the race as a whole. Free blacks enjoyed a modicum of personal liberty, but their collective status was that of slaves to the community.[2]

Many of the Europeanized Africans, who had spent their entire lives under Caucasian rule, seemed to accept with little question the idea that Africa and her darker peoples were barbarous. Common sense—really no more than an accumulation of prejudices—dictated that Anglo-Saxon Christendom was the most excellent civilization ever devised by man. Uncomfortable with such a perception, they began to seek a historical explanation for the relative status of white and black peoples, and, more importantly, to search for a means of altering the balance of power. Thus may black nationalism be seen as a byproduct of the slavery experience. Like many other nationalisms it was the reaction of a formerly disunited group to a sense of mutual oppression and humiliation. During the millennia that Africans had been isolated from Europe, there had been no need for such concepts as black nationalism or the unity of all African peoples. African peoples, like their barbarian European counterparts before the Roman Empire, were organized around local cultural loyalties and traditions.[3] In "primitive" or traditional societies, like those of Africa during the eighteenth century, or Europe before the coming of Mediterranean civilization, life is past-dominated. Tradition, as embodied in the wisdom of living elders or revered ancestors, is sacred. The myth of progress, as it is entertained in Western societies, is unknown. As the Westernized Africans came to accept the ideas of progress and civilization, they found it necessary to rationalize the indifference to such ideas in traditional Africa.[4]

Slavery was, in a sense, the cause of black nationalism. It destroyed the ethnic loyalties of those whom it enslaved; it disastrously eroded traditional culture within a generation or two. But while it tended to strip slaves of their local traditional cultures, it endowed them with a sense of common experience and identity. The slavery experience was shared to some extent by most English-speaking blacks. It was not an experience to be proud of, but it was an experience held in common; therefore, it was the basis of a racial unity, unknown among the various traditional peoples of Africa before the slave trade. Pan-Africanism seems to have originated with the awareness of Westernized Africans that all black people were suffering from the slave trade which tended to confer an inferior status upon all black people, whether slave or free, and regardless of the continent upon which they lived. To say that black nationalism was caused by slavery is not, however, to argue that slavery was a good thing. Nationalism has often been bred by evil circumstances.

Nationalism during the late eighteenth and early nineteenth centuries can be attributed to two broad sets of aspirations. Often it resulted from the desire of a subject people to break away from foreign rule; in other cases it represented the desire to unite traditionally disunited peoples.[5] Black nationalism has historically conformed to both of these patterns. The ideological basis of nationalism is the idea that the people concerned are tied to a geographical region which they have either traditionally possessed or which they feel entitled to possess. The national group are seen as organically united by language. Black nationalism differs from most other nationalisms in that its adherents are united neither by a common geography nor by a common language, but by the nebulous concept of racial unity. It seeks to override the numerous differences among the dark brown-skinned peoples whose ancestors lived in sub-Saharan Africa before the age of European expansionism.[6] It attempts to unify politically all of these peoples whether they are residents of African territories or descendants of those Africans who were dispersed by the slave trade. It is essentially a trans-Atlantic phenomenon, but occasionally it has involved the darker peoples of the South Pacific. Black nationalism has sometimes, but not always, been concerned with the quest for a nation in the geographical sense. But often it has been "nationalism" only in the sense that it seeks to unite the entire black racial family, assuming that the entire race has a collective destiny and message for humanity comparable to that of a nation. For this reason it is impossible to speak of black nationalism without simultaneously speaking of Pan-Africanism.

In his essay, "The Classification of Nationalism," K.R. Minogue identifies a phenomenon he calls "macro-nationalism". This includes the "pan" movements such as "Pan-Germanism" and "Pan-Slavism," both of which have aimed to unite various independent ethnic groups under the banner of collective nationalism because of assumed similarities in their cultures and histories.[7] These movements, like Pan-Africanism, have sometimes involved the idea of geographical and political unity; sometimes only the idea of cultural and spiritual unity. Ideological Pan-Africanism had been traced back to the eighteenth century by such scholar-activists as C.L.R. James and George Padmore.[8] The writings of these two West Indian authors provide an introduction to Pan-Africanism, both as an historical development and as a vital political ideology. Its roots, as a mass movement, are in the maroon revolutions of Haiti, Jamaica, and Surinam, during the seventeenth and eighteenth centuries, and in the rebellions of Denmark Vesey and Nat Turner in the nineteenth. Pan-Africanism is also manifest in the struggles against imperialism and neocolonialism among the African peoples of the present age.

Among the principal spokesmen for classical Pan-Africanism in the nineteenth century were the Americans Alexander Crummell, Martin R. Delany, and James T. Holly; the West Indian Edward Wilmot Blyden; and the West African Africanus Horton. Pan-Africanism was given classic summation in the Constitution of the African Civilization Society, which stated in 1858, that the purpose of that institution was to carry out "the intention of the Divine Mind towards Africa." Practically stated, the objects of the society were "the civilization and christianization of Africa, and of the descendants of African ancestors in any portion of the earth, wherever dispersed. Also the destruction of the African Slavetrade, by the intoduction of lawful commerce and trade into Africa: the promotion of the growth of cotton and other products there, whereby the natives may become industrious producers as well as consumers of articles of commerce: and generally, the elevation of the condition of the colored population of our country, and of other lands."[9]

Clearly, Pan-Africanism is not confined to the continent of Africa, itself. Indeed, before the twentieth century, it would have been impossible to define Pan-Africanism as an ideology that was solely, or even primarily concerned with the political unification of the continent. Such an emphasis has been present, however, in recent years. The goals of political and economic solidarity have been explicit aims of the Organization of African Unity founded in 1963.

The history of Pan-Africanism as an ongoing institutionalized movement can be traced through a series of congresses, the first of which was called by Trinidad barrister Sylvester Williams in London in 1900. Williams was aided in organizing the Congress by Alexander Walters, a leader of blacks in the United States and a bishop of the African Methodist Episcopal Zion Church. Pan-African Congresses were organized by W.E. Burghardt Du Bois in 1919, 1921, 1923, and 1927. The movement was widely publicized by Marcus Garvey, whose singular contribution was to make Pan-Africanism—which was for a time limited to the urban elite—accessible to the masses of working people. Donning the gaudy finery of empire-building militarism, Garvey headed the Universal Negro Improvement Association (UNIA) which he founded "to promote the spirit of race pride and love; to reclaim the fallen of the race; to administer to and assist the needy; to assist in civilizing the backward tribes of Africa; to strengthen the imperialism of independent African States; to establish Commissionaries or Agencies in the principal countries of the world for the protection of all Negroes, irrespective of nationality." The fifth (some call it the sixth) Pan-African Congress of 1945 was the first Congress to be dominated by Africans rather than by New World blacks, although W.E.B. Du Bois did attend, "greying, ascetic-looking, at seventy-three very much the Grand Old Man." Known as the Manchester Conference, the meeting of 1945 was attended by representatives of a new generation of African leaders including Kwame Nkrumah, Nnamdi Azikiwe, and Jomo Kenyatta. At Manchester, a sixth congress to be held in Africa itself was planned, but the conference which actually took place in Accra, Ghana in 1958, was held under the name of the "All Africa Conference." Pan-Africanism persists today as a movement of all African peoples throughout the world, who believe that all black people have interests in common. Its adherents accept as axioms the ideas that no black person is free until all are free, and that the liberation and unification of Africa is essential to the dignity of African people everywhere.[10]

Black nationalism has many forms, then. In Africa, it has meant simply the desire to be rid of foreign domination. In the United States it has often meant either the desire to return to Africa and establish a modern black state, or to establish a separate black nation in the Americas. Black nationalism has often been indistinguishable from the idea of Pan-Africanism, in which cases it has not necessarily been concerned with the establishment of a geographical state but only with asserting a sense of kinship among the African peoples. If there is one *essential* quality of black nationalism, however, it is the feeling on the part of black individuals that they are responsible for the welfare of other black individuals, or of black people as a collective entity, simply because of a shared racial heritage and destiny.

When we turn to its history in the United States, we can see that black nationalism has been a changing phenomenon, adapting to the changes in the American life and culture that are its environment; still, there are consistent elements. The nineteenth century cycle of black nationalism, from the late 1700s to the early 1900s was dominated by the idea of progress, the doctrine of *racial uplift* or "Negro Improvement"—sometimes taking the form of an African civilization movement. Other important ideas were unity (or collectivism), separatism (or self-containment), and a mystical racial chauvinism. These ideas do not represent different varieties of black nationalism; rather they are ingredients common to all black nationalism. Furthermore, these ideas are present in varying degrees in the public pronouncements of all persons who aspire to leadership in the black community.

Racial uplift, Negro improvement, African Civilization, race progress, African development, were all ideas that made appearances in the rhetoric of black leaders during the nineteenth century. Clearly the ideas are related, if not synonymous, all of them having to do with the assumed need to civilize the Negro race. "Civilization" is a word that became fashionable during the late eighteenth century, although Samuel Johnson, despite Boswell's promptings, refused to include it in his dictionary. French writers apparently began using the word around the 1750s, and English writers apparently began to adopt it during the 1770s. By the early nineteenth century—the idea that history could be divided into stages or phases, the idea that human society was in the process of improvement, were the central ideas in the concept of civilization. "Civilization," as developed in the writings of such social thinkers as Guizot and Gobineau, came to imply the concept of progress.[11] The idea was European, not African. Indeed, since African societies were traditional and organized largely around the principle of ancestor veneration, the concept of progress was antithetical to most African cultures. The Anglicized African in the nineteenth century had little appreciation for such facts. He was cut off from the values of his ancestral society and surrounded by people who were themselves just in the process of discovering progress. Civilization was their culture. In other words, Englishmen were so involved in the myth of progress, and so delighted with the progress of their own society as to be unaware of their ethnocentrism.[12]

Westernized Africans were exquisitely conscious of the differences between African societies and the self-confident, civilized, Anglo-Saxon culture. Thus did they begin to advocate African civilization, which embodied a sense of obligation to aid in the uplifting of the continent and its "backward" peoples as an initial step in the elevation of black people everywhere. If the internal life of the continent could be upgraded, black folk in England and America would experience a corresponding elevation in status. Africa's lack of civilization was not only a source of shame for the Anglo-Africans, it was used as the justification for the slave trade. If Africa could be uplifted, the slave trade would cease. Africans living abroad could take pride in their homeland. The humanity of the Negro would be vindicated and the link between blackness and slavery would be destroyed, once an African civilization had been established.

Civilization was to be achieved through unity among all black people. An authoritarian collectivist ideal was evolved, a belief that all black people could and should act unanimously under the leadership of one powerful man or group of men, who would guide the race by virtue of superior knowledge or divine authority towards the goal of civilization. Ortega y Gasset called collectivism "the characteristic creation of the nineteenth century."[13] Indeed it was a basic ingredient of nationalistic theory as espoused by Herder, Schleiermacher, Hegel and von Treitschke. In England, a variety of organic collectivism was developed in the writings of Burke. With the air full of such ideas, it should not be surprising that black nationalists of the nineteenth century, influenced as they were by the European nationalisms, should likewise develop the idea of organic racial unity. Edward Wilmot Blyden thought of races as "great organic types of being," which represented aspects of the divine personalitiy. Alexander Crummell called them "the organisms and the ordinance of God." Racial obligation was an important theme in the writing of black nationalist pamphleteers, Robert Young and David Walker, who urged subordination to the worthy messianic leader who they assumed was to come.[14]

The idea of organic collectivism under authority was not solely the result of the intellectual climate, however. There were factors in the experience of the masses of black people that led to the development of an authoritarian and collectivist ethic. These factors were discussed by E. Franklin Frazier in *The Negro Church*, which is far more than a study of Afro-American religion; it is actually a study of leadership and community organization. Frazier attributed the growth of an authoritarian political tradition within the black community to the peculiar role served by the Negro church.[15]

> As a result of the elimination of Negroes from the political life of the American community, the Negro church became the arena of their political activites. The church was the main area of social life in which Negroes could aspire to become the leaders of men. It was the area of social life where ambitious individuals could achieve distinction and the symbols of status. The church was the arena in which the struggle for power and the thirst for power could be satisfied. This was especially important to Negro men who had never been able to assert themselves and assume the dominant male role, even in family relations, as defined by American culture. In the Baptist churches, with their local autonomy, individual Negro preachers ruled their followers in an arbitrary manner, while the leaders in the hierarchy of the various Methodist denominatioins were czars, rewarding and punishing their subordinates on the basis of personal loyalties.

The authoritarian tendencies are easily witnessed in the black leadership class, many of whose members were, more than incidentally, preachers. Alexander Crummell, Edward Wilmot Blyden, Henry Highland Garnet, J.T. Holly, and such Methodist bishops as Daniel A. Payne, Alexander Walters, William H.

Heard, and Henry M. Turner were among the clergymen who, during the nienteenth and early twentieth centuries, hammered out the principles of devotion to duty and subordination to the group ethic that became the hallmarks of black nationalism.

Black separatism, or self-containment, which in its extreme form advocated the perpetual physical separation of the races, usually referred only to a simple institutional separatism, or the desire to see black people making independent efforts to sustain themselves in a provenly hostile environment. Black separatism has usually been contradicted by the assimilationist attitudes of the separatists. I say this because most separatists during the nineteenth-century cycle were also civilizationists, that is, they were committed to the doctrine of uplift which assumed that black people were, as a whole, backward. Separatists often strove to build black institutions that were imitations of white institutions. They were contemptuous of African institutions and they tended to think of the Afro-American masses as degraded. Their dream of renascent Africa, like their dream of a reconstructed black America always implied making blacks more like whites. In almost every case, for example, blacks who spoke of returning to Africa also spoke of carrying with them the Christian religion, whose blessings they hoped to bestow upon the natives. Nonetheless, the theme of black separatism was a strong one, sometimes involving plans for an African emigration, at other times advocating the establishment of black schools, churches, and newspapers. The more extreme black nationalists have accepted with little resistance the illogical argument that they have no right of access to the American institutions upon which all other American ethnic groups depend, and that they should therefore create their own.

It would be unfair to characterize black separatism as if it were born solely of a spirit of accommodation, however; elements of racial chauvinism were also involved. Black chauvinism during the nineteenth century occurred in both religious and secular forms and in combinations of the two. The religious form most commonly referred to is "Ethiopianism." The Ethiopian tradition derives from the Biblical verse, "Princes shall come out of Egypt; Ethiopia shall soon stretch forth her hands unto God." White abolitionists in England and America had early sought to apply the verse to the situation of the black slave.[16] Among black writers it made repeated appearances during the nineteenth century and by World War I, Ethiopianism had become not only a trans-Atlantic political movement, but a literary movement well-known among all black people from the Congo basin to the mountains of Jamaica to the sidewalks of New York. Ethiopianism involved a cyclical view of history—the idea that the ascendency of the white race was only temporary, and that the divine providence of history was working to elevate the African peoples. Prince Hall revealed a typically "Ethiopian" view of history when he wrote in 1797:

> My brethren, let us not be cast down under these and many other abuses we at present are laboring under,—for the darkest hour is just before the break of day. My brethren let us remember what a dark day it was with our African brethren, six years ago, in the French West Indies. Nothing but the snap of the whip was heard, from morning to evening. Hanging, breaking on the wheel, burning and all manner of tortures, were inflicted on those unhappy people. But, blessed be God, the scene is changed. They now confess that God hath no respect of persons, and therefore, receive them as their friends and treat them as brothers. Thus doth Ethiopia stretch forth her hand from slavery, to freedom and equality.[17]

Another chauvinistic religious tradition similar to Ethiopianism was the convention of comparing the plight of enslaved blacks to that of the Israelites in Egypt. And so the slaves sang, "Go down Moses! Tell old Pharaoh to let my people go." Miles Mark Fisher, in his *Negro Slave Songs in the United States,* traces the tradition of subtle resistance found in the religious music of Afro-American slaves.[18] Sometimes the spirituals mythologized a longed-for return to Africa.

> Don't you see that ship a-sailin'
> A-sailin'- a-sailin'
> Don't you see that ship a-sailin'
> Gwine over to the Promised Land?

The chauvinistic element in such songs is, of course, the implicit claim that blacks are the chosen people of a God who works not only in the hereafter, but in human history, his wonders to perform.

In its secular form, black chauvinism derives, ironically enough, from European racial theory. Like the concept of civilization, racial chauvinism can be traced back to the writings of Hegel, Guizot, Gobineau, and other continental racial theorists of the nineteenth century. Indeed it was the German, Herder, who in the eighteenth century, developed the theories of organic collectivism upon which Blyden and Crummell later built their own brand of ethnic chauvinism. Strangely, the black nationalists of the nineteenth century tended to accept the descriptions of the various races and their innate characteristics almost exactly as they had been described by the European philosophers. Martin Delany, Alexander Crummell, Sutton Griggs, and W.E.B. Du Bois—to name some of the more prominent—all seemed to agree with Gobineau that blacks as a race were sensual, emotional, and "feminine", as opposed to the hardy, aggressive and "masculine" Anglo-Saxons. Racial chauvinism therefore often consisted of arguing that nature had actually been kinder to the sensitive and gentle African than to the stolid, frigid European.[19]

Black nationalism by general consensus originated in the late eighteenth century. Since it was developed in the climate of the slave trade and was largely a reaction to attitudes of white supremacy, it is impossible to conceive of its existence outside the context of Western civilization. Black nationalism and Pan-Africanism were adaptations to social environments. As the world view of Europe and America underwent a series of changes from the age of reason to the First World War, the pattern of nineteenth-century black nationalism developed. The wonder and admiration which the black nationalists felt for European culture in the late eighteenth century had been replaced by attitudes of criticism and doubt by the early twentieth. A brief survey of the transformations of black nationalism, as it responded to the shifting patterns of Anglo-American thought, may be of use.

The period from 1787 to 1817 is sometimes referred to as the period of proto-Pan-Africanism.[20] These years were marked by the appearance of abolitionist writings by Olaudah Equiano (Gustavus Vassa), and Ottobah Cugoano, both of them ex-slaves concerned with the problem of African uplift. It was a period during which literate blacks became interested in such activities as the art of letter writing and neoclassical poetry which we see in the productions of Ignatius Sancho and Phillis Wheatley. Enlightenment ideology penetrated the thinking of Benjamin Banneker, who was a student of mathematical and mechanical theories as well as political philosophy. Freemasonry was adapted to an Afro-American context by Prince Hall, whose successors were to argue that the first Masons had been black men in ancient times. The spirit of the French Revolution spread rapidly in the black world, its most dramatic applications finding expression in the Haitian Revolution. News of the Haitian Revolution spread rapidly among the slaves and freemen in Europe and the colonies, especially in urban areas. Revolutionary activity was also frequent in Jamaica and Surinam. Jamaican maroons were resettled first in Nova Scotia, later in Sierra Leone, where they and other "Anglo-Africans" established the first colony of Europeanized blacks in West Africa. Sierra Leone was no hotbed of nationalism in the early nineteenth century, but it did serve as a beacon to African redemptionists like the black American Quaker, Paul Cuffe, who hoped to establish a colonization project for some of his own countrymen. Colonization of Africa, it was hoped, would lead to the establishment of black "civilizations," which would give evidence of the black man's capacity for self-government, and gradually bring about abolition of the slave trade.

The early nineteenth century saw the establishment of the American Colonization Society and its colony, Liberia, which became independent in 1847. No sooner had the Colonization Society been formed, however, than black Americans began to protest against the idea of being resettled. Black thinkers and political activitists found themselves working in concert with white activists like William Lloyd Garrison for the immediate abolition of slavery. They found congenial the transcendentalism of New England radicalism, which tended to emphasize the universal brotherhood of man and the commonness of the human experience. Because they found a sympathetic hearing among the New England intellectuals, black thinkers in the early nineteenth century tended to phrase their appeals in a rhetoric that was similar to that of the transcendentalist movement. Frederick

Douglass and Charles Remond, the principal black public figures of this period, tended to emphasize the unity of the human family and eschewed the rhetoric of racial separatism and Ethiopian mysticism.

The passage of the Fugitive Slave Law in 1850 led to a resurgence of the spirit of black nationalism. Emigration schemes proliferated; sometimes under the auspices of the American Colonization Society, sometimes under the leadership of state colonization societies, and sometimes as a result of independent black efforts. Africa was not the only potential site under consideration. A plan to colonize Haiti was offered by the British abolitionist James Redpath and even some of the committed integrationists like William Wells Bown and Frederick Douglass were willing to listen to his proposal. The decade preceding the Civil War was the high-water mark of classical black nationalism, not only in terms of the renewed interest in colonization, but also in terms of the philosophical writing produced. The call to racial duty was a recurrent element in Afro-American writing during these years. Black chauvinism as reflected in writings by the proponents of nationalism echoed the sentimental Christian racism of Harriet Beecher Stowe, Hollis Read, and Frederick Freeman. Like these white gradual emancipationists, black nationalists attributed to the Negro the possession of innate Christian instincts which would suit him well for the founding of a new civilization that would stand as a shining example to the prodigal Christians of Europe and America.

During the late nineteenth century, black nationalism was influenced by Darwinian science and by Victorian conceptions of domestic virtue. Sutton Griggs, a black minister of Memphis, Tennessee, was steeped in the theories of Darwin and other evolutionary theorists—Benjamin Kidd, Piotr Kropotkin, and Herbert Spencer. His novels represented a merger of archaic social science and sentimentalism, an attempt to create a humane theory of biological and social evolution within the framework of a national literature. Booker T. Washington's writings, and those of Alexander Crummell, refer to black people as a "new people," still in the process of being elevated to a status of equality with the other nations. Mary Church Terrell tells of how, as a child, she was demoralized by the application of Lamarckean theories to African peoples.

Late Victorian sexual attitudes also had a strong effect upon black social thought and institution-building. The novels of Sutton Griggs and W.E.B. Du Bois attempted to encourage Victorian standards of genteel courtship and premarital chastity. The National Association of Colored Women saw as its primary work the promotion of the social purity movement in the Afro-American community. Mrs. Terrell and her co-workers in the National Association of Colored Women revealed a total inability to comprehend the peasant morality of many black women in the rural South. The quest for gentility despite the many obstacles erected by the white majority is one of the important themes of Afro-American life in the Victorian age.

The turn-of-the-century years, 1895-1915, may be identified as the age of Booker T. Washington. These years were characterized by a technocratic black nationalism. Washington hoped to build a business and industrial technocracy among black people. He hoped that by responding to the demands of the age for skilled industrial workers and competent businessmen, black Americans could make themselves sophisticated contributors to the new industrial revolution. Washington's rival, W.E.B. Du Bois also hoped to establish a black technocracy, which he called the "Talented Tenth." The Du Bois technocrats were to be social scientists and humanists, rather than industrial workers. But Du Bois, like Washington, was in step with those main currents of American thought which were at the time extolling the virtues of professionalization and the creation of reformer elites. Black progressivism can be detected not only in the writings of Booker T. Washington and W.E.B. Du Bois but in writings of many black leaders during the period, concerned as they were with helping to form the new industrial democracy and with institutionalizing reform. Populism, Free Silver, the single tax theories of Henry George, all found their way into black separatist ideologies and institutions during these years. The social gospel was preached from the African Methodist pulpit of Richard Wright and Christian socialism was defended by Reverdy C. Ransom.

Something beyond the watch and guard of America happened to black people during the years around the First World War. S.P. Fullinwider has suggestively hinted that the rise of social science in the first three decades of the twentieth century encouraged attitudes of social relativity. As the Victorian sexual ethic was eroded, white Americans found it easier to accept the freer lifestyle of the black American. Black American intellectuals found it easier to accept the moral conventions among the masses of their own community. The World War itself influenced the development of black nationalism, as colored peoples all over the world lost their admiration for the civilization of Europe which had perpetrated such brutality upon itself. For over a century, black intellectuals had been predicting the decline of the West, which now, even respected Western intellectuals foresaw with fear and trembling. European loss of prestige was neither immediate nor complete, of course. Nineteenth-century patterns continued to exist in black nationalist movements and in separatist institutions. So, for example, Marcus Garvey continued to employ the rhetoric of redemptionism with respect to Africa. Christian messianism continued to exist in the black cults of the metropolis, despite the declining influences of the Christian church in the larger world. The old patterns of mythology have not died easily because they have continued to serve as an inspiration for the black masses among whom the traditional black nationalist longings are still strong.

Black nationalism has often been incorrectly viewed as a phenomenon restricted to lower classes, but during the period from 1850 to 1925, even the most educated and Anglicized black Americans were denied access to the mainstream institutions in American cultural and intellectual life. An Afro-American bourgeois genteel culture therefore evolved, which emphasized black self-sufficiency, group self-consciousness, and spiritual allegiance to Africa. The black middle classes, like the toiling masses, required a variety of ethnic chauvinism. Black bourgeois nationalism was not a fantasy, nor was it an escape from reality; it was a rational attempt to manipulate the hostile environment in which it was conceived. Black bourgeois nationalism began to lose force even before the 1920s, which saw the abortion of Garvey's throwback movement. The new cosmopolitanism affecting American intellectual traditions and the urbanization of black people caused by the Great War made black nationalism less attractive to the black leadership class. They were beginning to find American social insitutions more accessible, not only because they had become more culturally assimilated, but because Anglo-American culture was becoming less ethnocentric.

E. Franklin Frazier criticized black bourgeois separatism, and rightly so, for he recognized that black separatism has often served the interests of only a small class of blacks who seek to preserve segregated institutions which they can organize as their own private satrapies. This idea dominated his studies, *Black Bourgeoisie,* and *The Negro Church in America.* Given the tradition in American thought of ridiculing the black middle class and portraying black intellectuals as incompetent buffoons, it is not surprising that *Black Bourgoisie* was almost universally applauded by American academics. The few who protested were shouted down and because of Frazier's acceptance by whites, he came to be accepted by most blacks. But *Black Bourgeoisie* is a diatribe, a polemic. Overstatement and irony are its principal rhetorical devices; it cannot be read without a sense of bitter humor. For black bourgeois nationalism is only partially an escape from participation in the larger society. It has evolved into an alternative structure, a functional tradition created for the purpose of publicizing black aspirations, giving them political force, and institutionalizing them in forms that might ultimately transform American civilization.[21]

The reform panaceas of most Afro-American leaders during the nineteenth century embodied paradoxical compromises between cultural assimilationism and political nationalism. Their programs were aimed at achieving assimilationist ends through separatist means. Typical examples of these contradictory programs were to be observed in such black institutions as Hampton and Tuskegee, where the educational philosophy was neither truly separatistic, nor truly integrationistic. The goal of Tuskegee Institute, founded by Booker T. Washington in 1881, seemed to be to create a new Negro, thoroughly imbued with mainstream values, although produced in a segregated environment. Other black leaders seemed to agree with Washington that in order to advance the status of the Afro-American, it would be necessary to complete the "civilizing" process, assumed to have begun during slavery. It would be necessary to teach him the gospel of efficiency, work and wealth and make him a useful cog for the new industrial democracy. Social integration would have to be preceded by cultural assimilation. If black people would become thoroughly Anglo-Saxonized, they would become acceptable to society in spite of their racial differences.

It is difficult to imagine whether black social reformers of the nineteenth century would be dismayed or pleasurably astonished by a glimpse of our present age, in which the scientific and moral axioms that once sustained Victorian civilization on both sides of the Atlantic are no longer capable of sustaining themselves. They would rejoice at the discovery that proud England has fallen while her former colonies are seizing the initiative in determining world events. They would be disturbed by the realization that, faced with a crisis of industry and ecology, the human race can ill afford to perpetuate the energetic gospel of work and wealth. They would be shocked to witness the decline of the Victorian sexual ethic, accompanied by steady intrusion of "primitive" and "oriental" ideas into a formerly smug Christian universe. Of course, nineteenth-century black nationalists had no means to predict these developments, and they therefore thought that the best way to secure the fortunes of Afro-Americans was to make them into "civilized" people.

Chapter Two

Black Nationalism
on the Eve of the Civil War
Patterns of Anglo-
African Conservatism

A startling feature in the rhetoric of black institutional leadership on the eve of the Civil War was the popularity of the term, "Anglo-African."[1] The term is a useful one for the historian to remember because it recalls the ambivalence of early black nationalists, and minimizes the often overstated distinction between nationalism and assimilation. Its popularity, especially among black nationalists, indicates the extent to which black Americans identified with the history and culture of Europe and desired to merge their destiny with it, despite their repeated forecasts of the decline of the West. By 1900, "Anglo-African" had been replaced by "Afro-American" and such variants as "Euro-African," and "Negro-Saxon." The persistance of compound names symbolizes the reluctance of even the most racially assertive black Americans to divorce themselves spiritually from the white American mainstream.

Black nationalism on the eve of the Civil War is usually discussed as if the most important indicators of its presence were support or rejection of territorial separatism in the forms of the various colonization and emigration movements. Howard Brotz, Harold Cruse, and Theodore Draper are among those who have tended to equate black nationalism with participation in the territorial separatist movements.[2] Not all historians have been comfortable with this approach, however. John Bracey, August

Meier, and Elliot Rudwick have recognized that black nationalism does not always imply territorial separatism, and have tended to emphasize the phenomenon of "cultural nationalism." These scholars have loosely identified cultural nationalism as "interest in the race's past and in creating a racial literature. . . . "[3] They do well to broaden the definition of black nationalism beyond mere emigrationism, but they accept too readily the rhetoric of the cultural nationalists, who see themselves as forging a distinctly African civilization and creating a culture that is distinctly black. The argument of this chapter is that it is not valid to distinguish between nationalists and assimilationists on the basis of their attitudes toward emigration; in any case, the distinction between nationalism and assimilation is a false one, since the two ideas are not mutually exclusive.

The colonization movement must be distinguished from black nationalism, not because whites were involved in the movement as is sometimes suggested, but because many black nationalists refused to leave American soil. Nonetheless, the colonization schemes had among their advocates some black nationalists, as well as whites. The whites may be divided into two categories for the sake of convenience. Some were benevolent conservatives who were sympathetic to black people and hoped to see them become free and prosperous people—far from the shores of America. Other proponents of colonization were hostile to the libertarian aspirations of Afro-Americans. These men, led by their spokesman Henry Clay, forced the Society to include an anti-abolitionist plank in its constitution. The society, as a result of their efforts, was to concern itself solely with the expatriation of emancipated blacks. It would not seek to encourage abolition in even its most gradual form, nor would it advocate the freeing and expatriation of slaves. The founding of the Society led to the establishment of Liberia, and to thirty years of half-hearted experimentation in African Colonization.[4]

In the meantime, certain black entrepreneurs, who made their fortunes in the maritime trades, were seeking to encourage African colonization as a means of gradual emancipation and Negro improvement. Paul Cuffe, a man of black and native American ancestry had carried a few dozen freed men and women to Sierra Leone in 1817, encouraged by his friend James Forten, a sailmaker.

Their aim seems to have been to establish a booming shipping trade in anticipation of the black star line that was to be advocated by Marcus Garvey a century later. Correspondence exchanged between Forten and Cuffe indicates that their plan did not have much support among the masses of the free people of color. Forten wrote to Cuffe describing a meeting in Philadelphia of three thousand people who turned out to condemn colonization. The predominant feeling was that slaveholders wanted to get rid of the free Africans so as to make their property more secure. "My opinion," said Forten, "is that they will never become a people until they come out from amongst the white people. But as the majority is decided against me, I am determined to remain silent, except as to my opinion which I freely give when asked."[5]

In 1829 the able, dedicated John Russwurm lost a number of friends when he sailed to Liberia under the auspices of the Maryland affiliate of the American Colonization Society. He was roundly denounced by Samuel Cornish, his old associate at *Freedom's Journal,* and letters to the editor of *The Liberator* accused him of adopting a pro-colonizationist stance for pecuniary reasons:

> Mr Russwurm tells us, he knows no other home for us than Africa. If he were in Philadelphia, and would make this assertion to me, I would tell him it was a palpable falsehood, and would prove it by his former editorial documents. I would ask whether Mr. R. would have gone to Africa even on a visit, had he been in flourishing circumstances? I answer, no. I am too sensible to this fact, that he would as reluctantly fall a victim to the lion, the tiger, the serpent, or the climate, as any of us: it was real necessity that drove him to seek in Africa an abiding home, as he terms it; and as his usefulness is entirely lost to the people, I sincerely pray that he may have the honor to live and also die there.[6]

During the 1830s and 1840s, many black Americans came to think of the American Colonization Society as a wolf in sheep's clothing. The National Negro Convention movement during those same years took a strong stand against colonization, and while taking an occasional interest in emigration, was careful to disassociate itself from the aims of the Society. By the 1850s, many black leaders found themselves in a strange dilemma. On the one hand they were committed to opposing the aims of the American Colonization Society, and yet they were supporting a number of schemes to settle black Americans in such various sites as Upper Canada, Haiti, Mexico, and even the Niger Valley. They made attempts to distinguish between voluntary emigration projects controlled by blacks and involuntary projects controlled by whites. Their arguments reiterated those of John Russwurm, and they were just as unconvincing to those who were opposed to expatriation under any guise.

Martin Delany and Henry Highland Garnet are representative of those leaders who condemned the American Colonization Society and found it necessary to rationalize away the similarities between colonization and emigration rhetoric. Delany heaped abuse upon both the Society and the Republic of Liberia while simultaneously forwarding his own proposals for emigration to South America. His principal criticism of Liberia was, in his words, that:

> Liberia is not an Independent Republic: in fact, it is *not* an independent nation at all; but a poor *miserable mockery*— a *burlesque* on a government—a pitiful dependency on the American Colonizationists, the Colonization Board at Washington city, in the District of Columbia, being the Executive and Government, and principal man called President, in Liberia, being the echo—a mere parrot of Rev. Robert R. Gurley, Elliot Cresson, Esq., Governor Pinney, and the other leaders of the Colonization scheme—to do as they bid, and say what they tell him. This we see in all of his doings.[7]

But Delany's position was inconsistent. Although in 1852 he had argued not only against Liberian colonization, but against any scheme to emigrate outside the Western hemisphere, he was to reverse his position by 1859, to make friendly overtures towards the Liberians and to consider migration to the Niger Valley as well.

The celebrated voyage of the Niger Valley Exploring Party, led by Martin Delany and Robert Campbell in 1859 pointed up the contradictions in the position of those who attempted to rationalize a distinction between emigration and colonization.[8] For the Niger Party was almost as dependent upon the good will of whites as were the colonizationists and missionaries to Liberia. Delany was incensed by the fact that some white citizens of Philadelphia were able to undercut his authority in the black community and to limit his ability to raise funds for the exploring project. Delany would certainly not have been so bitter as he was over the interference of whites if he had not felt that white attitudes could affect his success in securing funds for the project. On the eve of his departure, Delany, Campbell, and their agents were soliciting the goodwill of Robert Gurley and other A.C.S. officers and actually approaching the American Colonization Society for financial assistance. It seems to have annoyed Delany that he was forced to depend upon the usual sources of white philanthropy—British and American—to finance his trip to West Africa. But he was not able to claim that the project was totally black-controlled, and indeed he was forced to make peace with Liberian colonizationists like President Benson and Father Crummell, whom he visited in Cape Palmas.[9]

On arriving in Nigeria, Delany discovered that those blacks with whom he felt the strongest sense of comradship were not the most independent African leaders. In fact the friendly relations that Delany established with Africans were with the urbanized creoles and puppet chiefs. It has been said that a black man needs to leave the United States in order to discover how much of an American he is. Delany seems to have been forced to re-examine some of the workings of his own mind during the months he spent out of the country; in any case his report on the expedition certainly reveals that his head was full of Anglo-Protestant biases—which he was forced to confront during his African sojourn. He was appalled by the barbarous customs of the un-Christian populations, for he considered Protestantism to be the most advanced stage of civilization. He penned the slogan "Africa for the African race, and black men to rule them." But a few paragraphs later he called for British intervention in African affairs as he reported with dismay the sanguinary predelictions of the king of Dahomey.

His majesty Badahung, King of Dahomey, is about to make

the 'Grand Custom' in honor of the late King Gezo. Determined to surpass all former monarchs in the magnitude of the ceremonies to be performed on this occasion, Badahung has made the most extensive preparations for the celebration of the Grand custom. A great pit has been dug which is to contain human blood enough to float a canoe. Two thousand persons will be sacrificed on this occasion. . . . Would to God this might meet the eyes of some of those philanthropic Englishmen who have some feeling for Africa![10]

One of the institutions that aided Delany and Campbell in funding their African venture was the African Civilization Society. This organization, which claimed to be black-controlled and totally opposed to the American Colonization Society, actually had an overlapping membership with the latter institution. And some white officers of the A.C.S. were also officers of the African Civilization Society.[11] The Civilization Society's approach to African affairs did not emphasize sending black Americans back to Africa; it did have as its object "the civilization and Christianization of Africa, and of the descendants of African ancestors in any portion of the earth wherever dispersed." Its doctrine therefore was an incipient Pan-Africanism similar to that which was later to be advocated by Du Bois, Garvey, and other advocates of Universal Negro Improvement. The fact that there was an overlap between the two associations and their supporters suggests that not all supporters of the Colonization Society were cynically committed to deporting free black militant leadership. And there was apparently some sincere philanthropic motivation in the activities of many white members of the Colonization and Civilization Societies.[12]

Henry Highland Garnet was the most prominent black spokesman of the Civilization Society. Like Delany, he displayed shifting attidudes and ambivalence towards national separatism. In 1848 Garnet had stood unequivocally opposed to emigration. He believed that the western world was destined to be filled with a mixed race, and wrote:

America is my home, my country, and I have no other. I love whatever good there may be in her institutions. I hate her sins.

I loathe her slavery, and I pray Heaven that ere long she may wash away her guilt in tears of repentance. I love the green hills which my eyes first beheld in my infancy. I love every inch of soil which my feet pressed in my youth, and I mourn because the accursed shade of slavery rests upon it. I love my country's flag, and I hope that soon it will be cleansed of its stains, and be hailed by all nations as the emblem of freedom and independence.[13]

But his attitude was to shift noticeably within the next few months, and in February of 1849 he wrote, "I am in favor of colonization in any part of the United States, Mexico or California, or in the West Indies, or Africa, wherever it promises freedom and enfranchisement. Other people became great and powerful by colonization."[14] By the early 1860s, he was working with Delany to promote a comfortable relationship with white colonizationists. And in 1859, he had attacked Frederick Douglass, who refused to support the activities of the African Civilization Society. His arguments anticipated the rhetoric of "blacker-than-thou" during the 1960s. He challenged Douglass to state what objection he had to the civilization and Christianization of Africa. Douglass's reply was that he had no objection to either, nor had he any objection to others embarking upon African expeditions, but that he chose not to go.[15] The African Civilization movement was, as Douglass charged, supported by white colonizationists, describing their crusade as "African colonization under another name . . . except that it professes to be anti-slavery."[16] Douglass recognized that emigration and colonization were more closely related than the emigrationists cared to admit. Douglass was certainly as good a black nationalist as many of his contemporaries, but his ephemeral support of emigration, when it occurred, was half-hearted. Douglass belonged to that tradition of black nationalists who militantly asserted their right to American citizenship. It was the tradition represented by David Walker, whose case exemplifies the distinction between nationalism and emigrationism.

David Walker, like most black nationalists of the nineteenth century, blended radical and conservative elements in his philosophy, advocating violent means to achieve fundamental changes in the nature of American life. He was a fervent black nationalist, yet he opposed emigration under any auspices. Walker's black nationalism was evident in his view of history. He thought of Afro-Americans as a distinct people with a divine mission which was as important as that of the ancient Hebrews or Christian Europe. American black people were viewed not as Americans in the truest sense, but as a separate nation in bondage. He spoke to the people of the United States as if he viewed them as a people distinct from his own:

> I tell you Americans! that unless you speedily alter your course, you and your *Country are gone*!!!!!! For God Almighty will tear up the very face of the earth!!![17]

But Walker claimed that he did not wish the destruction of white Americans, nor did he desire the perpetual separation of the races. He hoped that black and white Americans would eventually become "a united and happy people," and therefore saw the Colonization Society as a principal source of Afro-American wretchedness. No one has yet denied that David Walker was a black nationalist, but he opposed colonization, emigration, racial separatism, and laws prohibiting intermarriage.

Frederick Douglass, although not quite as volatile as Walker, fit into the same pattern of black nationalism. Douglass, too, opposed colonization and the doctrine that the races should be perpetually separate, and yet his thought and writings conform to certain patterns of nationalism. Douglass's debate with Garnet has been overemphasized to the point that Douglass is often misinterpreted as being totally opposed to nationalism.[18] Actually, the Douglass/Garnet debate, despite Garnet's attempt to confuse the issues, had nothing to do with the questions of nationalism, African regeneration, anti-slavery, or racial solidarity. The debate was really over the question of emigration and not much else. Douglass was as good a nationalist as most; he referred to Afro-Americans as an "oppressed nation" on more than one occasion. He participated in and defended the right to institutional separatism, and he flirted with the idea of Haitian emigration. Like others among his contemporaries, Douglass was given to discussing black Americans in terms of Jewish analogies, both ancient and modern. The American Negroes were advised to follow the example of the modern Jews in Europe and the United States who, through a spirit of unity and community discipline, were constantly improving their status.[19]

Douglass was strongly individualistic, yet he recognized the need for group solidarity. At the Colored National Convention of 1848, he participated in the drafting of AN ADDRESS TO THE COLORED PEOPLE OF THE UNITED STATES:

> In the Northern states, we are not slaves to individuals, not personal slaves, yet in many respects we are the slaves of the community. . . . It is more than a figure of speech to say, that we are as a people chained together. We are one people—one in general complexion, one in a common degradation, one in popular estimation.—As one rises, all must rise, and as one falls all must fall. Having now, our feet on the rock of freedom, we must drag our brethren from the slimy depths of slavery, ignorance, and ruin. Every one of us should be ashamed to consider himself free, while his brother is a slave.[20]

This is the essence of black nationalism, and we must understand that this is more than a metaphorical mode of expression; it is an accurate description of a social condition. The preceding excerpt from the *Address* was really only a more direct statement of what the Dred Scott decision would proclaim ten years later. The convention called black people "slaves of the community"; Judge Taney said that Negroes were "a subordinate and inferior class of beings, who had been subjugated by the dominant race, and whether emancipated or not, yet remained subject to their authority and had no rights or privileges but such as those who held the power and the government might choose to grant them." Douglass and the committee who drew up the 1848 *Address* and had it printed in the *North Star* office were being very realistic about the status of black people in the United States. They recognized the fact that Afro-Americans were a subject people; they felt the de-individualizing pressures of being classed together with others solely on the basis of color; they saw the need for unity, because all black people would be forcibly lumped together regardless of individual preferences or personal merits.

Douglass's approach to black nationalism may seem to some to be negative, for he never found much consolation in the breast-beating chauvinism that characterized the rhetoric of Alexander Crummell and Martin Delany. He always perceived his blackness as a burden thrust upon him from outside—an attempt to distort his self-perception and obliterate his individuality. His position may seem contradictory, as his contemporary William Whipper pointed out, for Douglass sought to use nationalistic means for integrationist and assimilationist ends. Although Douglass consistently favored assimilation throughout his life, he was not above pragmatic separatism to suit his personal ends, nor was he totally immune to any sense of racial feeling.

If there was a contradiction between Douglass's means and his ends, there were contradictory patterns among the classical nationalists as well. While the flamboyant racial enthusiasts conjured up such shibboleths as "Negro nationality," and "African Civilization," they showed little readiness to divorce themselves from the institutional and moral support of whites in England and the United States. A case in point was Alexander Crummell, a Cambridge-trained missionary to Liberia who left England for Monrovia in 1853 and endured the rigors of colonial life for the next twenty years. Crummell was not content to impose hardship upon himself and his family; he began to argue that all black men had a duty to contribute to the civilization and Christianization of Africa. He was passionate and romantic, but at the same time, iron-willed and ruthlessly puritanical. His ties were to the Episcopal church which he preferred because of its orderly liturgy and hierarchical structure. He had little understanding of the culture traits of freed slaves and crusaded zealously against "Gree-Greeism," "Obeaism," noisy church services, and all attempts to adapt Anglicanism to the culture of its Liberian practitioners. His crusade against Africanisms in West Africa was paralleled by the similar concern of Bishop Daniel A. Payne in the United States with stamping out "heathenish" and "disgraceful" extravagances in Afro-American religion.[21]

Crummell tended to equate the progress of African civilization with the spread of the English language and culture along the coast. He saw black people themselves as having little, if any, culture or intellectual heritage worth preserving. He described the typical freedman in Liberia as "ignorant, benighted, besotted and filthy both in the inner and the outer man." Crummell took an inflexible approach to governmental reform. He quarrelled constantly with his fellow ministers in Liberia. He had no tolerance for the free and easy sexual morality of many former slaves, and denounced governmental and community leaders who condoned drinking and divorce. His philosophy of African regeneration did not grow organically out of the Liberian experience, but was rather an attempt to transplant Anglo-African ideals to the Fatherland whether the citizens desired such ideals or not.

Crummell was forced to admit that his African mission was a failure after twenty tedious years of attempting to "civilize" his brethren. Toward the end of his sojourn he began to call for a greater assertion of American authority along the coast. He even suggested an American protectorate be established over Liberia. He gazed wistfully at British imperialism in Nigeria and the Gold Coast and was convinced that European colonization had done more for black civilization and advancement than had the establishment of Liberia as a sovereign state. Crummell's philosophy of African regeneration was not an aberration. West Indian migrants to Africa, like Edward Wilmot Blyden and Robert Campbell, showed little more abiding respect than Crummell for the customs of indigenous peoples. While they might marvel at some isolated instances of barbaric splendour, or praise the warrior virtues of the various traditional nations, they still viewed Africa as a diamond in the rough. Native West African intellectuals differed little from those who were born in the new world. With the resurgence of interest in black nationalism in the late sixties, it became fashionable to emphasize the elements of nationalistic thought in such nineteenth century African spokesmen as Edward Wilmot Blyden and Africanus Horton. But we should recall that these men hardly favored the idea of a precipitous withdrawal of British influence from the coast.

Africanus Horton, the Sierra Leone nationalist, was a devoted British subject. It is "through Brittannic influence," said Horton in 1868, that Africa "is free of foreign slavery." He endorsed a House of Commons Africa Committee resolution "to encourage in the native the exercise of those qualities which may render it possible for us more and more to transfer to the natives the administrations of all the Governments, with a view to our ultimate withdrawal from all, except probably Sierra Leone." He admitted that it was a glorious idea to contemplate that "the sun never sets on the British Empire," although he felt that an even greater idea would be for England to encourage Africa along the road to self-government. But Horton did not encourage an aggressive self-assertiveness for blacks; he felt that it would be necessary for West Africa to undergo the civilizing processes of technical and Christian training.[22] Edward Wilmot Blyden, a West Indian migrant to Liberia and another person often identified with the "fathers of black nationalism," proposed to the British government that it establish a protectorate extending outward from Sierra Leone to encompass all of West Africa. He had little respect for the culture of the peoples of the hinterland, who were neither Christian nor Muslim, but "besotted pagans."[23] Even much later in his career, after spending some thirty-seven years of study and travel in West Africa, Blyden had not shaken loose from the idea of civilizationism. He came to display an ambivalence concerning the respective merits of Christianity and Islam—the two most rapidly growing faiths in Africa. Of one thing, however, he was certain: Africans would be better off as soon as they replaced their indigenous religions with either of the more respectable newcomers.[24] He hoped to call the attention of the English government to unenlightened areas, saying that as certainly as England stood "foremost among nations as the energetic promoter of whatever concerned the welfare of the African continent," so was she particularly qualified because of her control of the colonial government of Sierra Leone "to contribute largely towards rescuing tribes . . . from their present abject condition."[25]

There were elements of assimilationist thought in the philisophies of pioneering black nationalists, then, just as there were elements of black nationalism in the philosophies of such assimilationists as Frederick Douglass. The attempts to divide black thought during the pre-Civil war decade into discrete categories of nationalism and assimilationism creates a false dichotomy. But the creation of such false dichotomy is not a distortion of modern analysis. Nineteenth-century spokesmen promoted similar distortions in their own time. One noted anti-slavery advocate announced that members of his society were "not colonizationists, but abolitionists," as if the two categories were mutually exclusive. It is probably as true today as it was in the 1850s that all black people harbor some assimilationist daydreams along with black nationalist fantasies.

So far this discussion has been limited to a focus on Africa. There were, of course, colonizationists and emigrationists who rejected Africa as a possible Zion, holding out for Haiti, or some other New World site. James T. Holly was the most articulate spokesman for Haitian emigration and a great believer in the destined greatness of Haiti. He may be contrasted with Frederick Douglass and William Wells Brown, who entertained the idea briefly although neither retained an interest long. Ironically, Holly's belief in Haitian potential was based on a firm belief in English cultural supremacy. While the Haitian people were certainly the heroic vanguard of the spirit of black pride and independence, providence had suited Afro-Americans for leading Haiti toward her destiny as a leader of the western world. Haitians had discovered the revolutionary spirit; Afro-Americans had discovered, in Holly's words, "the arts, sciences and genius of modern civilization," tutored by "this hardy and enterprising Anglo-American race."[26] Holly was the first black Bishop of the Anglo-Catholic church; he maintained a loyalty to the mother institution throughout his life. Holly's philosophy contained the usual trappings of Christian nationalism. He believed in manifest destiny and he thought he could see Providence directing the destinies of blacks in the New World. Despite his ethnic chauvinism and commitment to the idea of a separate national destiny for African people, he was very much the Anglophile. His attitudes paralleled those of J. Dennis Harris, who added to Holly's Anglocentrism a defense of mulattoes and of the term Anglo-African as the best description for the new nation he wished to found.[27]

Black nationalism on the eve of the Civil War meant various things when applied to its various adherents. To the classical black nationalists—Blyden, Crummell, Holly, Horton—black nationalism was a mystical system of beliefs. It had to do with dreams of competing with and excelling the white man—beating him at his own game. Black nationalism often assumed a self-confident, optimistic stance, but sometimes was pragmatic and defensive. The rhetoric of the Colored National Conventions was not one of strident racial chauvinism, a rejoicing in blackness. Emigration was considered a necessity by most proponents; separate institutions were advocated as defense mechanisms. Most of the ideological black nationalists never made a serious attempt to resettle outside the United States. Indeed this gives some credence to the position argued by John Hope Franklin that black nationalism on the eve of the Civil War was simply a reaction to the fugitive slave law and the Dred Scott Decision.

Of black nationalism before the eve of the Civil War, we would say, in summary, the following:

1. It was a pragmatic movement, an adjustment to the reality of rejection. It was an attempt to bring about a unity based on a common heritage of oppression. It was not based on sympathy of belief or on commonality of spiritual aims.
2. The distinction between black nationalism and emigrationism needs to be more carefully drawn. Many emigrationists—especially among the newly emancipated—could not have cared less for the high-flown rhetoric of Crummell and Blyden.
3. There was no clear-cut distinction between black nationalism and assimilation. Black chauvinists, like Delany, were dedicated to Christianizing and "civilizing" the African continent and actively solicited the support of whites to accomplish this goal. Avowed integrationists, like Douglass, were willing to participate actively in all-black institutions, and defended their right to do so.
4. The distinction between colonization and emigration was not as clear as the emigrationists would have liked it to appear. Colonizationists and emigrationists mingled freely in such organizations as the African Civilization Society, which admitted white members and encouraged a tolerant attitude toward white advocates of colonization.

What all of this suggests is that black nationalists on the eve of the Civil War, despite their fierce rhetoric of independence, despite their declamations about God-given mandates to develop a separate destiny, were hardly eager to remove themselves from white society, and were reluctant to contemplate a future severed from the values of Anglo-American civilization.

Just as they failed to question the cultural values of English-speaking societies, so too did the black nationalists fail to question racial stereotypes. This tendency is readily observable in the writings of Martin R. Delany, eminently respectable in black nationalist circles. Delany was clearly impressed by the material development of Anglo-Saxon commerce and industry. He attempted to argue, however, that the black race was endowed with a natural aestheticism and congenital morality and that the colored races possessed, in short, "the highest traits of civilization" among all peoples. This was similar to the strain of condescending romantic racialism running through the thought of many white abolitionists. Delany referred, as black nationalists often do, to the legendary superiority of Negroes in the artistic and aesthetic areas of life, claiming for black people a self-evident excellence in the areas of music and oratory. And yet the whites "probably excel in mathematics, sculpture and architecture. . . . commerce and internal improvements."[28] On another occasion, he spoke of the "living truths" that characterized English-speaking civilization, the "mighty trains flying with the velocity of a swallow . . . the great and massive buildings" and other "living monuments of industry rebuking us with scorn."[29]

Late in the century, Frederick Douglass rebuked Afro-Americans at a meeting of the Bethel Literary Society for their failure to develop a more sophisticated technological civilization. Blacks would become equal in actuality and not only potentially equal, he argued, if they had, like the whites, "built great ships, sailed around the world, taught the sun to take pictures, [and] the lightning to carry messages."[30] Such thinking as Delany and Douglass articulated was endorsed by large numbers at both the antebellum and the post-Civil War Colored Conventions. It was at the root of the idea that industrial training of the Negro masses would positively guarantee an improvement in the well-being of blacks in the new world. Toward the end of the century, Alexander Crummell, Booker T. Washington, Frederick Douglass, William Hooper Council, and others became convinced of the importance of technical training as almost a panacea for Negro problems.

This was mainly because they conceived of blacks as a languid, dreamy, "feminine" race, that could well benefit from the training associated with the tough and masculine industrial sciences.

It cannot be overstated that Delany, Blyden, and Crummell failed to challenge racial stereotypes. It is also important to note that white Americans who were sincere friends of the Negro shared essentially racist conceptions of the Negro with his confirmed enemies. George Frederickson has identified the tendencies to racial stereotyping in the thought of such respectable abolitionists as Harriet Beecher Stowe, Hollis Read, Theodore Parker, and Lydia Maria Child, all of whom conceived of American blacks as predisposed toward "feminine" languidity and softness.[31] This resembled the thinking of continental racialists, like Gobineau, who identified the black race with sensual and artistic gifts, the yellow race with stability and fertility, and the white race with the noble, vigorous, and manly traits most needed for the building of civilization.[32]

Black nationalists characteristically believed that the technological aspects of civilization were destined to develop collaterally with Protestantism. No other form of Christianity could conduce to the civilization of Africa, felt Alexander Crummell, and he attributed the shortcomings of the Haitian experiment to the influences of Roman Catholicism.[33] Anti-Roman Catholic sentiments are among the most interesting features of some early works of black nationalist propaganda. David Walker's *Appeal*, for example, was as vehemently anti-Catholic as it was anti-Spanish and anti-Portuguese. The *Appeal* roundly denounced Bartholomew Las Casas as "that very, very avaricious Catholic priest," as if either Roman Catholicism or Las Casas's efforts had been the cause of the African slave trade.[34] Martin Delany's anti-Catholicism was also obvious, as, for example, in his 1854 publication describing an expedition to the Niger Valley. While it was certainly apparent to him that Christianity was "the most advanced civilization that man had ever attained to," it was just as certainly apparent that "slavery was the legitimate successor of Roman Catholicism." Although he represented a people who were victims of Anglo-Protestant culture, he chose to direct his vitriol in the direction of Roman Catholicism, while in adjacent paragraphs praising the Protestants as foes of slavery.[35] Clearly he was well under the influence of that same Anglo-Protestantism that was being used throughout North America as a justification for slavery.

Protestant Christianity was an essential, rather than an accidental quality of Anglo-African nationalism. Martin Delany recognized that religion was a potential source of conflict within the Pan-African revolution since so many of the Caribbean blacks were Catholic; still, he insisted upon Protestantism as an aspect of African redemption. He would not have been willing to reconcile religious differences within Pan-Africanism by making it a totally secular movement. The rigidity of his religious attitude can be seen in his novel, *Blake*. In one scene, which describes the utopian striving after unity often desired by blacks of many diverse cultural backgrounds, a woman confesses to being "bred Catholic" and to believing in "the doctrine of the Romish Church." She admits to some misgivings about participating in Pan-Africanist meetings because "a portion of our ceremonies consist of prayer and other formalities."[36] The hero attempts to reassure her with the unconvincing argument that Pan-Africanism is an interdenominational movement and that the religious services are non-sectarian. Of course, to Catholics in the 1850s the distinction between a Protestant and an interdenominational meeting would have been totally incomprehensible. The tone of *Blake* is decidedly anti-Catholic. According to the guidelines offered in Delany's didactic novel, Catholic blacks were to show their good faith by participating in non-Catholic religious services, and accepting the stridently Protestant rhetoric of the universal African civilization movement.[37]

African civilizationism, as described in the previous paragraphs, implies a goal of African political independence as a vindication of the right of the Ethiopian race to self-determination and freedom. The separatist strain in black thought was rationalized by a Christian mysticism. The voluntary institutional separatism, which originated in the eighteenth century, had by the 1850s taken on all of the trappings of romantic racialism. Romantic racialism on the European continent has signified the idea that every national group manifests distinctive talents and peculiar traits of personality which may be spoken of as its racial genius.[38] This variety of thinking came into fashion during the late eighteenth century when it was formalized by the German theorist, Johann Gottfried von Herder. Herder rejected the idea associated with Enlightenment rationalism that nationality was only a figment of the imagination, and argued that each nation was an organic entity. "Each nationality was," according to one scholar's interpretation of Herder, "a part of the divine plan in history. In the development of each nationality he saw the unfolding of the divine will."[39] Friedrich Schleiermacher, who thought similarly, wrote:

> Every nation is destined through its peculiar organization and its place in the world to represent a certain side of the divine image . . . for it is God alone who directly assigns to each nationality its definite task on earth and inspires it with a definite spirit in order to glorify himself through each one in a peculiar manner.[40]

Parallel developments were present in the thinking of Anglo-Africans and the following, by Edward Wilmot Blyden, has a familiar ring:

> As in every form of the inorganic universe we see some noble variation of God's thought and beauty, so in each separate man, in each separate race, something of the absolute is incarnated. The whole of mankind is a vast representation of the Deity. Therefore we cannot extinguish any race either by conflict or amalgamation without serious responsibility.[41]

When Blyden visited the United States late in the century, he spoke to various black groups in several cities, admonishing them on the subjects of racial independence and divine mission.

Alexander Crummell accompanied Blyden on a tour of the United States in 1861, as an official representative of the Liberian government in order to encourage emigration to Liberia.[42] Crummell was occupied with racial ideas, similar in some respects to those of Blyden. "Races, like families, are the organisms and the ordinance of God", Crummell once said, "and race feeling, like family feeling, is of divine origin."[43] He was influenced, as were white Americans, by concepts of nationality then prevalent. His ideas of nationalism, like those of the European nationalists, emphasized a concept of each nation as "destined through its peculiar organization and its place in the world to represent a certain side of the divine image."[44] Indeed, there is in Crummell's writings, as in the writings of both European and American racial ideologues, a tendency toward the doctrine of racial superiority. This doctrine was advanced with the usual Christian rationalizations, and was accompanied by the theory of divine apportionment of Earth—the idea that each race was entitled to the hereditary realm in which God had originally placed it. The rhetoric of the colonization movement and other migrationist movements was thus rooted in prevailing Euro-American concepts of race and territoriality, and bore the usual mystical trappings of racial chauvinism. Crummell and Blyden spoke of the duty of Africans of the diaspora to support the work of civilizing the blacks of West Africa and elevating them to self-governing status; James T. Holly adapted the rhetoric of Christian expansionism to the black Caribbean.

The coming of the Civil War released a flood of emotion in the free Negro community. Many black citizens greeted the firing on Fort Sumter as the signal of a new day and expreseed the belief that the reign of slavery was drawing to an end. Nicholas Biddle, a sixty-five-year-old fugitive slave from Pottsville, Pennsylvania immediately attached himself to the Washington Artillerists, although he was not allowed to enlist officially. Biddle's eagerness was apparently not unusual; throughout the North, black men quickly formed volunteer companies and offered their services to the War Office.[45] In the South, as well, black Americans entered fully into the war spirit. Apparently in hopes that faithful service to the Confederacy might lead to the possession of full citizenship rights, the free colored people of Louisiana organized two regiments of "Native Guards" and offered their services to the cause. Although they were organized with the permission of the governor, the Native Guards were not allowed to see active duty under the Confederacy, but in 1862, when the Federals occupied

New Orleans, the first regiment was mustered into the Union Army.[46]

The free people of color were not unanimous in believing that the war necessarily meant the demise of slavery. William Wells Brown was to remember that the war seemed in those early days to be for the preservation of both the Union and the institution of slavery.[47] Five slave states fought on the Union side. Anti-Negro riots occurred in such Northern metropolises as Boston, New York and Baltimore. Lincoln and his generals seemed determined to conciliate the slaveholding Union states by taking a strong stand against the idea of universal abolition. Although some generals were inclined to free slaves in territories under their control, most were willing to abide by the Lincoln doctrine and return "contrabands" to their masters. For this reason, then, John S. Rock, a black physician of Boston, was convinced that "the present war is an effort to nationalize, perpetuate, and extend slavery in this country."[48] Frederick Douglass, however, was convinced that slavery could be abolished and the Union preserved. "The Government is aroused," he wrote, "the dead North is alive, and its divided people united. Never was a change so sudden, so universal, and so portentous." The change resulted, opined Douglass, from the fall of Sumter. If the South had not been so aggressive in her arrogance, the North would have come to terms, even as the urban industrialists and the pro-slavery clergy were urging. The South had lost its most faithful supporters and secured its own defeat with the defeat of Sumter, said Douglass. "They have completely shot off the legs of all trimmers and compromisers, and compelled every body to elect between patriotic fidelity and pro-slavery treason." The war, gradually but certainly, was evolving into a war aginst slavery, and Douglass began to reveal his plan for winning the war.[49] Slavery, the "primal cause" of the war, must be struck down by a proclamation from Washington. The slaves and free colored people should be called into the service and formed into a liberating army. Since the slaveholders had not hesitated to employ black workers in erecting the very fortifications that had silenced Fort Sumter, why should the North be squeamish about recognizing the military usefulness of the Negro? Douglass noted as a shameful irony that General Butler, a native of Massachussets seemed more interested in

putting down slave insurrections than in fighting rebels. The
North should be as conscientious in fighting for liberty as the
South was in fighting for slavery. He printed an anonymous letter
to the editor which defended the arming of the slaves and which
closed with the following note:

> France has some regiments of native Africans, who are
> incarnate devils on a field of battle. The Austrians had a touch
> of their quality in Italy. Nothing would please me more, and
> bring the race into favor, than to see Southern chivalry well
> whipped by an equal number of black men. It would, indeed
> be refreshing.[50]

By 1862 it had become apparent that black men were going to
fight in the war. Radicals in Congress were pressing for a change
in governmental policy toward arming black men. On July 16,
they passed a Confiscation Act, authorizing the President to make
military use of persons of African descent. Public opinion in
support of Negro enlistment slowly began to change, especially
among the working classes, resentful at the thought that free black
people were not allowed the risks of the battlefield. Early in 1863,
Thaddeus Stevens's bill calling for the mustering of black
regiments was passed in the House and the governors of Mas-
sachussetts and Rhode Island were authorized to recruit Negro
troops. This growing disposition toward the use of black troops
was viewed by Douglass as "the most hopeful sign of the times."
He called upon men of color to take up arms and win their own
freedom, so that their right to freedom would never be challenged.
A colored man should enlist because he was an American citizen
and had an obligation to put down the rebellion, but also "to learn
the use of arms, to become familiar with the means of securing,
protecting and defending his own liberty."[51] Enlistment in the
Northern armies would provide the black man with an occasion to
prove his manhood to the world and to bolster his own self-
confidence. "Once let the black man get upon his person the brass
letters, U.S.," reasoned Douglass, "let him get an eagle on his
button, and a musket on his shoulder and bullets in his pocket,
and there is no power on earth which can deny that he has earned
the right to citizenship in the United States."[52] Perhaps he spoke
too optimistically.

Martin Delany, whose ideas had seemed so remote from those of Douglass's just two years earlier, dramatically shifted his attention from the cause of gradual abolitionism by means of African regeneration to that of immediate abolitionism and the elevation of the African in America. He began to agitate for the formation of a black regiment, a "Corps D'Afrique". Like Douglass, he noted that French armies had found African troops nigh indispensable in their Old World campaigns. In 1864, Delany, who had been living in Chatham, Ontario, moved his family to Wilberforce, Ohio. He had already spent several months working as a recruiter, traveling to several states of the North; his son Toussaint L'Ouverture Delany had joined the Union Army in the spring of 1863. And Delany was to enter the service himself toward the end of the war. In February of 1865, Delany secured an interview with President Lincoln, and later recounted memories to his biographer, Frances Rollin. He proposed to Lincoln that in order to "prevent enrollment of the blacks in the rebel services, and induce them to run to, instead from, the Union forces—the government undertake—the commissioning and promotion of black men now in the army, according to merit." When the President asked Delany how he planned to overcome the objections of white officers and men to the commissioning of black officers, Delany revealed his plan for an all-black army:

I have the remedy, Mr. President, which has not yet been stated; and it is the most important suggestion of my visit to you. And I think it is just what is required to complete the prestige of the Union army. I propose, sir, an army of blacks, commanded entirely by black officers, except such whites as may volunteer to serve; this army to penetrate through the heart of the South, and make conquests, with the banner of Emancipation unfurled, proclaiming freedom as they go, sustaining and protecting and leaving a few veterans among the new freed men, when occasion requires, keeping this banner unfurled until every slave is free, according to the letter of your proclamation. I would also take from those already in the service all that are competent for commission [ed] officers, and establish at once in the South a camp of instructions. By this we could have in about three months an army of forty thousand blacks in motion, the presence of which anywhere would itself be a power irresistible. You should have an army of blacks, President Lincoln, commanded entirely by blacks, the sight of which is required to give confidence to the slaves, and retain them to the Union, stop foreign intervention, and speedily bring the war to a close."[53]

Delany was never to see this plan materialize, but he was to begin to implement it after receiving his commission as army Major. By contrast, Frederick Douglass was shabbily treated by the War Department, having been promised a commission and then peremptorily denied it in August of 1863. Major Delany continued his recruitment activities until the end of the war; afterward he would work with the Freedmen's Bureau, aiding the emancipated blacks to struggle manfully for their rights, and for the lands they had cleared and cultivated.

In the moment of truth, with the emancipation of the slaves and the acceptance of freedom into the army, Delany revealed the assimilationist and integrationist aspirations always basic to his personality. One cannot question the sincerity of his black nationalism during the 1840s and 1850s, or, on the other hand, fail to remark at the alacrity with which he devoted himself to the political and economic goals of reconstruction, which were essentially intergrationist. During the first phase of Reconstruction his goals as a black leader were not substantially different from those of Douglass. He sought by means of Republican party politics to bring black Americans into the mainstream of life in the United States, and encouraged them to defend their rights as citizens. He rejoiced in his status as a former officer of the United States Army. But after a checkered and embittering fifteen-year career in South Carolina politics, Delany emerged again as a supporter of emigration, cooperating with the American Colonization Society as an officer of the Exodus Association, which planned to resettle blacks in Liberia. He did not choose to migrate himself, however.[54]

Thus did the supporters of black nationalism tend to vacillate during the years of the slavery crisis—the first half of the nineteenth century. Most of them sought occasions to work out dignified compromises with white America, and they sought to enjoy all the benefits of American citizenship if possible. Crummell and Holly represented a minority among the articulate spokesmen for black nationalism who chose to risk their own fortunes by resettling in a new land, and Crummell was due to return to the States for good by 1873. Frederick Douglass's concern with colonization was only half-hearted, brought on by the evils of the fugitive slave law and the Dred Scott Decision. Likewise, William Wells Brown was relieved to discover that Haitian migration would not be forced upon him. He was not eager to follow Lincoln's suggestion that all Afro-Americans depart for the Caribbean. As they turned their attention to the task of reconstruction, most black leaders were to acknowledge by their actions that they thought of themselves as Americans. A sense of racial pride and identity would not prevent them from seeking cultural assimilation and economic and political integration in the United States.

PART TWO

Leadership and Programs
in the Nineteenth Century

All historic fact shows that force, that is authority, must be used in the exercise of guardianship over heathen tribes. Mere theories of democracy are trivial in this case, and can never nullify this necessity. You cannot apply them to a rude people, incapable of understanding the social and political obligations which belong to responsible humanity. "Force and right," says a brilliant writer, "are the governors of the world; force till right is ready. * * * *And till right is ready, force the existing order of things, is justified, is the legitimate ruler."

ALEXANDER CRUMMELL
Our National Mistakes and
the Remedy for Them,
(Liberia, 1870)

Chapter Three

Alexander Crummell
Civilizing Missionary

Alexander Crummell (1819-1898) has occasionally been mentioned as a founder of the black nationalist school, or as an influential person within the history of Afro-American thought.[1] Crummell's influences are not difficult to trace, but rather than call him influential, we should say that he voiced with eloquence and force several values that dominated Anglo-African thought and writing during the nineteenth century. These are seen in his commitment to Christian civilization; his manifest faith in the destiny of black African peoples; his authoritarian political philosophy; and his insistence on the importance of independent Afro-American institutions. Crummell typified the influences of Victorian civilization on the black nationalist ideology and gave voice to a common belief that Africans were universally lacking in "civilization," which they would have to acquire in order to avoid the fate of the American Indian and the Sandwich Islander.[2]

By "civilization," Crummell meant different things at different times. Like many of his contemporaries, he sometimes used the expression as a synonym for culture. It was not that Crummell was inconsistent; it was simply that the word was inconsistently and confusingly employed during the nineteenth century. Crummell, like many of his contemporaries, was influenced in his use of the term by the writings of Francois Pierre Guillaume Guizot, the French historian who headed the French parliament under Louis

Philippe, and who believed the political processes among the British to be the world's most civilized. Crummell's essay, "The Progress of Civilization Along the West Coast of Africa," delivered as an address several times during his 1861 tour of the northern United States, was prefaced in a printed edition of 1862 by quotations from Guizot's *General History of Civilization*[6]. Crummell's purpose in quoting Guizot seems to have been to support by reference to authority, and also on intellectual grounds, his sincere belief that history was moving toward a purpose and was guided by providence. Guizot mentioned providence numerous times in the *General History of Civilization*. He described providence moving "through time as the Gods of Homer through space,"[4] and held it to be self-evident that civilization is an ongoing process, the great end toward which world history moves, presumably under providential aegis. Now Guizot was not a metaphysical historian, nor, as a recent biographer has observed, did he wish to "resuscitate the theological historicism that had fallen from favor in the eighteenth century."[5] Still, he believed that history was guided by purpose, and that it evolved progressively toward an end. For this reason we may assume that when Guizot spoke of providence, it was something more than a formality. Providence was, at the very least, a metaphor for progress, and represented a mystical belief in the design and predictability of history.

Neither Guizot nor Crummell ever attempted a systematic or truly social scientific definition of civilization; Guizot argued that "scientific definitions are, in general, much narrower, and, on that very account, much less correct, than the popular significations given to words." While these sentiments may be understandable, they are not particularly helpful, and so in a footnote to the eighth American edition of the *General History*, editor C. S. Henry attempted to provide a concise definition of civilization as he understood Guizot to be using the term. "Civilization," he said, "may be taken to signify merely the multiplication of artificial wants, and of the means and refinements of physical enjoyment. It may also be taken to imply a state of physical well-being and a state of superior intellectual and moral culture."[6] Crummell used a similar definition in his pamphlet of 1898, *Civilization, the Primal Need of the Race:*

What he [the Negro] needs is CIVILIZATION. He needs the increase of his higher wants, of his mental and spiritual needs.[7]

Crummell came closest to clarifying what he meant by the word "civilization," in the late fall of 1895 at the famed Atlanta and Cotton States Exhibition. His address was delivered in connection with the Congress on Africa held under the auspices of the Stewart Missionary Foundation for Africa. It was entitled, "Civilization as a Collateral and Indispensable Instrumentality in Planting the Christian Church in Africa."[8] Crummell defined civilization as:

the clarity of the mind from the dominion of false heathen ideas, . . . the conscious impress of individualism and personal responsibility, . . . the recognition of the *body*, with its desires and appetites and passions as a sacred gift, and as under the law of divine obligation, . . . the honor and freedom of womanhood, allied with the duty of family development, . . . the sense of social progress in society, . . . the entrance of new impulses in the actions and policy of the tribe or nation, . . . an elevated use of material things and a higher range of common industrial activities, . . . [and] the earliest possible introduction of letters, and books, and reading, and intelligence to the man, his family, and his social circles.

Crummell argued that the missionary to Africa had the duty to follow up his Christianizing efforts with attempts to elevate the material life of his flock so that the convert to Christianity might experience "in all ways of life, a new creation." The missionary was to assume, in addition to his evangelical duties, a "secondary obligation," which was to lift the African "from the rudeness of barbarism." Crummell believed that Christianity had been an important cause not only of spiritual and intellectual development in Europe, but of material progress as well. Clearly, Crummell's Christian prejudices did not allow him to entertain an exalted view of indigenous African cultures. Like many of the early philosophers of black nationalism, he was a Christian clergyman, and had little appreciation of anything African unless it had first been washed in the purifying waters of Anglo-Christianity.[9]

The most prominent characteristic of Crummell's personality, aside from his religiosity, was the temperamental conservatism which his contemporaries found so remarkable. This conservatism was not an all-encompassing political reactionism—for he was, simultaneously, a committed abolitionist. It was a selective orthodoxy that supported only certain elements of the status quo. When John Greenleaf Whittier sent a volume of Crummell's sermons to Charlotte Forten in 1863, he described their author as "a churchman and conservative," a statement he did not explain, except to say that "his writings are a noble refutation of the charge of the black man's inferiority. They are model discources, clear, classic, and chaste."[10] William Wells Brown, in that same year, described him as "gentlemanly in all his movements, [with] language chaste and refined." Years later the same author referred to him a little less glowingly as "somewhat punctillious."[11] The young W.E.B. Du Bois, himself a trifle stuffy and stodgy, bowed instinctively before the man, so "tall frail and black . . . with simple dignity and an unmistakable air of good breeding."[12] The reputed formality of Crummell is a characteristic often attributed to bourgeois blacks, as, for example to W.E.B. Du Bois and Marcus Garvey. Possibly it was a defense mechanism, a form of overcompensation, affected as a means of self-protection and race vindication. The conservatism to which Whittier referred was probably a conservatism of temperament, a gothic coldness, a baroque formality which was apparent even in his writing.

He was born free in New York on March 3, 1819. Of his parents, little is known. His mother was descended from a New York family that was reported to have been free for several generations at the time of his birth. His father, Bostin Crummell, claimed descent from a prince of the Temne people who had inhabited that region of West Africa, eventually absorbed into what is now Sierra Leone. The reports of his youth are hazy and contradictory. George W. Forbes says that he was not a Temne, but a Vey, who came under the influence of missionaries while he was still a child in Africa, "through whom he had received some schooling and was afterwards brought hither to New York." William H. Ferris says that he was kidnapped by slavetraders while he was playing on the beach. At all events, the senior Crummell thrived in America and became active in black community efforts and abolitionist activities during the early 1800s. It was in his home in New York that America's first black newspaper was founded in 1827. As Forbes observed, "the boy Alexander appears from the outset to have had the care of kind and indulgent parents."[13]

Not only were the Crummells "kind and indulgent"; they were apparently prosperous, and able to give young Alexander the benefits of an education, which began at the African Free School, Number Two, sometimes referred to as the Mulberry Street School in New York City. In 1831, when Rev. Peter Williams, with the aid of Theodore S. Wright and the Tappan brothers founded the Canal Street High School, Crummell was enrolled in that institution, along with Henry Highland Garnet, to whom he was a lifelong friend. They continued at the Canal Street School until 1835, when abolitionists in Canaan, New Hampshire opened the Noyes Academy with some eighty students. The journey from New York to Canaan was undertaken by Crummell and Garnet in the company of another Negro youth, Thomas S. Sidney. In spite of the inclement weather, they were forced to spend the first leg of their journey on the deck of the steamboat from New York to Providence. They then proceeded from Providence to Canaan on the top of a stage coach. Crummell was never able to recall this journey without some emotion, and said in later years, "the sight of three black youths, in gentlemanly garb, travelling through New England was, in *those days,* a *most unusual sight;* started not only surprise, but brought out universal sneers and ridicule."[14] Garnet was at that time a semicripple, due to an infection that later resulted in the loss of a leg; Crummell, too, was of frail health. Finally, however, on reaching their destination, they were enrolled in the Noyes Academy, and soon demonstrated that they were the equals of any of the eighty or so white students already enrolled. But they were not to remain long in Canaan, for on July 4, 1835, they presumed to exercise their right of free speech by addressing an Independence Day gathering at Plymouth, New Hampshire. So excellent was the oratory of Crummell and Garnet that the crowds were willing to remain until much later that evening in order to hear Sidney speak. The local citizens organized a mass meeting that same evening, and another to be assembled on

July 13, and after nursing their feelings of hatred and envy, they notified other towns in the vicinity of their manly resolve to rid the community of the offensive three.[15] On August 10, 1835, three hundred stalwart New England yeomen, full of the spirit of seventy-six, hitched ninety yoke of oxen to the school building and dragged it into a swamp almost half a mile from its former site. Although Crummell was born a free resident of New York, he was in no way sheltered from the threats to life and limb traditionally employed to keep American Negroes from being educated.[16] While white youth, like Emerson and Thoreau, undoubtedly encountered hardship, their efforts at self-improvement were met with encouragement and applause. Crummell and Garnet were unable to acquire learning without risking their lives. Crummell's early experiences in the American democratic republic were not destined to endow him with a strong belief in the essential nobility of the human heart. His conservatism, his distrust of liberalism and democracy, his fear of the tyranny of the majority, resulted largely from his experiences as a New England Negro in Jacksonian America.

The following year, Crummell, Garnet, and Sidney entered the Oneida Institute at Whitesboro, New York, where Crummell remained for three years (1836-39). The Oneida Institute was founded in 1833 by Beriah Green, a Presbyterian minister. Known for his radical abolitionism, Green had been president of the Philadelphia convention at which the American Anti-Slavery Society was formed. The Oneida Institute emphasized manual training as well as education along more academic lines, although Greek and Latin classics were de-emphasized in favor of Greek and Hebrew Scriptures. Green encouraged Crummell to enter into holy orders, which he did before graduating from Oneida and seeking admission to the General Theological Seminary of the Protestant Episcopal Church. Being refused admission on the grounds of color, he undertook study with Rev. Alexander Vinton in Providence, Rhode Island, where he became involved in mission work among the colored population, but met with little success in his work among white Christians. He was raised to the order of priesthood in 1844, having acquired the necessary theological expertise as speedily as if he had been enrolled in the Seminary. Crummell was able to continue his formal education as a result of a fund raising trip to England in 1848. During this excursion he made a number of friends who, shocked by his treatment at the hands of the American church and eager to remove the stain of prejudice from their denomination, arranged for him to attend Queen's College, Cambridge, from which he took the A.B. in 1853.

The next twenty years of Crummell's life were spent in the land of his fathers; he became a missionary to Liberia, apparently hoping to do for others what Christian missionaries had done for his father a half-century earlier. The fifties, of course, represented the high point of American black nationalism. Even people like Frederick Douglass, ordinarily hostile to the idea, flirted with colonization schemes during these years of disaster for the free black population. Passage of the Fugitive Slave Law with all its potential for abuse, seemed a dire omen in 1850, and the Dred Scott decision of 1857 left black people defenseless before the law. George Washington Forbes suggested that the tense conditions at home and the frail state of Crummell's health might have contributed to his decision not to return to the United States. But Crummell was most certainly motivated by a sincere interest in Africa, for he did not return to the States, or renounce his black nationalism immediately after the Civil War. Nor did he become a Republican Party hanger-on, or a seeker of patronage. He remained in Africa for eight more years, which would seem to be proof of deep commitment. Crummell was not a successful missionary, however; his personality seemed to alienate the other nationals. At one point, members of his congregation were being lured away by a more popular and folksy preacher. His church was not given adequate support from the mother institution; his health was not good, and he had frequent bouts with fever. The youngest of his children died within a few months of his arrival in Africa. In short, his material existence during these twenty years does not seem to have been luxurious. Sermons published during the Liberian years gave little indication of the personal hardships he was undergoing, however. His public statements were characterized by an optimism that can be explained only in terms of religious faith. For cetainly there were few rational bases for his ardent belief in Liberia's potential for "noble national growth and ... future superiority." Indeed his private letters show that many of his public addresses amounted to whistling in the dark.[17]

The sermons published during the Liberian years were mostly political discourses, rendered on state occasions. It should not be surprising, for this reason, that most of these tracts reveal a political conservatism, a puritanical sexual ethic, an absolute faith in Anglo-Christian values, in short, an inability to question the values of Victorian civilization. Crummell often wrote on the subject of civilization, but while he may have understood some distinction between that concept and the concept of culture, this was not manifest in his writings. For Crummell, as for most people afflicted with Anglophilism, English speaking culture was a perfectly adequate synonym for civilization.[18] The English language was self-evidently superior, he felt, to any of the indigenous tongues of West Africa. On at least two occasions Crummell was ready to point out that "among the other providential events the fact, that the exile of our fathers from their African homes to America, had given us, their children, at least this one item of compensation, namely, the possession of the Anglo-Saxon tongue . . . and that it was impossible to estimate too highly, the prerogatives and the elevation the Almighty has bestowed upon us, in our having as our own, the speech of Chaucer and Shakespeare, of Milton and Wordsworth, of Bacon and Burke, of Franklin and Webster."[19] Aside from this there were other benefits accruing to Anglo-Africans by the loss of their mother tongues. The English language was "a language of unusual force and power." It was "characteristically the language of freedom" and the "enshrinement of those great charters of liberty which are the essential elements of free governments." But finally and most importantly, the English language was seen to have a "peculiar identity with religion" and it seemed to Crummell a self-evident truth that the language of King James was so undeniably a source of freedom-inspiring ideas that the blacks of non-English-speaking countries would never be able to achieve democracy on the scale of his prognostications for Liberia. Was it not obvious that Haiti, Catholic and French-speaking, in spite of "all our hope for and pride . . . in her history" had not learned and was not destined to have learned, the ways of progress and freedom?[20]

Crummell saw hope for Africa in the prospects of the continent's "complete evangelization," which could be predicted by means of "secular evidences" and "temporal providences." For the Negro possessed "strong vital power," and had not been destroyed by either the "ravages of the slave trade" or the horrors of the "mid passage." On the contrary, the slave trade was in the process of being abolished, black men were raising themselves to positions of authority and respect throughout Europe and America. Africa was soon to awake and arise after centuries of slumber, and stretch forth her hand to Christianity and Civilization.[21]

And why was Christianity so important to the growth and development of African Civilization? "If a people think that God is a Spirit, that idea raises, or will raise them among the first of nations," was Crummell's answer. "If, on the other hand, they think that God is a stone or a carved image, or a reptile, they will assuredly be low and rude. A nation that worships shocks, or ugly idols, can never, while maintaining such a style of worship become a great nation." Crummell was an idealist, an admirer of Plato, suspicious of the senses and of the material world.[22] He lived in a world of ideas where he was a functional isolate. Unlike his contemporaries, Blyden and Horton, he was not a scientist by nature. His mind worked deductively from the general to the specific. He made efforts, but still found it difficult to see the world from more than one perspective. And his views of Africa, as expressed in 1860, read like a racial horror story. How painful it must have been for this sensitive and orderly person who wanted such great things for his people, to have suffered under the burden of his own conception of Africa as a dark continent:

> Darkness covers the land, and gross darkness the people. Great evils universally prevail. Confidence and security are destroyed. Licentiousness abounds everywhere. Moloch rules and reigns throughout the whole continent, and by the ordeal of Sassywood, Fetiches, human sacrifices, and devil-worship, is devouring men, women, and little children.[23]

Strangely, some years later, in 1882, Crummell was to venture the assertation "that any one walking through Pall Mall, London, or Broadway, New York, for a week, would see more indecency in look and act than he could discover in an African town in a dozen years." He avowed that, "during my residence there, I only *once* saw an indecent act."[24] In the twenty-two years separating the two statements Crummell may have changed his opinion, or perhaps he simply tailored his remarks to suit his audiences. The 1860 statement was made in a letter to a fellow black nationalist; the 1882 statement was in defense of the Negro race after the attacks of a hostile critic. It must be acknowledged, however, that one of the more consistent strains in Crummell's writing is the severest criticism of black people. Throughout the bulk of his essays, regardless of date, the theme of civilizationism is strong. Black people are consistently seen as needing to be uplifted, civilized.

Crummell's faith in African peoples was nonetheless mighty. Not only did he believe that Africa could be civilized, he believed that blacks were in the fortunate position of being able to contribute to the world's civilization. Liberia could become an instrument for the abolition of the slave trade and the destruction of slavery in all quarters of the globe. What greater contribution could a rising Protestant state make to the world's civilization? The solution was not only religious and moral—it also involved a sophisticated economic and technological adjustment for Africans.

> You know the high value of COTTON, and its great demand: you know also how important the production of the article has become in the decision of that great moral question of the age—THE DESTRUCTION OF SLAVERY; and I need not pause here to show what a blessing we might become to our race and to the world, by the "disturbing element" of thousands of bales of cotton, competing with the oppressors of our race in the ports of Liverpool and Glasgow, and beating down their ill-gotten gains! It grows all around us here, amid the huts and villages, and the rice farms of our heathen neighbors, and by the use of bounties we can largely prompt its growth among them, as also by our labor lead to its extensive and profitable cultivation in our own fields.[25]

With the growth of the cotton trade Crummell also hoped to see the growth of great commercial houses in Liberia, and the rise of a class of "princely merchants" in West Africa. Crummell's spirit of otherworldiness did not prevent him from valuing the role of commerce in the growth of a nation. It seemed to him a "clear mandate of Heaven" that "the nations that will not hold intercourse with other peoples, in trade and barterings, and thus bless the world, they shall suffer and shall die!"[26]

So idealistic were Crummell's dreams that disillusionment was perhaps inevitable. In 1870, still three years before he was to return to the United States, he frankly stated some of his reasons for dissatisfaction with conditions in Liberia. His statement took the form of an address, "Our National Mistakes and the Remedy for Them." In particular, his remarks had to do with the "native problem." Neither had Liberians as individuals, nor Liberia as a nation discharged their duties to the black people still living according to tribal traditions. They had "ignored the *national* obligation to train, educate, civilize and regulate the heathen tribes around us!" Crummell also criticized his countrymen for their dependency on foreign imports "to the culpable neglect of our native resources and of native skill." The failure of Liberia to cultivate native resources—human or material—was at the base of the nation's deficiencies. It is ironic, then, that in the same essay, Crummell succumbed to years of frustration and fatigue and proposed the establishment of a protectorate in West Africa to be administered by the United States. Perhaps Crummell derived the idea from other West Africans, like Blyden and Horton, who proposed similar schemes for British protectorates, or perhaps Crummell was made optimistic by reports of activities of the Freedmen's Bureau on behalf of the newly emancipated in America.[27]

An African nation dominated by an emigrant elite and supported by a foreign power would not seem the very essence of democracy to most observers. Crummell, however, was no democrat. To the objection that perhaps the Liberians had "no right to command, or press such regulations upon our native population," Crummell had an answer:

> All historic fact shows that force, that is authority, must be used in the exercise of guardianship over heathen tribes. Mere theories of democracy are trivial in this case, and can never nullify this necessity. You cannot apply them to a rude

people, incapable of perceiving their own place in the moral scale, nor of understanding the social and political obligations which belong to responsible humanity. "Force and right," says a brilliant writer, "are the governors of this world; *force till right is ready.* . . . And till right is ready, force, the existing order of things, is justified, is the legitimate ruler."[28]

Crummell's later years, 1873 to 1898, were characterized by attempts to adapt his Christian nationalism to an American environment, and to the demands of a more secular age. He returned to the United States in 1873 due to the violence that came to dominate Liberian life. Crummell had given the Fatherland the twenty best years of his life and was fifty-four years old when he returned to the New World to take up an active ministerial and intellectual career. He was still representative of separatist, conservative black thought and still continued to exalt the values of Christian civilization; to assert the need for authoritarian control of the Afro-American world; and to rely on mystical or irrational visions of an Ethiopian awakening.

August Meier has hinted at "the close affinity between Crummell's Liberian nationalism and his later advocacy of racial solidarity."[29] Indeed, one might observe that there are definite connections between the African civilizationist schemes of the 1850s and the philosophies of racial uplift in America inaugurated from the rise of Booker T. Washington to the fall of Marcus Garvey. The years following Crummell's return to the United States in 1873 witnessed a rebirth of the black nationalist spirit which had languished during the optimistic period of post-Civil War congressional ascendancy.

During these years, any blacks who had been laboring under the delusion that emancipation would result in the sudden democratization of American society were rapidly enlightened. It was becoming apparent to the post-bellum generation of black leaders that individual accomplishments offered little protection from the threats and abuses of the caste-like American system. The middle class Negroes would remain victims of prejudice, so long as the masses remained untutored, impoverished, and demoralized. The goal of uplifting the freedmen was similar to the goal of uplifting Africa, and was to be carried on for the same purposes as the old antebellum African civilizationism. The building of an Afro-American culture would demonstrate to all the world that blacks were able and willing to make a contribution to American life, and were, therefore, fit to be United States citizens. As the masses were elevated, the bourgeoisie would rise correspondingly. Crummell, a veteran of the pre-war movement, and a black nationalist of impeccable credentials, was particularly suited to act as the philosopher of uplift in post-Reconstruction America.

The same elitist approach to reform that characterized Crummell's career in Liberia was to remain an important element in his pronouncements after returning to the United States. In 1865, he addressed the Pennsylvania Colonization Society on the importance of involving an educated black elite in the regeneration of Africa. He spoke on the need for an indigenous missionary agency for the evangelization of Africa in Atlanta in 1895, and although he came to modify his view that the Afro-American was well suited to African missionary work, his basic commitment to the idea that blacks should uplift blacks remained unaltered. Crummell's faith in the importance of an uplifting elite was applied to an American context in his commencement address at Storer College, Harper's Ferry, West Virginia, on May 30, 1885. The elitist principles he stated were to characterize black nationalism of the Right, well into the twentieth century. His position amounted to a denial of the political importance of moral suasion, agitation, and propaganda. It signified an acceptance of the idea that blacks should be more concerned with mastering the culture of the Anglo-American gentry than with protesting political and educational injustices either of the past or the present.

Crummell's approach to the problem of racial uplift after the Civil War was philosophically similar to the antebellum idea of gradual abolitionism through African regeneration and universal Negro improvement. What it presupposed was that blacks were oppressed because of some flaw in themselves, and not only because of a moral flaw in the hearts of their oppressors. Such an attitude was anathema to those blacks who were of the radical egalitarian school. Frederick Douglass, who was in the audience, rose to take issue with Crummell, as Crummell himself reported:

It happened that my distinguished neighbor, Hon. Frederick

Douglass, was one of the audience on that occasion. The leading thought of the address—the shifting of general thought from past servitude, to duty and service, in the present;—met with his emphatic and most earnest protest. He took occasion, on the instant, to urge his hearers to a constant recollection of the slavery of their race and of the wrongs it had brought upon them.[30]

Undoubtedly, Douglass, who had once been a fugitive slave, was somewhat offended by the claims of Crummell (born a free man) that the recollection of slavery was a waste of time. Crummell had never been committed to the agitationist, camp-meeting style of rabble-rousing abolitionism. Militant abolitionism had been Douglass's stock-in-trade. Crummell had cooperated in a scheme for gradual abolitionism to be brought about as the result of some mighty project of race vindication. Douglass had believed in immediate abolitionism, and had seen human freedom and dignity as natural rights, not as privileges to be earned. Finally, Douglass was certainly bothered by the idea that the uplift of the freedmen could be accomplished solely through the missionary activities of the black leadership class and without benefit of agitation, publicity, and the law. Until his death, Crummell clung to the idea that blacks themselves were responsible for their condition. "There are evils which lie deeper than intellectual neglect or political injury," he maintained. It was "the greatest unwisdom" to pass over these deeper maladies "to attend to evils less virulent in their effects." Crummell felt that political organization ought not to be the first concern of black leaders. Rather, they should turn their attention to strengthening "three special points of weakness in our race," which he apprehended as, "THE STATUS OF THE FAMILY"; "THE CONDITIONS OF LABOR"; "THE ELEMENT OF MORALS."[31]

These emphases cannot be attributed solely to the cleric's professional concern for public morality. They also stemmed from Crummell's belief that the burden of responsibility for the uplifting of black people rested with the people themselves. Had the black family been destroyed by slavery? Then it was up to black people to "attempt the repair of this, the noblest of all the structures of human life. For the basis of all human progress and of all civilization is the family."[32] Was the state of black labor degraded? Then let black labor become better educated in hand and in head, for without the solution of the labor question "neither individual nor family life can secure their proper condition in this land."[33] Crummell felt that the uplift of black family life and of black workers should become the duty of the educated blacks. The day was past for appeals to the conscience of white America. The emancipation of American blacks from "injustice and grinding tyranny" was to be effected by the development of personal thrift, energy, and manliness. "To bring about these results," said Crummell, "we need intelligent men and women, so filled with philanthropy that they will go down to the humblest conditions of their race . . . [carrying] all the appliances of school and industries, in order to raise and elevate the most abject and needy race on American soil."

> *Who* are to be the agents to raise and elevate this people to a higher plane of being? The answer will at once flash upon your intelligence. It is to be affected (sic) by the scholars and philantropists which come forth in these days from the schools. *They* are to be the scholars; for to transform, stimulate and uplift a people is a work of intelligence. It is a work which demands the clear induction of historic facts and their application to new circumstances,—a work which will require the most skillful resources and the wise practicality of superior men.[34]

The uplift of black people was seen as being dependent upon character building and the elevation of moral life. The program of character building and moral regeneration was to be carried out through the work of an educated black elite. This was the genesis of the idea of the American Negro Academy and consequently the origin of the philosophy of the "Talented Tenth."

Crummell founded the American Negro Academy in 1897 for the purpose of undertaking "the civilization of the Negro race in the United States, by the scientific processes of literature, art, and philosophy."[35] In his inaugural address as president of the academy, he revealed the ideology of elitist reform that he shared with other members of the academy. Black people as a race in

America required an indigenous missionary force, elite bearers of culture who would guide them in the creation of an Afro-American civilization. This was a plan for domestic nationalism which would somehow perform many of the cultural and economic functions of a nation, while lacking both land, and the political apparatus of a state. After his return to the U.S.A., Crummell still retained some of the ideas he had attempted to apply to black Africans. A nation of people has an obligation to contribute to the world's civilization, but black people, taken as a whole, had produced no art, no science, no philosophy, no scholarship. As individuals, some blacks, it was true, had been successful in each of these areas, "but mere individuality cannot be recognized as the aggregation of a family, a nation, or a race; or as the interpretation of any of them."[36] It was necessary for Blacks to be able to claim a body of intellectual production distinctly their own, and to take their "place in the world of culture and enlightenment."

As an admirer of Plato, Crummell was predictably opposed to materialistic theories of race relations. "Men are constantly dogmatizing theories of sense and matter as the salvable hope of the race," he lamented. But these are "blind men!"

> For they fail to see that neither property, nor money, nor station, nor office, nor lineage, are fixed factors, in so large a thing as the destiny of man; that they are not vitalizing qualities in the changeless hopes of humanity. The greatness of peoples springs from their ability to grasp the grand conceptions of being. It is the absorption of a people, of a nation, of a race, in large majestic and abiding things which lifts them up to the skies.[37]

This was, implicitly, a criticism of the Booker T. Washington school of race relations. It was an attack on those who, in Crummell's words, gave the "cautious, restricted, limiting . . . advice" to "start at the bottom" with industrial training, rather than with the training of the mind. Crummell answered those who suggested that the Negro needed to learn to work by saying that labor was a necessity of life, "And the Negro has had it for centuries; but it has never given him manhood." The Negro did not need to learn to work, so much as he needed to learn the value of his labor. He needed to learn "intelligent impatience at the exploitation of his labor, on the one hand; on the other hand courage to demand a larger share of the wealth which his toil creates for others."[38]

Crummell, however, was guilty of the same racial stereotyping practiced by many of his ideological opponents—Booker T. Washington, for example—and his white supporters. He tended to see blacks as an aesthetically gifted people, strongly enthusiastic, but lacking in discipline.

> The mind of our people seems to be a hot-bed of rich, precocious, gorgeous and withal genuine plants:—and if I mistake not, I discover in it all, that permanent *tropical* element which characterizes all the peoples whose ancestral homes were in the southern latitudes; and who may be called "children of the sun. . . . " I see, nowhere, any counterbalance of the hardier studies, and more tasking scholarship, which serve to give vigor, hardihood and robustness to a race.[39]

It was thinking on this order that led to the militarization of the black academic experience in such institutions as Hampton and Tuskegee, where not only were trades taught, but a thoroughgoing military-industrial organization of community life was enforced.

Whether or not the authoritarian collectivism found in Crummell's political writing is in any way peculiarly black, it is persistently recurrent in the writing of his contemporaries. William H. Ferris, a protege of Crummell, who described himself as a "sometime reader of papers before the American Negro Academy and other literary societies," was, like Crummell, a clergyman and an advocate of authoritarian collectivism. Ferris's later appearance in the fascist Garvey movement is not surprising if one remembers his persistent racial chauvinism and involvement in authoritarian movements among elitist blacks. Sutton Griggs, who was, like Ferris, a trained minister, also tended to see collectivist authoritarian schemes as panaceas for racial problems. The quest of Negroes for individual success was almost, if not quite, a violation of the laws of God and nature. Was it not apparent that "every man in the world is affected, not only by his own reputation, but by that of the race to which he belongs"? His proposed solution to the racial problem in America was similar to Crummell's; it involved the development of a national science, art and literature.[40] And, of course, there must be an elite to guide the mass, for "even as the bees are nonplussed when they have no superior voice to guide, just so groups of people fail of the desired progress whenever they have no man among them of exceptional strength."[41]

Crummell's idea that individual Negroes could not hope to rise solely on their own merits was echoed by Bishop Henry McNeal Turner, who admitted being influenced by Crummell.[42] He tended to think of Negro attainments in purely collective terms, and denounced assimilationists and individualists as scullions, would-be whites, and fools.[43] John E. Bruce, a militant black journalist and close friend and intimate correspondent of Crummell, tended to see the solution to the Negro's problems in terms of solidarity, collective effort, and race pride, "for race, as Disraeli says, is the key to history."[44] William Hooper Councill felt that Negroes, as individuals, had no rights at all. Echoing Martin Delany's advice of a half-century earlier, he submitted that if individual Negroes wished to enjoy the right to hotel accomodations, for example, they should await the day when the race as a whole could point to hotels that were black-owned. Councill had a grotesquely exaggerated idea of white racial solidarity. He assumed that the whites had a great sense of loyalty to and respect for one another, and especially for the weaker members of their race. "I honor the white man because he honors himself," said Councill. "I honor him because he places his mother, sister, wife and daughter on a platform up among the stars, gets a thousand Gatling guns, and decrees death to him who seeks to drag them down. I honor him because he throws his powerful arms around every little red-headed, freckled-face, poor white girl and boy in the land and makes the way possible for them to rise in the world."[45] This, of course, was pure nonsense in an age characterized by the degradation of labor and the exploitation of women and children by the forces of free enterprise.

We have seen that Crummell was representative of a number of black intellectuals who publicized throughout the nineteenth century the idea that civilization is a universal absolute toward which all peoples should strive and that it had found its highest expression among the Western European peoples. Crummell was also committed to the idea that in order to command the respect that is due to civilized people, Africans would have to make a collective effort under elite leadership to contribute to the world's cultural wealth in a way that could be described as definitely "Negro."

Some mention has been made of the religious influences on Crummell's brand of thought. Black religion before the Civil War had tended, at once, to foster a spirit of resentment and revolt among blacks, who realized that slavery was in no way consistent with a nineteenth-century Christian philosophy; and at the same time it was a principal vehicle through which mainstream American values were assimilated by the masses of black people. Afro-American religion had another function; it provided an extrarational basis for a belief in the future ascendancy of blacks. Racial chauvinism was thinly veiled in Crummell's essay of 1877, "The Destined Superiority of the Negro." The temporary degradation of a race was no proof of God's disfavor. God was known to chastise his chosen peoples from time to time. "The merciful aspect of God's economy shines out in human history as clearly as His justice and judgment. The Almighty seizes upon superior nations and, by mingled chastisement and blessings, gradually leads them on to greatness."[46] The truth of this hypothesis was evident, as, for example, in the history of Israel under Egypt which was "a process of painful preparation for a coming national and ecclesiastical responsibility." So too was "the feudality of Europe. . . a system of training for a high and grand civilization." From Crummell's vantage point, there seemed to be a pattern in world history since the rise of Europe. Crummell would have been amazed by our contemporary society in which the profound influences of the non-Christian world are recognizable throughout a formerly Christian West, for to him it seemed that Christian civilization was advancing almost everywhere. Heathen peoples the world over were being destroyed by Western civilization. Whole tribes—indeed whole civilizations—of American Indians had been destroyed in the Americas as well as whole nations in the islands of the Pacific. But while doomed people had departed before the advance of the civilized Europeans, the Negro was surviving wave after wave of a destruction that swept over his head, so that by 1877, even in the lands of his thralldom, the Negro had risen "taller, more erect, more intelligent, and more aspiring than any of his ancestors for more than two thousand years of a previous era." The Negro, like the Anglo-Saxon, was an imitative being, and, like the Anglo-Saxon, capable of being civilized because of this quality of imitativeness. What had been characteristic of Greek and Roman civilization seemed to be characteristic of all the great civilizations of the past; they had become "cosmopolitan thieves." They "borrowed" culture from every quarter. The Negro's peculiarity of imitativeness "is often sneered at," said Crummell. "It is decried as the simulation of a well-known and grotesque animal."[47] But the traducers of the Negro seemed to forget that imitation was a proof of intelligence, not of stupidity, and that imitation is the basis of culture. Sojourning under the auspices of the most advanced civilization that history had known, endowed with the quality of imitativeness, and living under the protection of a merciful providence, there could be no doubt that the Negro would soon be marching on "in the pathway of progress to that superiority and eminence which is our rightful heritage, and which is evidently the promise of our God!" I can think of no simple explanation for Crummell's optimistic view of history, his reliance on Providence, his belief in progress. Perhaps it was the influence of Guizot or some of the even more nationalistic Europeans; perhaps it was the influence of the manifest destiny myth, growing in the fertile soul of boundless America; perhaps it was due to the Pan-Africanist ideology he himself had helped to evolve. Probably it was a combination of all these influences that led Crummell to formulate his black nationalism in just the way he did.

Francis J. Grimke recalled the remark of a brother Washington, D.C. minister who had once observed of Crummell, "why, the Doctor is a perfect Tsar." Another associate of Crummell once referred to him as "a born autocrat."[48] Crummell was not, however, a mere authoritarian personality; he was authoritarian by ideological commitment because of what he believed about God, man and society. It was not that Crummell was opposed to a free system; it was simply that he defined a free system as one "which proclaims the *duties* of citizens as well as their rights;

which confers its franchises as *trusts* as well as prerogatives; which distinguishes calm Republicanism from wild and lawless Democracy." He believed that government should be concerned not only with its subjects' temporal interests, but that it should also "seek their moral elevation, and aim to strengthen their souls." He felt that government should "reverence law in the person of rulers," and should recognize "the authority of God in governors and magistrates." Crummell was more Hamiltonian than Jeffersonian, although Jefferson would have agreed with Crummell that government is "an ordinance of God; which holds all human law as subject to the higher law of heaven."[49]

At the time of President Garfield's assasination, Crummell again spoke of the evils of democracy, hailing Alexander Hamilton as "that great political prophet!" "Your president," he instructed his congregation, "is as much a ruler; he is as truly a potentate as the Emperor of Russia or the Queen of Great Britain. He is your ruler and grand magistrate and mine. And he sits in his chair of authority by the will of God, declared in governmental arrangements, as distinctly and positively as though he had been born to the office." Cynical with respect to Jeffersonian egalitarianism, and like his friend Francis J. Grimke, a "black puritan," Crummell was no believer in the essential goodness of man but spoke rather of the "pride and self-assertion of degenerate humanity."[50] For this reason, then, he said, "the theory of the Declaration is incomplete and misleading. Governments, my brethren, derive their just authority, *first* of all from the will of God; and then next, from the consent of the governed. It is because of the exclusion of this prime factor in this axiom that the governments of the earth are all more or less sick and diseased."[51] Crummell was revealing an emotion common to black people when he expressed disapproval of Jefferson, for certainly there are few black intellectuals who have not seen *The Declaration of Independence* as representing the ultimate in hypocrisy.

It is with caution that one suggests that Crummell may have been influential in any areas other than those already mentioned, to wit, in the development of black Nationalist ideology. One essay of Crummell's, however, does seem to have anticipated the direction in which much sociological writing in the twentieth century would move. Crummell was, of course, one of the first persons to attempt to write on Negro problems from a scientific rather than a purely rhetorical point of view. As early as 1846, we notice in Crummell's work an admiration for facts and statistics, and we notice that he, more than most other black authors of the nineteenth century, tended to use dates and census reports in his essays. While Crummell's methods were not sophisticated in any modern sense, they were certainly respectable considering that many white contemporaries were still under the influence of pseudoscientific social theories based on phrenology or physiognomic traits.[52] Crummell's pioneering efforts at sociological approaches to the white problem in America can be seen at work in an essay entitled, "The Black Woman of the South, Her Neglects and Her Needs," originally an address before the Freedman's Aid Society in Ocean Grove, New Jersey, delivered on August 15, 1883. "The Black Woman of the South" anticipated the work of E. Franklin Frazier in *The Negro Family* (1939). Of particular interest is Crummell's attributing black cultural disadvantagement to the heritage of slavery and its effects upon black womanhood and family structure. He argued that the exploitation of black female labor as well as the sexual exploitation of black women under slavery were not dead issues in 1883, but that their effects persisted after some twenty years. He anticipated Frazier's speculations on the nature of pregnancy and childbirth under a slave system, where the woman was forced to work "down to the period of those maternal anxieties, which in ordinary civilized life, give repose, quiet and care to expectant mothers."[53] She became the mother of children who were not her own, often fathered by a man with whom she could share no feelings even of temporary commitment. In her life, said Crummell, "there was no sanctity of family, no binding tie of marriage, none of the fine felicities and the endearing affections of home." The implications of this were largely left to the reader's imagination, but it was evident that Crummell believed that slavery had damaged black womanhood and the Negro family to an extent that the years since slavery had not erased.

The similarities to Frazier's *The Negro Family* should be obvious. Frazier knew of Crummell's work, and he too argued that the effects of slavery were still operative in the Negro family. Like Crummell, he believed that for the black slave woman, pregnancy and childbirth were traumatic, rather than pleasurable experiences.[54] Furthermore, the instability of the marital institution, which Crummell had found so remarkable, was seen as leading to a matriarchial family structure. Frazier's influences on Daniel Patrick Moynihan are so obvious and so often commented upon that we need only mention them here. It is interesting to note, however, that Moynihan (whose ideas have had some effect on American domestic and foreign policy) established his reputation on the basis of an idea admittedly borrowed from Frazier, but ultimately traceable to Alexander Crummell.

The long life of Alexander Crummell illustrates the continuity of the black nationalist tradition throughout the nineteenth century. A victim of the tyranny of the majority, forced to flee his republican birthplace to find greater freedom under the British crown, Crummell developed an early hostility to democracy. A devoted Platonist who "jokingly claimed to be a lineal descendant of the bee which tradition asserts lighted on the infant philosopher's lips to taste of that latent sweetness," he was hostile to Locke, to Jefferson and to the Enlightenment. Crummell was a racial romantic whose social theory derived from Guizot, Carlyle, and the Anglican philologist, Richard C. Trench. Crummell also seems to have been impressed by the German idealists, as his disciple, Du Bois, so obviously was. Like most black nationalists, Crummell was in no way dependent upon American social theorists for the underpinnings of his nationalistic philosophy.

In later years Crummell's antimaterialism led him to attack the industrial faddism of the day, although he consistently advocated training black youth to know the value of physical labor. He influenced W.E.B. Du Bois and William H. Ferris, who would later move in the direction of anti-Washingtonian positions. Crummell's attempt to write a descriptive sociology of the Negro and to explain social problems in terms of social facts was advanced for the times. His interest in Africa (persisting until his death and not terminating with his return to the United States) helped him to disseminate knowledge about Africa among the black intellectuals in his circle. But probably the most important thing that can be said about Crummell is that he provided a personal, as well as an ideological link between the African civilizationism of the nineteenth century and the separatist, authoritarian, mystical, Negro improvement movements that are preserved among Afro-Americans, until the present day.

Chapter Four

From Frederick Douglass to Booker T. Washington
The Reconstruction of the Negro

Frederick Douglass was born a slave in Tuckahoe, Maryland, around 1817; he never knew the exact date. Douglass was unaware of his father's identity, although he heard it whispered about the plantation that his master was his father. He never saw his mother "more than four or five times" in his life. As a slave, Douglass learned that the peculiar institution brutalized the slave and hardened the heart of the master. Even as a child, his reasoning led him to the belief that slavery was a sin, a crime against reason and Christian principles. First stealing the forbidden knowledge of letters, then clawing at such limited snatches of abolitionist literature as floated within his grasp, Douglass began to adopt the religion of the oppressed, saw God on his side, and became increasingly resentful over his condition. Escaping from slavery in 1838, he became an abolitionist lecturer, a journalist, and a spokesman for the black man. He allowed abolitionist friends to purchase his freedom, and his powerful skills as an orator and publicist brought him to national prominence as an advocate of reform causes. As a former slave, Douglass was a convincing representative of the aspirations of the masses of nineteenth-century black Americans. Of the principal black nationalist literati among his contemporaries—Crummell, Delany, Garnet, Holly—none had been adult slaves. They were not the authentic representatives of an enslaved people that Douglass was. Aggressive, tough, contentious, and self-confident, Douglass delighted in shocking the sensibilities of a racist society by promenading down New York City's Broadway in 1849 with an English lady on each arm.[1]

Douglass was the nineteenth century's most effective publicist for the doctrines of social equality and racial assimilation. Usually contrasted by scholars to the black nationalists among his contemporaries—Crummell, Delany, and Garnet—Douglass displayed considerable hostility to the idea of racial repatriation. Despite the fact that he was the best known apologist for the Afro-American people in his day, Douglass was hostile to the idea of racial pride, which he bluntly denounced as "ridiculous."[2] His second marriage, in 1884 to a white woman, Helen Pitts, has no doubt contributed to the opinion that he was antinationalistic.[3] Douglass has nonetheless claimed a place in the litany of black nationalist saints, and his essays appear in the best known anthologies of black nationalist writings. Although the general tenor of his remarks on black nationalism during fifty years of public life was negative, Douglass, like most black Americans, occasionally displayed nationalistic sentiment.

This took the form of a concern for ethnic self-assertion. In the premier issue of his first newspaper, *The North Star*, Douglass's editorial was characterized by a civilizationistic rhetoric that would have done Crummell proud:

> It is evident we must be our own representatives and advocates, not exclusively, but particularly—not distinct from, but in connection with our white friends. In the grand struggle for liberty and equality now waging, it is meet, right and essential that there should arise in our ranks authors and editors, as well as orators, for it is in these capacities that the most permanent good can be rendered to our cause. . . . Our race must be vindicated from the embarrassing imputations resulting from former nonsuccess.[4]

The inaugural editorial in *Douglass' Monthly* eleven years later showed dedication to the same principles of race vindication that the earlier journal had advocated. It was committed to publicizing the achievements of colored people and working to refute the prejudices against the black man's mental and moral attributes. It was to be a journal addressed both to the black and to the white community, concerned with directing "the colored minds of the country to the paths of wisdom and virtue."[5] Douglass always believed that the elevation of the colored minds in America should be assigned a higher priority than any African project; therefore, he remained a domestic, rather than an African, civilizationist.

Douglass felt it necessary to explain his reasons for founding a "colored newspaper." He did not want to be misunderstood as condoning institutional segregation, and he recognized that separate black institutions might be seen as maintaining "an odious and wicked distinction between white and colored persons." But, he argued, there was "neither good sense nor common honesty" in trying to forget the distinction between white and black. In order to remove this "odious distinction," it was necessary for blacks to become as successful as whites "in the race of improvement." While Douglass did not want to give his newspaper the character of a racially exclusive enterprise, he clearly saw himself as embarking on a project of racial vindication. Not only would he publicize the ethnic concerns of the black community, he would prove the abilities of colored men by means of his own success.[6]

The strain of authoritarian collectivism, which argued for the control of the destinies of black peoples under the leadership of civilizing elites, was not an aspect of Douglass's ideology. But Douglass was hardly devoid of a sense of communal feeling, a sense of solidarity with the masses of blacks, or a sense of sharing in their sufferings. He resented the attempts of the more extreme nationalists to impose duties upon him, but he was not reluctant to acknowledge a union with, and a sense of duty to his sable brethren. Disagreeing with his friend, William Whipper, a black businessman from Philadelphia who firmly opposed almost all racial separatism, Douglass supported the idea of a colored "National League" saying, "we wish colored men could be induced to make any kind of an issue. We want some signs of life—some evidence of a common desire to improve our present condition and to take some position in the moral world." Douglass reminded the readers of the *North Star* "that we are one, that our cause is one, and that we must help each other, if we would succeed." He protested, with greater credibility than most of the leading migrationists could muster, that he was a man of the people. "We have drunk to the dregs the bitter cup of slavery; we have worn the heavy yoke; we have sighed beneath our bonds, and writhed beneath the bloodly lash;—cruel mementoes of our oneness are indelibly marked in our living flesh."[7]

While Douglass was committed to racial uplift and ethnic solidarity, he was impatient with talk of emigration, as is often observed. That Douglass opposed the principles for which the American Colonization Society stood is hardly startling, since even among the principal black nationalist extremists, like Delany and Garnet, there was little support for that institution. Douglass safely assumed that he could speak for the vast majority of colored people when he asserted that even with financial support, "it is idle to think of inducing any considerable number of the free colored people to quit this for a foreign land."[8] On June 8, 1849, he gave a speech in Faneuil Hall decrying the objectives of the American Colonization Society, and denouncing its president, Henry Clay of Kentucky. The Society was an undemocratic institution which preached that color prejudice could never be overcome, that the Negro was inferior, and therefore that the two races were not capable of living together in harmony. "It is because the American Colonization Society cherishes and fosters this feeling of hatred against the black man, that I am opposed to it."[9]

For the efforts of the African Civilization Society, Douglass had little more admiration. One of his principal reasons for opposing the work of this ostensibly black-controlled group had to do with Douglass's own color consciousness. Like many Negroes who could not boast of unadulterated African ancestry, he was offended by much of the rhetoric of the civilizationists, which had to do with "keeping the black race black," and "preserving the identity of the black man." Some mulattoes, Douglass among them, felt that they had nothing to gain by associating themselves with chauvinists of either "pure race."[10] When challenged by Henry Highland Garnet, president of the African Civilization Society, to explain to the readers of *Douglass' Monthly* "what your objections are to the civilization and Christianization of Africa," Douglass responded that he had no objections whatsoever, but "the African Civilization Society says to us, go to Africa, raise cotton, civilize the natives, become planters, merchants, compete with the slave States in the Liverpool cotton market, and thus break down American slavery. To which we simply and briefly reply, 'we prefer to remain in America.'"[11] Douglass refused to cooperate with the Civilization Society because he saw it as encouraging the idea that Africa, and not America, was the home of the Black American. This is the "wolfish idea," said Douglass, "that elbows us off the sidewalk and denies us the rights of citizenship." It was an idea that would have died out long ago "but for the jesuitical and persistent teaching of the American Colonization Society."[12] The Civilization Society was not militant enough in the struggle for the abolition of slavery and the uplifting of Afro-Americans in the land of their birth.

The Haitian form of migrationism was no more acceptable to him than the African form. Although from November of 1860 to May of 1861, Douglass seems to have flirted with the idea of Caribbean black nationalism, his attitudes before and after that brief period were negative. An editorial in *Douglass' Monthly* for May of 1859 reads:

> Things in Hayti certainly do look at the present moment rather inviting to a certain class of our colored friends. But how long Hayti will wear its present *inviting complexion,* is rather uncertain. That country is French in its sentiments, French in its ideas and French in its sudden and violent changes. It is, to say the least, prudent in making up ones mind about going there to settle, duly to consider this fact, and the consequences arising out of it. It would be a sad thing to some of us, who have been hated and persecuted the first half of our lives for being too black, to go there and be hated and persecuted during the last half of life for being *too white.*

These sentiments were restated on another page of that same issue of *Douglass' Monthly.* The editor felt it more reasonable to assume that "the white and colored people of America can live here in the peaceable enjoyment of equal rights, than that the black and mulatto races can so live in Hayti." In that same issue, however, there appeared a letter from James Redpath who had made a trip to Haiti and seemed interested in continuing to investigate that nation's prospects. Redpath's articles over the ensuing twelve months presented a fairly positive image of the island republic.[13] The only instance in which Douglass showed even mild enthusiasm for migration was in May of 1861, when he announced on the first page of *Douglass' Monthly* his "dream fondly indulged," his "desire long cherished," to travel to Hayti. The purpose of the trip was to investigate the possibilities of resettling the black American population there. But on the second page of that issue Douglass announced the firing on Fort Sumter, saying, "this is no time for us to leave the country."[14]

Since his attitudes with respect to Haitian emigration had never been better than lukewarm, it is hardly startling that by June 16, Douglass had once again turned his back upon colonization. More surprising is the reversal of opinion among such African civilizationists as Daniel A. Payne, Henry Highland Garnet, and Martin Delany, who all developed renewed interest in the United States and the possibilities of becoming full-fledged citizens. Payne, who was one of many ministers connected with the African Civilization Society, revealed a less than enthusiastic reaction to the colonization proposal that Abraham Lincoln advanced before a group of free blacks in an audience of August 14, 1862. Payne held that it was "a moral and religious, as well as a political duty," to respect the legally constituted authorities of one's country. He felt that blacks would find it difficult to ignore presidential colonization which would obviously function with greater authority than had the nongovernmental program of the American Colonization Society. Payne observed that the opinions of the executive were "based upon the ideas, that *white men and colored men cannot live together as equals in the same country;* and that unless a voluntary and peaceable separation is effected *now,* the time *must come when there will be a war of extermination* between the two races." Since this was Lincoln's opinion, Payne advised his brethren neither to resist nor to comply, but to supplicate the throne of God in prayer. He did not speak in the tones of one who welcomed the presidential proposal.[15]

> To your knees, I say, O ye oppressed and enslaved ones of this Christian republic, to your knees, *and be there.*
> Before the throne of God, if nowhere else, the black man can meet his white brother as an equal, and be heard.

Douglass's reactions were, of course, more directly negative. He compared the President's thinking to that of horsethieves and highwaymen. Certain black citizens' meetings in several states also reacted strongly, which served to undermine the support given to Redpath's Haytian Bureau of Emigration by such notables as Brown, Garnet, and Holly.[16] By the end of the war, Brown and Garnet, but not Holly, had returned to the nativist fold. Garnet addressed the United States Congress on February 12, 1865, expressing his hope that the United States might contribute to civilization "the form of a model republic, founded on the principles of justice and humanity, and Christianity, in which the burdens of war and the blessings of peace are equally borne and enjoyed by all."[17] Martin Delany's nationalism began to focus more on domestic concerns with the outset of the war. He had an interview with Lincoln on February 8, 1865, at which he claimed to have proposed to the President "an army of blacks, commanded entirely by black officers."[18] For the remainder of his life, Delany showed greater interest in establishing himself in South Carolina politics than in establishing an empire in West Africa.[19]

Reconstruction provided opportunities for a new style of black leadership, making room for the practical politicians and allowing the more versatile man of letters to direct his skills towards pragmatic considerations. Sometimes concerns became too pragmatic: Delany seemed to have lost his moral compass, and by the election of 1876, had damaged his own credibility as well as his standing with the radical republicans through personal thoughtlessness and his decision to support the deceptive Wade Hampton.[20] New leaders like Robert Smalls and Robert Brown Elliott were committed, as was Delany, to effecting compromises whereby whites and blacks could live together peaceably but with dignity for both.[21] Alexander Crummell, who was perhaps the sincerest of all the ideological, idealistic nationalists, was acting out his commitments to Liberia, and the tradition of Ethiopian rhetoric languished during the reconstruction years. By the late 1870s however, the spirit of exodus was again asserting itself; this time, not only among a group of urban intellectuals, but among the masses of the people and their grass roots leaders. Migration out of the South in the directions of either Africa, the urban centers of the United States, or the western lands, was an accelerating trend that even Douglass's injunctions had no power to halt. Pap Singleton, an itinerant preacher, urged Negroes to migrate to Kansas and establish all-black towns.[22] Henry Adams organized a movement in several states to institutionalize black political protest throughout the black belt.[23] Edwin P. McCabe advocated that blacks take over the state of Oklahoma and elect black congressmen to both houses.[24] Henry McNeal Turner, gaining the aid of Blyden and the not quite moribund American Colonization Society, began his agitation for a new back-to-Africa movement.[25] Garnet accepted a Liberian ambassadorship, sailed for Africa, and died in the Fatherland in 1882.[26]

The same opposition to separatism that had typified Douglass's editorial policies during the antebellum years characterized his public statements during the later decades of the nineteenth century. He remained hostile throughout his life to the mystical, pseudo-Christian racial rhetoric of the Blydens and the Crummells, and he attacked the emigration proposals resurgent during his last years.[27] He believed in neither the sanctity nor the permanency of races, and seems to have wasted little time pondering the concept of racial genius. His selective support of all-black institutions was pragmatic rather than chauvinistic. Douglass felt that separate instituitons might, in some cases, be conscionable as temporary measures while the freedmen were adjusting to their new state and developing confidence and strength. For example, he was "heartily in favor of all educational institutions for the present education of colored people, even though they be separate institutions."[28] But he added, "present circumstances are the only apology for such institutions." Unlike the nationalists of the Crummell tradition, he had no dreams of developing a "black civilization" in the United States, no emotional or aesthetic attraction to any such ideal. In an interview with I. Garland Penn during the late years of his life, Douglass expressed the view that the molders of opinion in the black community should "say less about race and claims to race recognition, and more about justice, liberty, and patriotism."[29] Consistent on all really important matters, "Douglass, in his old age, still bravely stood for the ideals of his early manhood,— ultimate assimilation *through* self-assertion, and on no other terms."[30]

The public personalities of Frederick Douglass and Booker T. Washington are so often contrasted that one may easily overlook the points at which the two men's philosophies resemble each other.[31] Washington admirered Douglass and saw himself as the legitimate heir to the mantle of the older race leader. His opinions were, in many cases, logical extensions of Douglass's. Both were self-made men in an age of enterprise, and hoped to see the masses of black people catch the spirit of the times. Both were associated with the rhetoric of rugged individualism, rather than with the gospel of racial collectivism. Both were inclined to place a disproportionate amount of the blame for what was at that time called the "Negro problem" upon the blacks themselves for they were victims of the technocratic myth—the belief that the problems of African assimilation into American life could be solved simply by equipping the blacks with skills necessary to the larger society.

The optimistic faith that technical training could work miracles for the Negro's problems was a black manifestation of the prevailing trend in American life toward industrial and technological professionalization during the nineteenth century. In the white world this trend manifested itself in the establishment of mechanics' institutes and trade schools, which de-emphasized classical education in favor of industrial training. Typical was the Mechanics Institute of Cincinnati, founded in 1828, where instruction was offered in such areas as botany, chemistry, mechanics, geometry, and arithmetic. The idea of the institute was to provide training in the higher sciences that had hitherto been available only in the colleges and universities, and at the same time to offer practical experience in the mechanical arts. The opinion was that "those who are engaged in the mechanic arts and manufactures would make better progress by being acquainted with the scientific principles on which those arts are founded."[32] The interest among antebellum free blacks in the establishment of trade schools was an outgrowth of this movement. Interest was also stimulated by the fact that the apprentice system of industrial training, with its dependency upon ties of friendship and family, provided few opportunities for black youth to master industrial skills.

Frederick Douglass advocated industrial training for black

youth not only because of his exposure to the rhetoric of industrial education, which was already prevalent by the time of his escape from slavery, but also as a result of his work experiences. While still a slave in Baltimore, Maryland, he had "hired out" as an apprentice caulker in William Gardiner's shipyard, and had encountered the difficulties attendant upon a black man's securing a trade. During the eight months that he worked for Gardiner, Douglass learned little of the caulker's trade. His duties were to run errands for the seventy or eighty carpenters employed in the shipyard, all of whom seemed to demand his services at once, and most of whom resented his presence. Hostility between black and white workers was rife in Baltimore during the 1830s. White artisans feared, as Douglass observed, "that educating slaves to be mechanics might, in the end, give slavemasters power to dispense with the services of the poor white man." This led to a reluctance and in some instances to an outright refusal by white tradesmen to work side by side with blacks. Douglass's resentful manner led to his being beaten and ejected from Gardiner's shipyard. He was finally able to learn something of the caulker's trade while subsequently employed in the shipyard of Walter Price, where he was trained by fellow black workers.[33]

In a letter to Harriet Beecher Stowe, Douglass remarked that he could more easily get his son "into a lawyer's office to study law than . . . into a blacksmith's shop to blow the bellows and to wield the sledgehammer."[34] In the pre-Civil War decade, he argued that "a purely educational institution" could not meet the needs of the blacks and that the free colored people required training even more basic than that provided by the ordinary industrial school. What Douglass envisioned was "a series of workshops where colored people could learn some of the handicrafts, learn to work in iron, wood, and leather, and where a plain English education could also be taught." Writing in his own newspaper in 1854, he went so far as to suggest that those abolitionists who refused to support the trade school movement were really not true friends. The presence of a large population of free blacks, he argued, who were "*poor, ignorant*, and *degraded*," strengthened the arguments of those who would doom the race to perpetual bondage. Douglass capped his argument with the ringing aphorism, "*the free colored man's elevation is essential to the slave colored man's emancipation.*"[35]

Free people of color, meeting in conventions during the three decades preceding the Civil War, showed marked interest in the trade school movement. The Philadelphia convention of 1831 adopted a plan "that a college be established at New Haven as soon as $20,000 are obtained, and to be on the Manual Labour System, by which in connexion with a scientific education they [Young Men of Colour] may also obtain a useful Mechanical or Agricultural progession." The conventions were never able to follow through even on such modest resolutions as this, however, due to their inability to amass the required funds. Subsequent conventions, throughout the 1830s and 1840s continued to recommend the establishment of trade schools and to encourage business education. Douglass supported the trade school movement of the conventions and in 1848, he served on a committee of five who drew up a position paper stating that "every blow of the sledge hammer, wielded by a sable arm, is a powerful blow in support of our cause. Every colored mechanic, is by virtue of circumstances, an elevator of his race. . . . Trades are important. Wherever a man may be thrown by misfortune, if he has in his hands a useful trade, he is useful to his fellow man, and will be esteemed accordingly. . . ." A naive notion, but one that was to dominate the thought of Booker T. Washington and many other black leaders during the later years of the nineteenth century.[36]

When Booker T. Washington rose to speak in Atlanta on September 18, 1895, he did not see himself as the betrayer of a dream, nor was he abondoning the platform of Frederick Douglass, who had died on February 20 of that same year. Washington idolized Douglass, and with the aid of his friends, the S. Laing Williamses of Chicago, wrote a biography of his hero, in which he was reverential in all respects. "I heard so much about Douglass when I was a boy," he said, "that one of the reasons why I wanted to go to school and learn to read was that I might read for myself what he had written and said." One of the first books that Washington tells us he read was the *Life and Times*, which he said "made a great impression on me, and I read it many times." In spite of this great admiration, however, Washington felt that "the long and bitter political struggle in which he had engaged against slavery had not prepared Mr. Douglass to take up the equally difficult task of fitting the Negro for the opportunities and responsibilities of freedom."[37] Washington was aware of Douglass's efforts on behalf of industrial schools, both before and after the Civil War. He called attention to the fact that Douglass had helped in the founding of a trade school in Manassas, Virginia. Indeed, Douglass made a trip to Tuskegee to deliver a commencement address, saying, "When you are working with your hands they grow larger; the same is true of your heads. . . . Seek to acquire knowledge as well as property, and in time you will have the honor of going to Congress."[38]

Washington conceived of the differences between himself and Douglass not as fundamental differences of opinion, but as differences in emphasis. Washington tended to play down the militant agitationist elements of Douglass's message and to play up the rhetoric of self-criticism and self-sufficiency. Especially appealing to Washington were the aphoristic statements in Douglass's address before the Tennessee Colored Agricultural and Mechanical Association at Nashville, September 18, 1873. "If we look abroad over our country and observe the condition of the colored people," said Douglass, "we shall find their greatest want to be regular and lucrative employment for their energies. They have secured their freedom, it is true, but not the friendship and favor of the people around them. . . ."[39] This speech and at least one other address delivered in the early seventies were decidely Washingtonian in their appraisal of the Negro's prospects in the South.[40]

Booker T. Washington's "Atlanta Exposition Address" was certainly different in tone from what is commonly associated with Douglass, but there were points at which it definitely intersected with the ideas of the earlier leader. For example, the Atlanta Compromise displayed an open hostility to white trade unionism, and to the self-assertiveness of organized labor, a hostility that Douglass also felt. Washington's advice to "cast down your bucket where you are . . . in agriculture, mechanics, in commerce, in domestic service, and in the professions," is reminiscent of Douglass's statement at the Colored Convention of 1848. Douglass had, on that occasion, argued that blacks should accept whatever gainful employment it was necessary for them to accept—whether that consisted of domestic service, the sweeping of chimneys, or the practice of law.[41] The Atlanta Exposition Address resulted in the Tuskegeean's offices being flooded with letters and telegrams "demanding that I take the place of 'leader of the Negro people', left vacant by Frederick Douglass's death, or assuming that I had already taken this place." Washington was surprised at first, he claimed, but it was not long before he "began to find out what was expected of me in the new position into which a sudden newspaper notoriety seemed to have thrust me."[42]

Washington himself was fond of emphasizing the similarities of his economic doctrine to that of the older race leader:

> Mr. Douglass had the same idea concerning that importance and value of industrial education that I have tried to emphasize. He also held the same views as I do in regard to the emigration of the Negro to Africa, and was opposed to the scheme of diffusion and dissemination of the Negro throughout the North and Northwest, believing as I do that the Southern section of the country where the Negro now resides is the best place for him. In fact, the more I have studied the life of Mr. Douglass the more I have been surprised to find his far-reaching and generous grasp of the whole condition and needs of the Negro race.[43]

Washington resembled Douglass in one other significant area: like his predecessor, Washington gave the impression of believing that wealth was the ultimate solution to the black man's problems. Douglass once argued that "the want of money is the root of all evil to the colored people."[44] Douglass advised blacks to emulate the Jews, and to acquire wealth as the Jews supposedly did. "A Hebrew may even now be rudely repulsed from the door of a hotel; but he will not on that account get up another Exodus, as he did three thousand years ago, but will quietly "put money in his purse" and bide his time . . . "[45] At another time he said, with exceeding naivete,"the Jew was once despised and hated in Europe, and is so still in some parts of that continent; but he has risen, and is still rising to higher consideration, and no man is now degraded by association with him anywhere."[46] This statement was made ten years before the sentencing of Colonel Dreyfus to life on Devil's Island, and five years before the birth of Hitler. Washington, like Douglass, had great admiration for the Jews, whom he said blacks should consider "a bright and shining example. . . . They have a certain amount of unity, pride, and love of race; and as the years go on, they will be more and more influential in this country."[47] Washington observed that "notwithstanding the barriers in this country, one of the most noted banking firms in the United States is composed of Jews. Members of a despised race, they made up their minds that in spite of difficulties they would not stop to complain, but would compel recognition by making a real contribution to the country of which they formed a part."[48]

While both Douglass and Washington spoke occasionally of black unity, both men were individualistic by temperament. They rebelled against the organic collectivism of the Delanys, Blydens, and Crummells. "Individually," said Washington, "the Negro is strong, organically he is weak."[49] In 1889, speaking before the Bethel Literary Society, Douglass said, "I hold that our union is our weakness . . . colored men seem to forget that there are exceptions to all rules, and that our position in this country is an exeptional position. . . . There are times and places when separation and disunion are better than union, when to stand apart is wiser than standing together."[50] The Washington-Douglass conception of black economic development differed greatly from that offered by Elijah Muhammad. Black businessmen and tradesmen were not to isolate themselves from the larger society, selling only to blacks, nor were black consumers to patronize black artisans and merchants only because they were black.[51] The Negro in America was to advance himself by free competition on the open market. Their economic philosophies were essentially laissez faire formulae for black advancement through individual commitment by individual blacks to the gospel of work and wealth. Their ultimate goal was not to build a black counterculture. "A nation within a nation," said Douglass, "is an anomaly."[52] The purpose of Douglass and Washington was to encourage black unity and self-assertion on a political level, while encouraging cultural and economic assimilation.[53] This would theoretically result in integration of blacks into mainstream American society, after the manner in which the Jews seemed to be blending into European and American society.

Although there were similarities at certain points between the philosophies of Frederick Douglass and Booker T. Washington, there was an essential difference in their ultimate objectives. Douglass worked to make a new America; Washington worked to make a new Negro. Washington, like Douglass, worked for the assimilation of blacks into the American society and culture, but he resembled the antebellum traditionalists in his timidity with respect to changing the social system. He hoped to see blacks ultimately assimilated into the American system, but he seemed blind to many obvious failings of the system. He spoke of blacks as a "new race" or a "new people," as if Negroes still required some finishing touches of the evolutionary process.[54] Washington wanted to create a "a new Negro for a new century," a twentieth century black man particularly adapted to assume a new role in American life.[55] Douglass realized that it was in the nature of man to adapt his environment, not himself. This is what humanity is really all about. Washington seemed to forget that civilization is a process occurring not only in man, but also in his environment.

Washington was born a slave in Franklin County, Virginia, but was unsure of the place or date. It was around 1856, and "in a typical log cabin." He knew nothing of his father other than the rumor "that he was a white man who lived on one of the near-by plantations." He spent his boyhood in Malden, West Virginia, where he lived in poverty until the age of sixteen, when he walked back to Virginia to attend Hampton Institute. As founder of Tuskegee, Washington proved to be a humane and innovative teacher, who, like his contemporary, John Dewey, believed that people learned by doing. But like General Samuel C. Armstrong, the model of his youth, Washington had a grim, puritanical view of life. His goal was to make black people into a noble and Spartanlike caste—if caste apart they must be—humble, civic-minded, and duty bound. Du Bois observed in Washington "singleness of vision and thorough oneness with his age . . . the mark of the successful man," adding, "it is as though Nature must needs make men narrow in order to give them force."[56]

Washington's celebrated "Atlanta Exposition Address" is said to have moved the Negroes in the audience to tears; whether these were tears of joy at seeing a black man on the podium, or tears of dismay at hearing their rights compromised away by a black man is left to the historian's speculations. Rayford Logan has been of the opinion that "Washington's Atlanta Compromise Address consoled the consciences of the judges of the Supreme Court who, in *Plessy v. Ferguson*, the following year, wrote into American jurisprudence one of its least defensible doctrines, the constitutionality of equal but separate accomodations." Saunders Redding has said that if Douglass had not been dead for eight months at the time of the speech, he would have condemned it as "weasel, mealy-mouthed, and reactionary." C. Vann Woodward called the Atlanta Compromise Address "a renunciation of active political aspirations for the Negro," and said that "it had an important bearing upon the movement for disfranchisement."[57]

The address was actually a brilliant and subtle piece of Anglo-African chauvinism, and an artful statement of the assimilated Negro's case. Washington played upon the Anglo-Americans' xenophobic fears of Catholics and Jews, of southern Europeans and Slavs, "those of foreign birth and strange tongue and habits." He conjured up images of dirty-bearded and foul-breathed anarchy streaming into the cities of the North. He contrasted this with reminders of the passivity of the South's Negroes, who, he reminisced, had nursed the children, watched by the sickbeds of aged parents, and "followed them with tear-dimmed eyes to their graves." He promised:

> ... we shall stand by you with a devotion that no foreigner can approach, ready to lay down our lives, if need be, in defence of yours, interlacing our industrial, commercial, civil, and religious life with yours in a way that shall make the interests of both races one. In all things that are purely social we can be as separate as the fingers, yet one as the hand in all things essential to mutual progress.[58]

This was Washington's tour de force, his suggestion that Protestant English speaking blacks were culturally superior to non-American whites. And was it not true that black people who already had a place in the South were potentially less disruptive than immigrants, and less likely to contaminate society with radical ideas?

If the South appreciated the social implications of Washington's statements, Northern industrialists pricked up their ears at the economic implications. What Washington seemed to be saying was that Tuskegee was training black industrial workers to preserve their old traditions of mining the hills and building the railroads "without strikes and labor wars." Here was a labor force so loyal to management that they hid the old plantation silver from the Yankee troops. Here were workers whose fidelity and love had been tested when to have proved false would have meant the ruin of the hearthside. If Washington could produce such workers, with skill far above average, yet blindly loyal, he was indeed a friend of the American capitalist. White labor would have to fall into line with company policy, at the threat of being replaced with such an accomodating and efficient army. Washington was unable to view the labor problems of the South as a gestalt; he understood only that blacks were an exploited labor force. Among his contemporaries were those who, like Timothy Thomas Fortune, recognized that the labor problems of blacks required more complex solutions than Washington proposed.[59]

Fortune, like Douglass and Washington, was born a slave, and inherited Douglass's role as principal militant journalist and theorist of social change. Described by one biographer as "an author, a journalist, an agitator, and a lecturer," Fortune was a true radical.[60] Like Douglass, he had experienced the hostilities of the white working class, but his reaction to racial hostility was not so emotional as to blind Fortune to the importance of economic issues in race relations.[61] In 1884, Fortune published a sophisticated piece of journalism, and, for its time, a superior piece of sociology: *Black and White: Land Labor and Politics in the South.* The main purpose of the work was "to show that the social problems in the South are, in the main, the same as those which afflict every civilized country on the globe: and that the future conflict in that section will not be racial or political in character, but between capital on the one hand and labor on the other."[62] Fortune was not free of some of the myths that seem to predominate in black nationalist thinking, such as the one that "colored people are naturally sociable, and intensely religious . . . they are musical, humorous and generous to a fault."[63] He was inclined to nationalism, this sensitive, ectomorphic, fair-haired quadroon who attacked the migrationist, Bishop Turner, in his youth, but who served as an editor of Marcus Garvey's *Negro World* in his old age.[64] He provided an ideological link between the philosophies of Washington and Douglass, cooperating at times with the Tuskegee machine policies of accomodation, and at times speaking out in militant tones against government at the highest levels.[65] He supported Washington apparently because he saw the need for building up black interests in business, industry and education as Washington stressed, and perhaps it was this same element in Garveyism that attracted him to that movement. But he claimed to be more in agreement with the policies of Douglass than those of Washington, and a contemporary said, "he is the complement of Booker T. Washington. Each is doing his own work in his own way; the one supplements the other's work."[66]

Archibald H. Grimke (1849—1930) was older than either Fortune or Washington, but outlived them both. Grimke, a member of the American Negro Academy, and later a vice president of the NAACP was a Harvard-educated lawyer, and a militant integrationist married at one time to a white woman. True to the Douglass tradition, Grimke employed the military-industrial rhetoric of the Washington school when he spoke of the Negro's place in American life. He asked if blacks were to become "grist for the nation, or mere chaff, doomed like the Indian to ultimate extinction in the raging fire of racial and industrial rivalry and progress?" Grimke took pride in pointing to an assessment in the *Washington Post* which described blacks in tones similar to those Washington used in Atlanta, comparing them to white emigrants:

> We hold as between the ignorant of the two races, the Negro is preferable. They are conservative; they are good citizens; they take no stock in social schisms and vagaries; they do not consort with anarchists; they cannot be made the tools and agents of incendiaries; they constitute the solid worthy, estimable yeomanry of the South. Their influence in government would be infinitely more wholesome than the influence of the white sans-culottes, the riff-raff, the idlers, the rowdies and the outlaws. As between the Negro, no matter how illiterate he may be, and the poor white, the property owners of the South prefer the former.[67]

No, blacks were not to be exterminated. The Negro had "the

capacity for becoming one of the best all-round laborers and artisans in our industrial army of conquest." He was suited to be a model citizen in this "age of industrialism and democracy."

Not only could the Tuskegee rhetoric parallel that of the American Negro Academicians, at times it sounded more militant. W.E.B. Du Bois's conservative statement in the American Negro Academy *Occasional Papers* (1897), presented as an address at least a year after the Atlanta Compromise Address lauded the ideal of "two races" developing "side by side," and did not advocate "such social equality between these races as would disregard human likes and dislikes." Du Bois also opined that the way to alleviate "the present friction between the races" was to correct the "immorality, crime and laziness among the Negroes themselves." In view of the fact that such sentiments were being expressed by members of the American Negro Academy where the Talented Tenth philosophy originated, we can see that the issues surrounding the Washington-Du Bois controversy are often oversimplified.[68]

It has become common practice since the days of Kelly Miller to describe black leaders as if all were either Douglass radicals or Washingtonian conservatives. Earl E. Thorpe, who is typical of historians who have inherited this perspective, has said that "until 1895 Frederick Douglass was the best-known protagonist of his race's egalitarian sentiments and efforts. He died that year and soon W.E.B. Du Bois and the NAACP assumed the position which Douglass had held." Such a view is correct, however, only in the most general sense. It is true that Frederick Douglass, and later the NAACP, militantly advocated egalitarianism; and it is also true that Booker T. Washington discouraged open confrontation with whites over the issue of immediate social equality. But it does not follow that Du Bois, or anyone else who subsequently disagreed with Washington was a medium for Frederick Douglass, who may indeed have turned over in his grave as a result of Washington's Atlanta speech, but certainly was not killed by it.[69]

It is also something of an oversimplification to see Du Bois as the inheritor of Douglass's position within the intellectual tradition. During the years that he edited *The Crisis*, Du Bois was a crusader for integrationist principles, particularly in the areas of employment and politics, but Du Bois was profoundly influenced by an altogether different tradition in Afro-American thought than that represented by Douglass and the egalitarian radicals of the abolitionist school. Du Bois's roots were in the American Negro Academy, and his spiritual father was not Douglass, but Alexander Crummell, who Du Bois placed with Daniel A. Payne among the first rank of black leaders.[70] In many respects Washington represented the civilizationist tradition of Crummell, sharing with him such an idea as the advisability of encouraging industrial education for the masses to counteract the excessive aestheticism of the Negro's personality. There was, as August Meier has observed, considerable support for Washington among the Talented Tenth, and Du Bois was not the only classically educated man of letters who sympathized with Tuskegee objectives during the nineties.[71]

On October 15, 1895, twenty-seven days after the Atlanta Compromise, Booker T. Washington responded to a letter from Edna Dow Cheney, a reform-minded white woman of Boston, and Tuskegee supporter who asked for an explanation of his meaning. Washington replied that his remarks concerning the social separation of the races had only been meant to allay Southern fears that blacks wished to "intrude themselves into the social society of the South." By the "social society" of the South, Washington no doubt meant friendly and familial relationships. "I understand that there are a great many things in the South which Southern people class as social intercourse that is [sic] not really so," Washington continued to Mrs. Cheney. "If anybody understood me as meaning that riding in the same railway car or sitting in the same room at a railroad station is social intercourse, they certainly got a wrong idea of my position."[72] Such a statement, issued from the Tuskegeean's desk, gives credence to Kelly Miller's appraisal of Washington that "while he does not openly avow, yet he would not disclaim in distinct terms a single plank in the platform of Douglass."[73] Indeed, agreement between Washington's and Douglass's policies during the 1890s when their public lives overlapped is not difficult to find. Direct influences of radical Douglass upon radical Du Bois are less readily identifiable, as we shall see in a later chapter.

Chapter Five

Black Bourgeois Feminism versus Peasant Values
Origins and Purposes of the National Federation of Afro-American Women

The organizing leadership of the black women's movement in America was closer in ideological stance to the pragmatic nationalism of Frederick Douglass and the egalitarian radicals than to that of Alexander Crummell and the committed mystical nationalists. But like Douglass himself, women's leaders betrayed a subliminal commitment to some ethnocentric goals. Most of them accepted the idea that blacks as a group should be concerned about the problems of race recognition, self-help, and "Civilization." During the resurgence of black nationalism in the years following reconstruction, the National Association of Colored Women and its leaders included the most politically-minded black women in America. They showed a concern for such nationalistic values as collective effort, black uplift (or Negro improvement) and institutional separatism. With the exception of Ida B. Wells, no prominent member of the National Association of Colored Women became a Garveyite, however.[1]

The civilizationist element in the work of the National Federation of Afro-American Women and its successor, the National Association of Colored Women was the concern for the uplift of the black peasant woman and the improvement of Negro family life. Black women who were old enough to remember slavery interpreted the history of black women's enslavement just as Alexander Crummell had, and W.E.B. Du Bois and E. Franklin

Frazier would.[2] Slavery was a catastrophic experience under which sexual exploitation was common rather then exceptional. The sexual exploitation of the black woman was the cause of much of the marital and familial instability in black community life. The National Association of Colored Women was not obsessed with publicizing the sexual oppression of the black woman, although this was a part of their work. They were concerned with trying to introduce standards of genteel Victorian domesticity into the cabins of Georgia and Alabama peasant women. Domestic feminism among black women involved work of the settlement-house variety, albeit carried on in a rural, rather than an urban environment. It meant attempting to demonstrate a spirit of friendly solidarity with the culturally disadvantaged, "lifting as they climbed," to paraphrase the motto of the Association.

The history of the organization of the National Association of Colored Women demonstrates that even the most integration-minded of upper class Afro-American women were forced to confront the issues that nationalists introduced into community debate. Some women were committed to a nationalistic rhetoric, as can be seen in the debates over participation in the Chicago World's Fair and the Atlanta Exposition. The debate over whether the group should identify itself as "Colored" or "Afro-American" shows that nationalistic sentiment was not limited to male organizations. A survey of the organizational meetings of the National Federation of Afro-American Women and the National Association of Colored Women makes it possible for us to see such issues under discussion.

The involvement of Afro-American women in antilynching reform was the peculiarly "black" aspect of its work. But black women had some difficulty communicating their concern to their white friends, although lynching during the years of our study was a national disgrace. The NAACP publicized the fact that there were 3,224 lynchings in the United States between 1889 and 1918, of which 2,522 were perpetrated against blacks; fifty of these victims were women.[3] Popular mythology linked lynching in the public mind with the crime of rape, although as Frederick Douglass once said, "Thousands of white women were left for years in charge of Negroes, while their fathers, brothers and husbands were absent fighting the battles of the rebellion; yet there was no assault upon such women by Negroes, and no accusation of such assault. It is only since the Negro has become a citizen and a voter that this charge has been made."[4] Douglass's argument was to be repeated often by black women like Josephine St. Pierre Ruffin and Ida B. Wells throughout the period that Rayford Logan has called "The Nadir."

The National Federation of Afro-American Women (NFA-AW) was an organization of black women's clubs representing an attempt to unify the efforts of numerous local organizations. The club movement among Afro-American woman had its beginnings in the early 1800s with the formation of groups in those cities of the United States where the black middle class was large enough to provide a membership. "As a general rule," says Fannie Barrier Williams, "those who, in the proper sense, may be called the best women in the communities where these clubs were organized, became interested and joined in the work of helpfulness." Mrs. Williams saw this as a refutation of the charge that "colored women of education and refinement had no sympathetic interest in their own race."[5] Among the early clubs, the most prominent seem to have been the Phillis Wheatley Club of New Orleans, the Women's Loyal Union of New York and Brooklyn, the Women's Era Club of Boston, the Women's League of Washington, D. C., the Ida B. Wells Club of Chicago, and the Women's League of Kansas City, Missouri. The clubs were organized for various reasons and involved themselves in a wide assortment of activities. Some were purely social, while others were actively involved in community work. Most of the clubs were unaffiliated until 1895, when they convened in Boston at the call of Mrs. Josephine St. Pierre Ruffin to form the National Federation of Afro-American Women.[6]

There is some dispute as to when, exactly, the national organization originated. The Colored Women's League of Washington, D. C., founded in 1892, contended that they were the first of the clubs to become national in scope. Mrs. Mary Church Terrell was the most prominent member of the D.C. group. She wrote in 1893 of the need for "a national organization of colored women" and called on sister organizations in other states to unite with the league in their work.[7] By 1895, when the Woman's Era Club of Boston called the first national convention of black women's clubs, groups outside of Washington had become affiliated with the Washington league. By 1893, the league was publicizing its desire "to form like organizations throughout the country." Mrs. Terrell tells us, however, that while the Washington league was the first to "resolve that colored women of the United States associate ourselves together to collect all facts obtainable to show the moral, intellectual, industrial and social growth and attainments of our people, to foster unity of purpose, to consider and determine methods which will promote the interests of colored people in any direction that suggests itself", it was the Boston group that first actually assembled a gathering of women for the express purpose of creating a permanent national organization.

The First National Conference of Colored Women was held in Berkeley Hall, Boston, Massachusetts on July 29, 30, 31, 1895. It resulted primarily from the efforts of Mrs. Josephine St. Pierre Ruffin. Mrs. Ruffin was born in Boston in 1843. Her father was of full African and full Indian mixture; her mother, a white woman, was born in Cornwall, England. At the age of sixteen, she married George L. Ruffin—who was later to be appointed judge of the city court for the Charlestown district. Immediately after their marriage in 1859, the young couple sailed for England to escape from American tyranny. They returned during the Civil War and Mrs. Ruffin was involved in volunteer work and the sending of sanitary supplies to the soldiers. Even in her early twenties, Mrs. Ruffin had some idea of the responsibilities of her class. After the war, she organized the Kansas Relief Association to aid black people who were migrating to Kansas. She was responsible for the founding of *The Woman's Era*, which was the first magazine in the United States to be owned, published and managed solely by black women.[8]

Mrs. Ruffin, a woman of extraordinary beauty and vigor, buxom, silver-haired and majestic at the age of fifty, possessed of wealth, education and leisure, moved about Boston with a great deal more confidence than most women of color. Her opinions on the question of racial identity were pragmatic, intelligent, and clearly stated. Once, when a condescending Boston white woman expressed to her an abiding interest in the problem of her race, Mrs. Ruffin retorted, "which race?"[9] She clearly extended herself in the interests of colored people more conscientiously than have many vocal black nationalists. Mrs. Ruffin felt it important to make clear that the club movement among black women was not to be thought of as separatist, nor was it to be solely concerned with "our peculiar question." Rather, it was to be involved in "the general questions of the day . . . temperance, morality, the higher education, hygenic and domestic questions."[10] But while the Woman's Era Club was not to be "necessarily a colored woman's club," it was, more than incidentally, exactly that. There were, so *The Woman's Era* maintained, a number of white women's clubs "willing and anxious to receive colored women as members," and Mrs. Ruffin could easily have confined her participation to such groups, had her only intention been to involve herself in the women's club movement.

It was Mrs. Ruffin's intention that both the Woman's Era Club and the National Federation of Afro-American Women should stand not only for racial uplift, but for urban progressivism and the crusade for the rights of women. At an open meeting of the Woman's Era Club, held in the spring of 1893, Florida Ruffin Ridley, Mrs. Ruffin's daughter, read a report indicating that the organization was to be "a Woman's Club, not necessarily a colored woman's club, but a club started and led by colored women." White women were allowed to address this meeting, and at least one of them, Mrs. Laura Ormiston Chant, an English woman, expressed feminist sentiments. *The Woman's Era* reported her as saying that, "not all women are intended for mothers. Some of us have not the temperament for family life . . . clubs will make women think seriously of their future lives, and not make girls think their only alternative is to marry." The meeting was also addressed by Lucy Stone Blackwell, prominent abolitionist and feminist. The cover of the first issue of *The Woman's Era* was dominated by her portrait and obituary; she died in the interval between the open meeting and the appearance of the first issue in March of 1894. Ms. Stone's last words, "make the world better," were to become the motto of the Woman's Era Club. Other prominent women activists to address the meeting were Edna D. Cheney , Abby Morton Diaz, and Mrs. A. H. Spaulding, all of whom were white.[11]

Mrs. Ruffin was a member of several prestigious white clubs, and the first member of her "race" to become a member of the New

England Federation of Women's Clubs. She was capable of being pushy and intrusive when occasion demanded. In 1900 she attended the biennial meeting of the National Federation of Women's Clubs in Milwaukee, Wisconsin. She was a delegate of the Woman's Era Club, which had been admitted to membership before the executive committee realized that it was a black organization. She had also been elected a delegate by the Massachusetts State Federation which was, of course, predominatly white. An official statement by the Woman's Era Club summarizes the events of what came to be known as the "Ruffin incident":

> Upon arriving at Milwaukee, Mrs. Ruffin was forced into a humilating position for which she was wholly unprepared. The Massachusetts delegation was immediately notified that the Board had met and would not receive an application for membership of the Woman's Era Club. Mrs. Ruffin was informed that she could not enter the convention representing a "colored club" but would be received as a delegate from a "white club", and to enforce this ruling an attempt was made to snatch from her breast the badge which had been handed her on the passing of her credentials.
>
> Mrs. Ruffin refused to enter the convention under the conditions offered her, that is, as a delegate from the Massachusetts State Federation, for which she was also a delegate.

Mrs. Ruffin was not seeking "social equality," but rather a recognition of the collective efforts of all black women in the area of club work.[12]

While the Woman's Era Club was integration-minded, it was also race-conscious. The first issue of *The Woman's Era* publicized attrocities in the South. Florida Ruffin Ridley, Mrs. Ruffin's daughter, spoke of a "practical effort, put forth by the club," a leaflet issued to protest a lynching. Mrs. Ridley was not at all reluctant to criticize radical women's liberationists who were insensitive to the sufferings of black folk, an so, on June 1, 1894, *The Woman's Era* carried her open letter to Mrs. Laura Ormiston Chant, who would seem to have been the most radically feminist speaker at the open meeting of the preceeding year, saying, "Your name and that speech have been to us a refreshing memory; think then the shock it has occasioned us to hear that through your efforts, a resolution at the National Conference of the Unitarian Church denouncing lynching was defeated." An editorial in that same issue of the *The Woman's Era* read:

> Up to their ears in guilt against Negro women, they offer as their excuse for murdering Negro men, Negro women, and Negro children, that white women are not safe from the Negro rapist. . . . We are told that Francis [sic] Willard of America and Laura Ormiston Chant of England, have entered the lists as apologists. . . . Why did not the slaves, when their masters were away trying to shoot the Union to death and keep them forever slaves, out-rage the wives and daughters of these traitors confided to their care.

Interestingly, *The Woman's Era* emerged at this point as the defender of black manhood. The first editorial fireworks went off not in defense of women's rights, but on behalf of black males. Black women were defending black men in an area where they would have been uncomfortable defending themselves. The women recognized that the national pastime of lynching symbolized the entire system of sexist oppressionn of the black male, that he was being sexually victimized just as systematically as was the white woman.

As antilynching agitators, the Boston women claimed the inspiration of Ida B. Wells who, in the early nineties, was making a name for herself as a crusader against lynching. Born in Holly Springs, Mississippi in 1869, she lost both her parents at the age of fourteen, at which time she took over the duties of raising four younger brothers and sisters. She taught for several years in the public schools of Memphis, Tennessee, then resigned her position to become editor and half-owner of the Memphis *Free Speech*. Writing under the pen name of "Iola," she soon earned the nationwide respect of black people, and the open hatred of many whites. She was forced to flee Memphis when, in her editorials, she denounced the lynching of two black businessmen who had made the mistake of successfully competing with white merchants in their area. Eventually Wells settled in Chicago, where she married

Ferdinand Barnett, founder of Illinois's first black newspaper. The Barnetts came to represent the vanguard of the anti-Tuskegee forces in Chicago. They strongly believed in the development of black institutions, however, and sometimes rejected integration in favor of such. Midway in the tale of her years, one finds Wells in sympathy with Marcus Garvey, but she was never a racist or an escapist. She spoke out against the cheap and petty insults delivered against Mrs. Helen Pitts Douglass, Frederick Douglass's second wife and a white woman. She was a friend of Jane Addams.[13]

In spite of her impressive credentials as one of black America's most militant journalists, Mrs. Wells-Barnett did not occupy a formal position with *The Woman's Era*. She did occasionally contribute a letter to the journal, but the Chicago correspondent was Fannie Barrier Williams, wife of S. Laing Williams. Her husband, a former law partner of Ferdinand Barnett, and a strong supporter of Tuskegee, was the ghost writer of Booker T. Washington's biography of Frederick Douglass. Mrs. Williams, like Mrs. Ruffin had strong integrationist sentiments. She was known for her successful attempt to join the prestigious Chicago Women's Club in 1894. In its early days, the work of this white women's group had been "entirely literary, consisting of essays and discussions at the semi-monthly meetings on subjects connected with the work and study of the various departments." Practical work was in the areas "related to the interests of women" and consisted of such efforts as securing employment for women physicians in the Cook County Insane Asylum. After a battle of fourteen months, during which, said Mrs. Williams, "the whole anti-slavery question was fought over again in the same spirit and with the same arguments," she was finally admitted to the club.[14]

Other prominent correspondents of the *Era* and organizers of the National Association were Mrs. Mary Church Terrell, Mrs. Victoria Earle Matthews, Mrs. Margaret Murray Washington, and Mrs. Josephine Silone Yates. Mary Church Terrell was the Washington, D.C. correspondent of the *Era*; she was elected first president of the National Association of Colored Women (NACW) which evolved out of the NFA-AW in 1896, and served two two-year terms in succession from 1897 to 1901. Mrs. Terrell, whose mother had been a slave, was sent to school in the North from the time she was six years old by her wealthy and devoted father. She was a graduate of Oberlin and a student for three years in Europe. Fluent in French and German, she also knew Greek and Latin which she taught in the schools of the District of Columbia. She was the wife of Robert Herberton Terrell, who was a cum laude graduate of Harvard, and was later to become a municipal judge of the District of Columbia. Her editorials in the *Era* dealt with the problems of black women workers, among other things. In the December issue of 1894, she deplored the trend toward employing white cooks and housekeepers. (A few black women in Mrs. Ruffin's Boston set were guilty of this.) She encouraged the establishment of trade schools to train black girls for efficient domestic work. She recognized the displacement of black domestics as a serious problem "since the women wage earners of the race contribute as much at least to its support as the men, and when the women fail to find employment in domestic service many a family will suffer and much of the revenue enjoyed will be cut off." Mrs. Terrell was not a consistent supporter of Booker T. Washington, but she was favorably impressed by his work and she strongly believed in industrial education.[15]

The New York correspondent of the *Era* was Mrs. Walter E. (Victoria Earle) Matthews. Intelligent, forceful, and courageous, Mrs. Matthews was among the most active leaders among black women in the 1890's. An able politician, she was often responsible for whatever advanced thinking occured at the conventions. The daughter of a slave and born a slave herself, Mrs. Matthews was a member of the Women's Loyal Union of New York and Brooklyn and the founder of the White Rose Working Girls' Home, which was dedicated to the protection of black working girls and to providing a decent residence. During the winter of 1895, she toured the South investigating the conditions under which black women lived, her light complexion affording her some protection during her travels.

President of the NFA-AW was Margaret Murray Washington, wife of Booker T. Washington. Mrs. Washington was born in Macon, Mississippi at the close of the Civil War. At the age of seven years, upon her father's death, she was sent from her parents' home to that of a Quaker couple named Sanders who educated her and helped her to obtain her first teaching position at the age of fourteen. She attended Fisk University where, on graduation day in June of 1889, she was seated across the table from Booker T. Washington. Although she had originally planned to begin teaching in Texas, she decided to go to Tuskegee and become Lady Principal of the School. She married Mr. Washington in 1893 and became a sort of mother confessor to students and teachers at the Institute. In the late nineties she founded what she called a "Plantation Settlement," where she taught not only women and girls, but also boys the duties of maintaining a household. Booker T. Washington's statement that she was "completely one" with him in his work is of great interest, since she was committed to integration. Interesting also was her willingness to compromise with the segregation system, so long as the interests of middle-class blacks were protected. As did Booker T. Washington, she fought against Jim Crow legislation. On November 23, 1896, she wrote to Edna D. Cheney, the white Boston reformer, asking for greater support from progressive white women, who were at the time giving undue emphasis to the immigrant problem and ignoring black folk in the South:

> I can not tell you how I felt since Miss Willard has taken up the Armenian question, not that she should not do this but it is so strange that these people who have no special claims upon this country should so take possession of the hearts of northern women, that the woman of color is entirely over-looked.[16]

One can only speculate on what associations may exist between the nativism expressed here and in Booker T. Washington's *Atlanta Exposition Address*:

> To those of the white race who look to the incoming of those of foreign birth and strange tongue and habits for the prosperity of the South, were I permitted I would repeat what I say to my own race, "Cast down your bucket where you are." Cast it down among the eight million Negroes whose habits you know, whose fidelity and love you have tested in days when to have proved treacherous meant the ruin of your firesides.[17]

But it is most certainly consistent with the nativist sentiments of many Afro-American leaders in the late nineteenth century, such as those expressed in one of the *Woman's Era* editorials:[18]

> The audacity of foreigners who flee their native land and seek refuge here, many of them criminals and traitors, who are here but a day before they join in the hue and cry against the native born citizens of this land is becoming intolerable. No government upon earth would permit it but the United States, and all the signs of the times point to a time not far off where self defence and self protection will force this government to protect its own people and to teach foreigners that this land is for Americans black or white and that other men are welcome and can come here only by behaving themselves and steering clear of plots and schemes against the people and the citizens who are here by right.

The rhetoric was similar to that of white racist nativism, which opposed immigration on the grounds that alien influences would lead to anarchism. While whites feared the anarchism of Haymarket, blacks had learned to fear the anarchism of race riots and lynchings.

Mrs. Washington, like Mrs. Terrell, was among the black leaders who noticed the racism of the immigrant masses who competed with the black masses for work. Anti-immigrationism represented a self-interested bourgeois liberal attitude in the black community. It also represented a concern for the problems of the black masses. Mrs. Washington, who believed that pressure from white women's organizations could do something to combat segregationist legislation, also believed in self-help, as her columns in *The Woman's Era* reveal. In November of 1895, she outlined the sort of work she believed black women ought to engage in for racial uplift:

> Our poor need to be clothed. Our women must be taught to study for their own advancement. They need inspiration and encouragement to keep a brave heart. Homemaking must be though about, child rearing needs attention. Our girls need social purity talks. They must be warned of evil company.

They must be brought in closer touch with more that is good and pure. They must be taught to realize that they have a vital part to enact in developing the womanhood of their country.

Mrs. Josephine Silone Yates was the Kansas City, Missouri correspondent of *The Woman's Era*. Descended from the dark-brown Silone family of Long Island, who had been free before the Civil War, she was educated in Philadelphia and Newport, Rhode Island; there she entered the high school and became valedictorian of her graduating class. She was graduated from the Rhode Island State Normal School in 1879, and was a schoolteacher for many years. Mrs. Yates was a pioneer activist on behalf of black prison convicts and a publicizer of inequities in the judicial systems. When a colored woman was sentenced to be hung in Kansas City in June of 1893, her league circulated a petition "which was signed by a large number of the most prominent men and women of both races." As a result, the governor commuted the sentence to fifty years.[19] Believing that the position of women in a race is "always an index to the real progress of a people," she placed a high priority on training for women "along the line of education, the professions, the industrial arts, etc."[20] Mrs. Yates was second president of the NACW from 1901-1906.

The first National Conference of Colored Women in Boston in July of 1895 grew quite naturally out of the communications network maintained by *The Woman's Era* and its correspondents during the preceeding sixteen months. Mrs. Ruffin began to work for a national conference in May of 1894 when she wrote in her magazine, "the especial work of this paper is the binding together of our women's clubs. . . . To this end *The Woman's Era* urges the holding of a convention."[21] In that same year she began to mail a flyer to prominent black women and to women's clubs around the country, entitled, *A Call. Let Us Confer Together*. She urged "all clubs, societies, associations, and circles to take immediate action, looking towards the sending of delegates to this convention."[22]

While the subject of a national organization had been a matter of serious concern among black women for some time, the call for a conference was immediately precipitated by a specific incident in 1895. Miss Florence Balgarnie, an Englishwoman, Honorable Secretary of the Anti-Lynching Committee of London, received "a most indecent, foul and slanderous letter" from one Mr. Jno. W. Jacks, and forwarded it to *The Woman's Era.* [23] Mrs. Ruffin enclosed the Jacks letter with the *Call*, and mailed it to the women's clubs with the caution that it not be given general circulation or publication.[24] The ladies apparently took these instructions quite seriously and copies of the letter are rare, as the Jacks letter was never printed in *The Woman's Era*, nor did it appear in either of the two histories of the NACW. Copies are still in existence, however, such as the one found by the present author. The following excerpts will provide some sense of the letter's tone and contents:[25]

> Out of some 200 [Negroes] in this vicinity it is doubtful if there are a dozen virtuous women or that number who are not daily theiving from the white people. To illustrate how they regard virtue in a woman: one of them, a negro woman, was asked who a certain negro woman who had lately moved into the neighborhood was. She turned up her nose and said, "the negroes will have nothing to do with 'dat nigger', she won't let any man, except her husband sleep with her, and we don't "sociate with her."

We may speculate that either Jno. W. Jacks or some friend of his, well-acquainted with the prostitute population, had questioned the first woman about the character of the second. It might be reasonable to speculate further that upon discovering that the second woman was virtuous, and therefore not available to him, Jacks was so spiteful as to take out his frustrations on all Negro women. Jacks also attempted to assail the character of those northern and British women who worked for anti-lynching reform:

> Your plea seems to us to take the form of asking us to make associates for our families of prostitutes, liars, thieves, and lawbreakers generally, and to especially condone the crime of rape if committed by a negro. Respectable people in this country not only decline to form such associates, but naturally infer that those who ask them to do so and place themselves on a level with such characters must either be of

the same moral status themselves, or else wholly ignorant of the condition of affairs here, and consequently do not know what they are talking about.

Jno. W. Jacks was the editor of a newspaper in Montgomery City, Missouri, and president of the Missouri Press Association. He was a Sunday school superintendent and the son of a slaveholder. The editors of *The Christian Educator,* organ of the Freedman's Aid and Southern Education Society, reported to *The Woman's Era* that "he has never printed a disrespectful word in his paper here against the colored people. It is safe to say from what is known of the man, that he would never be even courageous enough to print the whole letter in his own paper, and look his neighbors in the face the same week."[26] The letter was in very poor taste, if not quite pornographic by the standards of the times, and it certainly would have violated the clubwomen's sense of good taste to have circulated it openly.

The first meetings of the convention were given up to the discussion of racial issues as well as "general questions of the day." Among the papers read were those by Mrs. Libbie C. Carter, "Industrial Training"; Mrs. Booker T. Washington, "Individual Work for Moral Training"; Mrs. Victoria Earle Matthews, "Value of Race Literature"; Mrs. Agnes Adams, "Social Purity." Mrs. Ruffin addressed the convention at an evening session on July 29, 1895:

The reasons why we should confer are so apparent that it should seem hardly necessary to enumerate them, and yet there are none of them but demand our serious consideration. In the first place we need to feel the cheer and inspiration of meeting each other; we need to gain the courage and fresh life that comes from the mingling of congenial souls, of those working for the same ends. Next, we need to talk over those things that are of especial interest to us as colored women, the training of our children, openings for our boys and girls, how they can be prepared for occupations and [what] occupations may be found or opened for them, what we especially can do in the moral education and physical development, the home training it is necessary to give our children in order to prepare them to meet the peculiar conditions in which they shall find themselves, how to make the most of our own, to some extent, limited opportunities. Besides these are the general questions of the day, which we cannot afford to be indifferent to: temperance, morality, the higher education, hygenic and domestic questions. If these things need the serious consideration of women more advantageously placed by reason of all the aid to right thinking and living with which they are surrounded, surely we, with everything to pull us back, to hinder us in developing, need to take every opportunity and means for the thoughtful consideration which shall lead to wise action. . . .

Now for the sake of the thousands of self-sacrificing young women teaching and preaching in lonely southern backwoods for the noble army of mothers who have given birth to these girls, mothers whose intelligence is only limited by their opportunity to get at books, for the sake of the fine cultured women who have carried off the honors in school here and often abroad, for the sake of our own dignity, the dignity of our race, and the future good name of our children, it is "meet, right, and our bounden duty" to stand forth and declare ourselves and principles, to teach an ignorant and suspicious world that our aims and interests are identical with those of all good aspring women.

Mrs. Ruffin, in a way that was characteristic of black leaders of the period, tried to remain loyal to the doctrines of racial solidarity and self help, but, at the same time, her sense of justice compelled her to avoid anything that would sound like a renunciation of the *right* to full participation in American life:

Our woman's movement is woman's movement in that it is led and directed by women for the good of women and men, for the benefit of all humanity, which is more than any one branch or section of it. We want, we ask the active interest of our men, and, too, we are not drawing the color line; we are women, American women; as intensely interested in all that pertains to us as such as all other American women; we are not alienating or withdrawing, we are only coming to the front, willing to join any others in the same work and cordially inviting and welcoming any others to join us.[27]

One interprets these lines as revealing a great deal of interest in social issues—a sophisticated, self-interested, bourgeois spirit. At the same time there is a feeling of loyal dedication to some vaguely conceived *Volk* idea, an almost religious commitment to the uplift of the "black masses."

The convention passed a resolution endorsing the "noble and truthful advocacy of Mrs. Ida B. Wells Barnett, defending us against the lying charge of rape,"[28] and a committee was appointed to draw up resolutions relating to lynching, to the Georgia convict system, and to the Florida state school segregation law.[29] The venerable Alexander Crummell "was invited to make some remarks and a rising vote of thanks was tendered to him by the Convention."[30]

On Thursday, August 1, 1895, an extra session, the fourth and last, was held. At that time a constitution was drawn up and a permanent organization was formed to be known as the National Federation of Afro-American Women. The objects of the Federation were stated in Article II of the constitution:

The object of this organization is (1) the concentration of the dormant energies of the women of the Afro-American race into one broad band of sisterhood: for the purpose of establishing needed reforms, and the practical encouragement of all efforts being put forth by various agencies, religious, educational, ethical and otherwise, for the upbuilding, ennobling and advancement of the race; (2) to awaken the women of the race to the great need of systematic effort in home-making and the divinely imposed duties of motherhood.[31]

Race-consciousness and a rather conservative brand of feminism were to be the dominant ideological features of the organization. The work of women was generally seen as lying within the province of the home, although Mrs. Terrell, viewing things realistically, did see the masses of black women as important breadwinners. The work of middle-class colored women was to be carried out among the women of her own race; it would consist of establishing firmly the middle class bourgeois morality of Victorian America. Elections were held, and the first president of the NFA-AW was Mrs. Booker T. Washington. Mrs. Ruffin was elected treasurer but positively declined to serve. The ladies adjourned after expressing their desire to form a union with the Washington Colored Women's League.[32]

Some months after the First National Conference of Colored Women that was held in Boston in 1895, black America passed the important milestone of the Cotton States and International Exposition in Atlanta, Georgia. The Atlanta Congress of Colored Women met during the Atlanta Exposition at the urging of Mrs. Blanche K. Bruce, President of the Ladies Auxiliary to the Negro Department of the Exposition. Later to be described as "the first Congress of Colored Women [and] the first Congress of Women in the United States"[33] it was neither of these, and Mrs. Ruffin was coolly indignant at such a claim. It was, however, an occurrence of some interest for one who wishes to understand the attitudes that prevailed among bourgeois Negroes at the time of Booker T. Washington's so called "Atlanta Compromise."[34]

Before attempting to evaluate the role of the colored people in Atlanta in 1895, we should recall that in 1893, in celebration of the one-hundredth anniversary of the discovery of America, the World's Columbian Exposition had been held in Chicago, Illinois. Because black people were not represented in the Exposition, some leaders, among them Ida B. Wells, launched a campaign for a separate black exhibit, but they were opposed by other black leaders, indignant at the idea that the color line should be drawn at a national exposition in a major northern city. This opposition felt that they were as American as anyone and that acceptance of a separate Negro exhibit would be a capitulation to racism.[35] It was because the idea of a separate exhibit was opposed by this faction of integrationist radicals, some argued, that blacks were not represented at all. The protests continued, but when the managers of the exposition responded by setting aside August 25, 1893 as Negro day, some militant blacks were offended at the offering of a sop and boycotted the fair. Frederick Douglass, however, in his role as principal speaker of the day, took occasion to excoriate those who had perpetrated the insult, thereby vindicating himself in the eyes of the militants.[36]

Black representation at world's fairs and international expositions was a divisive issue, then, and responses from the black community were varied when directors of the Cotton States and International Exposition offered a building to the black people of the United States. Mrs. Ruffin opposed the idea from the start; she recognized that there were "good reasons why the colored people should be represented there and take advantage of the new and large opportunities of vindicating themselves."[37] But still she opposed the project partly because she was a radical integrationist and felt that it was "as impossible to separate the whites and the blacks as it is to separate the work of those who have Irish or German blood."[38] She continued, "We do not see how the colored exhibit can escape being very meager, and the world should know the reason for it."[39]

In spite of the opposition of Mrs. Ruffin and others, the colored participation in the Atlanta Exposition was something of a success. Mrs. Ruffin herself grudgingly admitted that the Atlanta exhibits had won a great deal of praise from the press and had brought some credit to the race; however, she seems to have stood by her integrationist principles, and was never convinced that a separate exhibit was the best thing.[40]

Booker T. Washington gave his famous "Atlanta Exposition Address" on the opening day of the exposition, September 18, 1895. In this address he made numerous statements that were later to provoke controversy. Among them was his declaration that "whatever other sins the South may be called upon to bear, when it comes to business pure and simple it is in the South that the negro is given a man's chance in the commercial world; and in nothing is this Exposition more eloquent than in emphasizing this chance."[41] Perhaps Washington was remembering that there had been no "negro building" in Chicago in 1893. The most cursory study of the two expositions will reveal that Washington was correct in his observations, at least insofar as they pertained to the chances given black people at the Atlanta Exposition. Radicals, like Ida. B. Wells, would forget that they had endorsed "separate but equal," in effect, at the Columbian Exposition, and would begin to think of the Atlanta speech as a capitulation by the early 1900's.[42]

During the Atlanta Women's Congress, certain issues pertaining to the eventual unification between the NFA-AW and the Colored Women's League were discussed. The Chicago exposition had earlier been the scene of some efforts at unifying the work of Afro-American women. Miss Hallie Quinn Brown had approached the chairperson of the Woman's Board of Managers, Mrs. Potter Palmer, asking for membership of the Board "where she could, like Esther of old, make supplication, officially, for her people." Mrs. Palmer informed her that representation on the board was by organization and not by individual. Miss Brown traveled to Washington, D.C., where she met with "a most representative audience" at the fifteenth Street Presbyterian Church, in hopes of being appointed as their representative to Chicago. Her hopes were not realized, but the interest generated by her visit did lead to the formation of the Colored Women's League of Washington, D.C. Mary Church Terrell informs us that this association pretended to national ambitions but never actually took steps toward the calling of a national convention. It was the Atlanta Congress which would provide a setting for the calling of a national convention which would include both the Washington league and the NFA-AW, founded in Boston, the previous summer. Mrs. Booker T. Washington of the Federation and Mrs. Helen Cook of the Washington league had conferred earlier, deciding that two committees of three, headed by the presidents of each organization should hold Conference Committee in Atlanta. Three delegates from the Atlanta Congress joined them at the meeting, but unfication was not brought about at that time.[43]

The most important development at the Congress was the passage of a series of resolutions that provide some insights into the nature of Afro-American conservatism during the Progressive Era. Of particular interest is the resolution endorsing the Cotton States Exposition "in giving the Negro a chance to show what he is doing," but resolving further, "that we condemn in strongest terms the sale of liquor and all intoxicants in the lunch room of the Negro Building of the Cotton States Exposition and consider it a direct reflection upon the intelligence and character of our race."[44]

This resolution is of interest because it reveals that the Congress was devoted to encouraging the adoption of genteel bourgeois values. It also shows that these women were very concerned about their public image, and that they wanted to be remembered as upholders of puritan morality. Another resolution condemned the convict lease system of which, the congress saw it, "the indiscriminate mixing of males and females has been the most abhorrent feature."[45] Certainly the convict lease system had many abhorrent features. It was based upon a system of false arrest and false conviction. Mere children were arrested on trumped-up vagrancy charges, then hustled into work houses after hasty trials by kangaroo courts. Convicts could be leased by local legitimate entrepreneurs, or they could be put to work by the county or a local municipality. The chain gang was a significant factor in the labor history of the New South. The convict lease system was essentially a labor problem, then, and not a sexual problem. The mixing of male and female convicts has often been suggested, during more recent decades, as a progressive reform. Given certain humane guidelines and controls, such reforms could be healthy and beneficial for all society. In the context of 1895, however, especially when we remember the sorts of insults to which black women were constantly being subjected, it was impossible for black women to entertain progressive views on the question of mixing male and female prisoners. The black community was—as it still is—very defensive on the question of sexual morality, as any reader of *Muhammad Speaks* during the 1960's must surely know. The NFA-AW, in typical black nationalist fashion, was determined to present to the world a "strait-laced" image.

The Congress also resolved to condemn every form of lawlessness and miscarriage of justice and demand, without favor or compromise, the equal enforcement of the law for all classes of American citizens."[46] It was reported in *The Woman's Era* of February, 1896 that an addition to this resolution reading, "be it resolved that in denouncing lynch law we also condemn the crime that provokes lynch law," was also proposed.[47] Victoria Earle Matthews reported to *The Woman's Era* in the same issue that:

> The addition was not beheaded or purposely lost, as some were disposed to think, but after fearless intelligent direction by the committee, on the ground that mob law execution follows *suspicion of guilt, if the culprit or suspected one be*

colored, so swiftly that a crime is never proven, it was decided
that there was no tenable ground for the acceptance even of
the injurer's apology, much less a condemnatory resolution
based on no other evidence than the word or reports of even
those who support by non-interference crimes against law,
humanity and God.[48]

The controversey over the adoption of a resolution condemning
rape reveals that a given issue may have one meaning in the white
community and an entirely different one in the black. The NFA-
AW was very much opposed to all forms of sexual deviancy: they
were also strongly condemning of all forms of lawlessness.
However, in the context of 1895, it was impossible for the Atlanta
Congress to adopt a resolution denouncing rape, mainly because
Southern white men and women were attempting to identify rape
as a Negro crime in the minds of the public. The rejection of the
resolution by the Congress should be seen as an act of defiance, an
assertion that black men and women, not white women, were
being sexually victimized in the South. It required some daring for
the black woman to publicly assert such a position during the era
of the Great Pogrom.

A "Social Purity" resolution was also passed, "that we require
the same standard of morality for men as for women, and that the
mothers teach their sons social purity as well as their daughters."[49]
The social purity resolution is interesting in view of the fact that
the club movement was provoked into being by a sexual slander of
the black woman. A study of the southern black woman, con-
ducted under the auspices of the John F. Slater Fund in 1896
reveals that such matters were of great concern to black people at
this time.[50] While black leaders were well aware of the high
incidence of forcible rape of black women committed by white
men over the years, they also recognized the effects that this
brutalizing oppression had had on black womanhood. Alexander
Crummell, speaking on "The Black Woman of the South: Her
Neglects and Her Needs," once said:

This is the state of black womanhood. Take the girlhood of
this same region, and it presents the same aspect, save that in
large districts the white man has not forgotten the olden times

of slavery, and, with, indeed, the deepest sentimental abhorrence of "amalgamation," still thinks that the black girl is to be perpetually the victim of his lust! In the larger towns and in cities, our girls, in common schools and academies, are receiving superior culture. Of the fifteen thousand colored school teachers in the South, more than half are colored young women, educated since emancipation. But even these girls, as well as their more ignorant sisters in rude huts, are followed and tempted and insulted by the ruffianly element of Southern society, who think that black *men* have no rights which white men should regard, and black *women* no virtue which white men should respect![51]

With this in mind, and with an awareness of the "support by noninterference" of Southern white women, black women were interested in exposing the nature of American sexism. At the same time, they endorsed the post-reconstruction attempts, carried out at Tuskegee and elsewhere, to improve the moral tone of life among the black peasantry.[52]

The Atlanta Congress also resolved to "call upon the Southern legislators, in the name of the common womanhood, to adopt a first and second class [train] fare, so that the womanhood of the race may be protected from every outrage and insult."[53] This was a pet project of Mrs. Booker T. Washington, who held the office of First Vice President of the Congress and was a member of the Committee of Resolutions.[54] On November 23, 1896, she wrote to Edna D. Cheney, the Boston reformer, asking for her help in getting up a petition for a first and second class fare.[55] In *The Women's Era* in February of that year, she had published an open letter to the women's clubs which asked for their cooperation in circulating such a petition:

Argument is not needed to portray the evils of this system in the matter of forced indiscriminate contact, nor the illegality of the extortionate tariff placed on all who have to ride in the notoriously filthy, ill-ventillated "Jim Crow" cars. With others, I had hoped for greater harmony among our women at this time, so delayed the matter. Delays are dangerous.[56]

If Mrs. Washington was, indeed, as her husband said, one with him in his work, then we must acknowledge the presence of elitism in the Tuskegee machine. We realize that understanding and condoning are not the same thing, and we are able to recognize that, from a certain perspective, Mrs. Washington's approach to the Jim Crow question is understandable, if not exactly praiseworthy. She objected to being forced into association with a certain kind of black person whose behavior was offensive to her. However, this did not mean that she was ashamed of her race or that she despised her own kind. Mrs. Washington's motivation, moreover, could not have been primarily a desire to avoid contact with lower-class blacks, since she had chosen to devote her life to working among them. There was at least one other reason for seeking a two-class system. The Jim Crow car, located as it often was next to the saloon or smoking car, was sometimes invaded by a nasty, dull, and brutish type of white passenger. Charles Chesnutt describes such an incident in his novel, *The Marrow of Tradition:* Captain McBane, who has come into the colored passengers' car to smoke a cigar, is asked by the conductor to leave:[57]

> "The hell you say!" rejoined McBane. "I'll leave this car when I get good and ready, and that won't be till I've finished this cigar. See?
> He was as good as his word. The conductor escaped from the car before Miller had time for further expostulation. Finally McBane, having thrown the stump of his cigar into the aisle and added to the floor a finishing touch in the way of expectoration, rose and went back into the white car.

Who can blame a refined middle-class woman, in late Victorian America for recoiling in disgust from such a situation, even if to do so meant acceptance of a two-class system of Jim Crow? Jim Crow *was* a fact of life. On the other hand one also recognizes here a disturbing tendency of the black bourgeoisie, which, like every bourgeoisie, becomes most militant when protecting its own short-sighted class interests.

We ought not to leave the Atlanta Congress without further comment upon its conservatism. The two-class Jim Crow resolution, as well as the resolution denouncing the "crime that provokes Lynch Law," and another resolution which condemned the "universal prodigality of the race," must be recognized as accommodationist. If these resolutions represented the attitudes of a substantial portion of the black bourgeoisie, then Booker T. Washington's address of September 18, 1895 was fairly liberal. The "Cast Down Your Bucket!" speech was a masterpiece of doubletalk and did not involve—as Washington himself reminded Edna D. Cheney—the renunciation of any of the Afro-American's rights.[58] Nor does the speech seem conservative when compared to the position of the American Negro Academy in whose bosoms the Talented Tenth philosophy first quickened. W.E.B. Du Bois, one of the younger members of the Academy, articulated in 1897 the following position:

> We believe that the first and greatest step toward the settlement of the present friction between the races—commonly called the Negro Problem—lies in the correction of the immorality, crime and laziness among the Negroes themselves, which still remains as a heritage from slavery. We believe that only earnest and long continued efforts on our own part can cure these social ills.[59]

While such a statement reveals definite concern for the welfare of the masses and a commitment to uplifting them it does not reveal a willingness to accept the masses on their own terms. Major Afro-American bourgeois reform institutions such as the Tuskegee Machine, the American Negro Academy, the Universal Negro Improvement Association, and the NACW have tended to see their function as "uplifitng" the masses and preparing them for life in the twentieth century. The tendency to romanticize the culture of the folk—a tendency that is disturbingly persistent in contemporary black thought—was only beginning to make itself felt in black intellectual circles during the 1890's.

In July of 1896, the Colored Women's League of Washington, D.C. held its national convention in Washington. Mrs. Mary Dickerson of Newport, R.I., was sent by the NFA-AW to present fraternal greetings. The major development at this meeting was the tendering of an offer to the Federation that a joint committee be appointed to work toward a meeting between the two groups so that "they might go before the country with but one national organization of Colored Women."[60] While the two groups were eventually able to accomplish a successful merger, their hopes of achieving monolithic unity among Afro-American women were doomed to disappointment. The new organization that came into existence as a result of the Washington meetings was called the National Association of Colored Women. This group was the major national organization of Afro-American women until 1935, when Mary McLeod Bethune, one of its past presidents, founded the National Council of Negro Women which, along with other groups, now shares that role.

The name of the National Federation was changed to National Association of Colored Women, partly as a concession to the Washington league, and partly because some of the ladies objected to the name Afro-American.[61] An editorial in *The Woman's Era* had opposed use of the hyphenated term because it was too cumbersome. Victoria Earle Matthews, a friend of T. Thomas Fortune, who was editor of the *New York Age* and reputed author of the term's fashionablilty, sought to preserve its use:

> Mrs. Matthews gave the audience to understand that she had African blood in her veins and was of African descent, which entitled her to the name Afro. While this was true, having been born in America, she was an American citizen and entitled to all the privileges as such, although many of these rights are constantly denied, she was entitled to the name American, therefore she claimed that the Negro in America was entitled to the name Afro-American as much as the French, Franco-American, or the English, Anglo-American; as for the name "colored," it meant nothing to the Negro race. She was not a colored American, but an Afro-American.[62]

This debate over a change of name for the organization reveals that black people were involved in a full-swing debate over what to call themselves as early as the 1890's. The term "Afro-American," while historically and culturally more descriptive than "colored," "black," or "Negro," suffers from being a hypenated word. Furthermore, its acknowledgement of Africa has often been deemed inappropriate during times when the black community has sought to emphasize its Americanness. "Afro-American" had some unfortunate connotations in the Boston area, where it was the term employed by some middle-class light-skinned Negroes to distinguish themselves from lower-class blacks.[63] The term may also have been considered too political, as it implied a connection with T. Thomas Fortune's militant Afro-American League.

Fifty clubs were in attendance at the first convention of the NFA-AW, which was the same convention at which it merged with the Washington league and voted to change its name to the National Association of Colored Women. The keynote address was given by Mrs. Rosetta Douglass-Sprague, the daughter of Frederick Douglass:[64]

> Our wants are numerous. We want homes in which purity can be taught, not hovels that are police-court feeders; we want industrial schools where labor of all kinds is taught, enabling our boys and girls to become skilled in the trades; we want the dram shops closed; we want the pool rooms and gambling dens of every variety swept out of existence; we want reform schools for our girls in such cities where the conscience of the white Christian is not elastic enough to take in the Negro child.

The resolutions passed in Washington in 1896 were somewhat more commendable than those approved in Atlanta seven months earlier. They included resolutions endorsing the industrial school movement, encouraging "mothers" meetings throughout the country, where the mothers of our race be taught the necessity of pure homes and lives and privacy in home apartments." The work of the W.C.T.U. was endorsed; the *Plessy* vs. *Ferguson* decision was deplored. One resolution stated:

> That as "the gods help those who help themselves," we hereby condemn unreservedly the excursions and picnics of our race which patronize the railroads in the states where the separate car law is in operation, and pledge ourselves to do everything in our power through the press and pulpit to educate race public sentiment on this point. The recent decision of the U.S. Supreme Court convinces us that we must depend upon ourselves in this matter.[65]

The convention passed a resolution heartily endorsing the work of Mrs. Ida B. Wells-Barnett "in arousing the civilized world to the horrors of lynch law as it now stands in our country." It also heartily endorsed the work of Booker T. Washington, thereby advocating both agitation and self-help. The ladies dealt with one issue relating specifically to women's rights. The legal status of women (and children) was to be "looked into," but, interestingly, no resolution was passed taking a strong stand on women's rights.

When Josephine St. Pierre Ruffin called the First Conference of Negro Women in 1895, she clearly intended to form an organization that would deal with the race problem, but one that would deal just as conscientiously with the "general questions of the day." Even at the first conference, however, a strong racial concern was clearly dominant, and in 1896, when the year-old NFA-AW and the Colored Women's League of Washington, D.C. united to form the NACW, they brought into existence something more than a women's organization that was incidentally black. The obvious desire of the NFA-AW and the NACW to function primarily as racial organizations during the years of this study, may be attributed to a number of factors.

First, it seemed impossible for middle-class Afro-American women to separate their concerns as women from their concerns as black people. To have done so would have been unrealistic since they were victims not only of sexism, but of racism as well, and since the conditions of life for bourgeois colored women were drastically different from those for bourgeois white women.

Second, the Tuskegee Machine, with its well-publicized position of self-help for racial advancement, made its influences felt in the women's clubs through Washingtonian sympathizers, like Mary Church Terrell; through active agents, like Fannie Barrier Williams; and, through Mrs. Booker T. Washington. There is reason to believe that the campaign for a two-class system of Jim Crow was an extension of Tuskegee policy.

Third, conflicts with white women's groups worked to augment separatist tendencies. Separatism was in its origins, the fault of white women who, with a few notable exceptions, refused to associate with black women. Also, the misguided feminism of Frances Willard and others who apologized for lynching, was highly offensive to women of color.[66]

Fourth, it was a concern for the public image of black women that had led to the organization of the NFA-AW. The cowardly backstabbing of Mr. Jno. W. Jacks had been the catalyst for Mrs. Ruffin's *Call*. The Woman's Era Club had been committed by its consitution to the publicizing of racial progress. The NACW was organized because of an awareness that black women needed to unite in order to defend themselves and their men from white racist sexism.

While the NFA-AW and the NACW were self-help institutions, certain members gave strong indications of integrationist militancy. Josephine Ruffin and Fannie B. Williams participated in the activities of white women's groups. These women, along with Mrs. Terrell, Mrs. Wells-Barnett, and Mrs. Booker T. Washington, maintained contacts with white women reformers, both British and American, throughout the turn-of-the-century years. These contacts provided an area of communication between the white and the black bourgeoisie during an era when the doctrine of "social equality" was not at all fashionable. The tradition of self-help and interracial cooperation, inaugurated during the nineties, was carried on throughout the early decades of the twentieth century.

The women of the NACW had a genuine concern for the problems of the black masses. They adopted as their watchword the slogan, "lifting as we climb. This paralleled the Talented Tenth spirit of *noblesse obliqe* as represented in the philosophy of the American Negro Academy and in the writings of Alexander Crummell and W.E.B. Du Bois. Local activities of the clubs were directed towards providing community services for less fortunate brothers and sisters. Prison reform was a common concern of many local clubs throughout the country. Orphanages were established in St. Louis and New Orleans, and a home for working girls, set up in Brooklyn. The Richmond Women's League, the Kansas City, Missouri League, and the Atlanta Women's Club provided legal services for black men and women who needed them, but had no money to pay.

While certain prominent clubwomen, like Mrs. Ruffin and Mrs. Terrell, had feminist leanings, the NACW does not seem to have challenged as a matter of policy, traditional conceptions of a woman's role. Indeed, a great part of the work of the NACW seems to have been the encouragement of the masses of black women to accept the sexual morality of the Victorian bourgeoisie. The two organizational conventions passed what they called "social purity" resolutions. The women also took a strong stand in favor of temperance. What all this indicates is that the NACW, like its white counterpart, the General Federation of Women's Clubs was fervently committed to the maintenance of genteel bourgeois morality. The Afro-American clubwoman was conservative in terms of our own late twentieth-century values, but cooperative with the progressivism of her own times. The conservatism of the NACW, far from indicating an isolation from the concerns of the masses, shows a deep concern for the problems of ordinary blacks. The NACW was dedicated—as its members would have put it—to the work of uplift.

Uplift is the key word, for the middle-class Afro-American woman, like her white counterpart, viewed the masses as victims of cultural and social retardation. She had little sense of fellowship or identity with the masses. Her attitude was often one of crusading, uplifing zeal. The masses were to be prepared for the responsibilities of citizenship; they were to be Anglo-Americanized, it was hoped; they would be assimilated into mainstream American life. While this philosophy of assimilation may have been optimistic and premature, it was not silly or selfish. No worse, really, than a black adaption of the settlement house philosophy, which hoped to make Anglo-Saxons out of Armenian Catholics and Russian Jews. I feel comfortable with the generalization that the attempts of bourgeois black women to organize as bourgeois women were salubrious and praiseworthy. Indeed, the activites of the NACW and the contents of *The Woman's Era* reveal that a significant number of middle-class black women at the turn of the century were socially responsible and politically aware, a far cry from the pejorative stereotype.

Chapter Six

W.E.B. Du Bois
and Traditional Black
Nationalism

On March 9, 1895, the young William Edward Burghardt Du Bois participated in a memorial service at Wilberforce University in honor of Frederick Douglass, who had died seventeen days earlier. Addressing the convocation on "Douglass as Statesman," Du Bois acknowledged the inspiration of Frederick Douglass, the universal reformer, who, "as an advocate of civil rights . . . stood outside mere race lines and placed himself upon the broad basis of humanity." Douglass had carried the struggle outside the realm of racial chauvinism and self-interest, arguing, as Du Bois himself was known to do, not that black men should be honored "merely on account of their blackness," but that all men should be respected on the basis of their character. Strange it was, then, that Du Bois should climax his oration with a statement that was much closer to the spirit of Alexander Crummell than to that of his old rival Douglass, contending that, "Douglass and his race strive to say not only may individuals of a race arise, but races in the family of nations may also rise."[1]

Du Bois must be associated with the tradition of militant black journalists represented by Frederick Douglass, T. Thomas Fortune, and William Monroe Trotter, if by this we mean that he was more in agreement with their methods than with those of Booker T. Washington. But there is a difference between method and ideology, and to say that a certain group of writers were in agreement on the question of the importance of agitation and propaganda is not to imply that they shared the same political values. Unlike Douglass, Du Bois was never a radical assimilationist; he was influenced by the racial metaphysics that had flourished before the Civil War and would revive with the flamboyant Garvey movement. If Du Bois was not a chauvinist for black skin, or an advocate of biological separatism, he certainly wished to conserve races as organic cultures; in this sense, at least, he was conservative. Unlike either the egalitarian Douglass or the practical Washington, Du Bois was fascinated by race which he conceived as a mystical cosmic force. He did not view the concept of race as a mere figment of depraved imagination, or as the fabrication of oppressor classes. The young Du Bois called the idea of race "the vastest and most ingenious invention for human progress."[2]

Du Bois's similarities to the German racial theorists have been commented upon by A. Norman Klein, who sees his rhetoric as similar to the "superheated prose of central European nationalism," which is to Klein more in harmony "with a utopian *Volksgeist* and a German nationalist tradition than with the political rhetoric of a Garvey or any later American black nationalist leader."[3] Klein overlooked the fact that Garvey also resembled the German nationalists, not only in his rhetoric, but in his public style as well. Along with Garvey, Du Bois represented the culmination of a tradition that conceived black nationalism in European terms. As a young man, Du Bois heroized Bismarck, who "had made a nation out of a mass of bickering peoples."[4] Later, he studied with Heinrich von Treitschke and seems to have had some regard for the "fire-eating Pan German," whom he called the "most interesting of the professors."[5] But while it is probably true that Du Bois was influenced to some extent directly by German nationalism, it is just as likely that his ideas on race were informed by direct and indirect contacts with the ideas of such early Christian black nationalists as Blyden and Crummell, who admitted to European influences themselves.

Some months after the Douglass memorial service, Du Bois met Alexander Crummell at the Wilberforce commencement excercises. His own description of this first encounter, in which he describes his instinctive respect for the man, leads one to suspect that Du Bois found in Crummell a spiritual father to take the place of the natural father he had never known.[6] A year or two later, Du Bois was among the forty black intellectuals enlisted in the American Negro Academy of which Crummell was the first president. In the Academy's *Occasional Papers,* Du Bois published his Crummellian essay, "The Conservation of Races," showing that he was hardly out of step with the conservative Crummell during his years with the American Negro Academy.

"The Conservation of Races," published two years after Booker T. Washington's "Atlanta Exposition Address," reveals that by 1897, Du Bois had hardly emerged as an uncompromising integrationist. In this essay, Du Bois placed the responsibility for racial elevation upon the blacks themselves and strongly discouraged individualism because of his belief that "the history of the world is the history, not of individuals, but of groups, not of nations, but of races, and he who ignores or seeks to override the race idea in human history ignores and overrides the central thought of all history." Like Crummell, Du Bois showed an irreverence for American democratic traditions, especially those associated with the thought of Thomas Jefferson. The trait of authoritarian collectivism, often associated with black leadership, is strong in the address. Du Bois's discourse revealed an idea recurrent throughout his writings, that "closed race groups made history," a fact difficult to accept by Americans "reared and trained under the individualistic philosophy of the Declaration of Independence and the laisser-faire philosophy of Adam Smith."[7]

Du Bois defined a race as "a vast family of human beings generally of common blood and language, always of common history, traditions, and impulses, who are both voluntarily and involuntarily striving together for the accomplishment of certain more or less vividly conceived ideals of life." This was a dimly perceived definition, and its illustration did little to clarify exactly what Du Bois saw as the essential characteristics of a race. The twenty-nine year old Du Bois identified eight different races:

> They are the Slavs of eastern Europe, the Teutons of middle Europe, the English of Great Britain and America, the Romance nations of Southern and Western Europe, the Negroes of Africa and America, the Semitic people of Western

Asia and Northern Africa, the Hindoos of Central Asia and the Mongolians of Eastern Asia.[8]

This was faulty parallelism at its worst—a thoughtless concatenation of non-comparable entities, a wrenching together of religious, racial, geographical and linguistic groups. Why were the English, but not the Spanish and the French, assigned the status of races? Du Bois revealed here an Anglo-chauvinism that was to be bitterly disclaimed in later years.[9]

Du Bois's use of terminology in "The Conservation of Races" was disgracefully inconsistent. He interchanged such terms as "race" and "nation" with reckless abandon, and unsqueamishly assigned two different meanings to "civilization" within the same paragraph, thereby confusing it with "culture." The basis of Du Bois's raciological theory was not rational, but mystical; it was not grounded in reason, but in something akin to faith. Du Bois believed that racial growth was historically characterized by "the differentiation of spiritual and mental differences between great races of mankind and the integration of physical differences." This process had led to the clustering of mankind into the "present division of races as indicated by physical researches." And this was accompanied by the deepening of intraracial divisions between sub-races or "race groups." Each of these race groups or nations was striving "each in its own way, to develop for civilization its particular message, its particular ideal . . . " The German nation stood for science and philosophy; the English nation for "constitutional liberty and commercial freedom." It was manifest that some of the great races, "particularly the Negro race," had "not as yet given to civilization the full spiritual message which they [were] capable of giving." In 1897 Du Bois considered the issue of whether or not the Egyptian "civilization" was black "a mooted question." But whether or not Egypt had been a black culture, it seemed obvious that the "full, complete Negro message of the whole Negro race" had not yet been donated to civilization.[10]

The classical black nationalist traits of mysticism, authoritarianism, civilizationism and collectivism were strong elements in "The Conservation of Races." Du Bois called upon the Academy to exercise a firm leadership and to become "the epitome and expression of the intellect of the black-blooded people of America." The black leaders were not to organize for such mundane purposes as the stealing of political spoils, nor "merely to protest and pass resolutions." Black leadership should be united in its efforts to improve the black masses, to fight against loafing, gambling, crime, and prostitution. Black leadership should be committed to a firm belief in "our high destiny" to strive for "the rearing of a race ideal in America and Africa, to the glory of God and the uplifting of the Negro people."[11]

In 1903, Du Bois published *The Souls of Black Folk,* which is often viewed as an assimilationist manifesto. Actually, the book forcefully reiterates a theme carried out in "The Conservation of Races," where blacks are characterized as "that people whose subtle sense of song has given America its only American music, its only American fairy tales, its only touch of pathos and humor amid its mad money-getting plutocracy." In *The Souls of Black Folk* Du Bois similarly referred to black people as "the sole oasis of simple faith and reverence in a dusty desert of Dollars." In both the essay and the book, the black American was viewed as having a particular message to contribute to American life, just as the Negro race had a particular message to contribute to world civilization. His suffering had made him a seer.

> After the Egyptian and Indian, the Greek and Roman, the Teuton and Mongolian, the Negro is a sort of seventh son, born with a veil, and gifted with second-sight in this American world,—a world which yields him no true self-consciousness, but only lets him see himself through the revelation of the other world. It is a peculiar sensation, this double-consciousness, this sense of always looking at one's self through the eyes of others, of measuring one's self through the eyes of others, of measuring one's soul by the tape of a world that looks on in amused contempt and pity. One ever feels this twoness,—an American, a Negro; two souls, two thoughts, two unreconciled strivings; two warring ideals in one dark body, whose dogged strength alone keeps it from being torn asunder.[12]

This ambivalence makes it impossible to neatly pigeonhole Du Bois into either the black nationalist or the radical assimilationist tradition.

Two chapters of *The Souls of Black Folk* were devoted to
appraising black leadership as represented by Alexander Crummell and Booker T. Washington. The attack on Washington
involved more than a dispute over philosophies of education. It
was the attack of a conservative anticapitalist upon the values of
an upstart burgher class. Booker T. Washington represented "the
spirit of the age which was dominating the North . . . the speech
and thought of triumphant commercialism, and the ideals of
material prosperity."[13] The reason for the opposition of Du Bois
to the leadership of Booker T. Washington was linked to the
materialism that Washington represented. Du Bois's affinity to
Crummell probably stemmed from his appreciation for the
nonmaterial world in which the ascetic elder statesman of racial
mysticism had dwelt. Du Bois—and certainly Crummell before
him—had naturally recognized the importance of entrepreneurial
values to the programs they wished to launch, but neither wished
to see black leadership pass from the educated ministers and
professionals to the businessmen and administrators. Du Bois
identified with the older generation of ministerial leadership and
considered Alexander Crummell and Bishop Payne to be more
important than even the more respectable class of black politicians, with whom Washington was linked in his mind.[14] For Du
Bois, as for Crummell, the essential prerequisites for human
fulfullment were neither wealth, nor cheap political savvy, but
character and spiritual values:

> The old leaders of Negro opinion, in the little groups where
> there is a Negro social consciousness, are being replaced by
> new; neither the black preacher nor the black teacher leads as
> he did two decades ago. Into their places are pushing the
> farmers and gardeners, the well-paid porters and artisans, the
> businessmen,—all those with property and money. And with
> all this change, so curiously parallel to that of the Other-
> world, goes too the same inevitable change in ideals. The
> South laments today the slow, steady disappearance of a
> certain type of Negro,—the faithful, courteous slave of other
> days, with his incorruptible honesty and dignified humility.
> He is passing away just as surely as the old type of Southern
> gentleman is passing, and from not dissimilar causes,—the

sudden transformation of a fair far-off ideal of Freedom into the hard reality of bread-winning and the consequent deification of bread.[15]

Such a sentimental, racist, and unscientific appraisal of black leadership was, if not a justification of slavery, then at least an apology for the old Bourbon estate. In its approach to the problems of land, labor, and capital, *The Souls of Black Folk* was not as radical as T. Thomas Fortune's *Black and White,* published twenty years earlier.

When he wrote *The Souls of Black Folk,* Du Bois, who was capable of writing perfectly good sociology, sometimes lapsed into a wholly unscientific frame of mind. Confronted with a value judgement between the ideals represented by Washington and those represented by the Old South, his opinions were imbued with an "ottantottist" nostalgia for a world that never was.[16] Du Bois was an anticapitalist long before he was a socialist. Only late in life did he come to believe "that private ownership of capital and free enterprise [were] leading the world to disaster."[17] Du Bois is remembered as one of the great socialists of the twentieth century, and it is easy to forget the conservatism of his intellectual origins. He became a socialist by gradual stages. An imperious intellectual, a graduate of Harvard with a sense of *noblesse oblige* and a conservative, classical view of education, he was not ready to accept in 1903 what he called "a cheap and dangerous socialism." In 1907 he called himself a "Socialist-of-the-Path," meaning that he favored the socialization of certain naturally monopolistic industries which he felt were "no more private than God's blue sky."[18] Du Bois attacked capitalist business enterprise which preyed on the black peasantry, but his position was not radical or revolutionary. He cautioned Americans lest they "force moderate reformers and men with new and valuable ideas to become red radicals and revolutionists."[19] What Du Bois found most appealing about socialism was neither its opposition to private ownership, nor its leveling tendencies, but rather its war on the values of upstart bourgeois culture. Also congenial was socialism's insistence on collectivism, planning, and control.

Du Bois's twenty four year editorship of *The Crisis* was

characterized by mingling of the supposedly alien elements—racial chauvinism and social egalitarianism. This was linked with a pseudo-Christian mysticism, reminiscent of Emerson, but wholly of Du Bois's own creation. It was a personal mythology in which the collective consciousness of mankind, striving for world brotherhood, became a godlike demiurge, addressed in apostrophic voice and memorialized in heroic verse. During the early teens, transcendental and egalitarian elements were dominant in Du Bois's published writings. In both his national and international life, Du Bois worked for brotherhood among the races. In the first issue of *The Crisis*, he promised that the editorial page would stand for "the rights of men, irrespective of color or race, for the highest ideals of American democracy, and for reasonable but earnest and persistent attempt to gain these rights and realize these ideals."[20]

His early years with *The Crisis* fall into the period when Du Bois toyed with the idea of non-revolutionary white-collar socialism of the domestic American variety. He remembered this as a period when he had "conceived an inter-racial culture as superseding our goal of a purely American culture."[21] Before World War I, Du Bois worked in close cooperation with a group of liberals, progressives, and reform socialists including Jane Addams, Mary White Ovington, William English Walling, and Charles Edward Russell. In 1910, Du Bois joined the Socialist Party, but resigned in 1912, hoping to support the Progressive Party of Theodore Roosevelt, who was hardly committed to an ideal vision of world brotherhood. Du Bois proposed a plank for the party platform which he sent to Chicago, and asked the party to demand for American blacks "the repeal of unfair discriminatory laws and the right to vote on the same terms on which other citizens vote." It was taken to Chicago by Joel V. Spingarn, advocated by Henry Moskowitz and Jane Addams. "Theodore Roosevelt would have none of it. He told Mr. Spingarn frankly that he should be 'careful of that man Du Bois,' who was in Roosevelt's opinion a 'dangerous' person."[22]

Angered by Roosevelt's rejection, Du Bois threw the weight of *The Crisis* behind Woodrow Wilson, though he actually preferred the Socialists with their "manly stand for human rights irrespective of color."[23] Even as late as 1912, at the age of forty-four, Du

Bois had not become a commited radical, but was still an optimistic Progressive. He claimed in his autobiography that Marxism began to influence him during student days in Berlin and that its influences became increasingly strong after World War I. Nonetheless, Du Bois continued to display a distrust of the mob and a belief in the right of the educated to exclusive exercise of the voter's franchise as late as 1919 and the publication of *Darkwater.* Such compromises with egalitarian ethics would be acceptable at least temporarily, "until the ignorant and their children are taught; or to avoid too sudden an influx of inexperienced voters."[24] When he spoke of socialism, he removed it from the context of unqualified democracy, expressing a fear of the "tyranny of the majority" akin to Crummell's. If he favored democracy at all, it was a technocratic democracy resembling that advocated by Frederick Winslow Taylor or Thorstein Veblen. His socialism was still cautious; the transformation of society was not to be effected by instant revolution, but would advance step by careful step.

Du Bois was influenced throughout his life by both the conservative tradition of Crummell, and the radical transcendental principles of Douglass. Even when he urged Communism, the aging Du Bois did so on black nationalistic rather than on Marxist grounds. He was similar in this respect to Crummell, who had encouraged Victorian morality with a black nationalistic rhetoric, generalizing that "in West Africa, every female is a virgin to the day of her marriage," and that "the harlot class is unknown in all their tribes."[25] It was in such a spirit that Du Bois referred in *The Souls of Black Folk* to "ancient African chastity" and it was in such a spirit that he spoke of "the ancient socialism of Africa," and said of Ghana in 1962 that:

> Socialism blossoms hold
> On Communism centuries old.[26]

Du Bois's involvement in the Pan African Conference in London in 1900 has been frequently alluded to in recent years. Often overlooked is his more cosmopolitan interest in the Universal Races Congress in London in 1911, which was of equal importance to his development. The Pan African Conference was called by Trinidad Barrister, H. Sylvester Williams, "to bring into closer touch with each other the peoples of African descent throughout the world," to establish better relations with the whites, and to work towards "securing to all African races living in civilized countries their full rights, and to promote their business interests." Du Bois, as chairman of the Committee on Address to the Nations of the World, submitted a position paper that was signed by dignitaries of the conference. The paper was written in a spirit of interracial cooperation:

> Let not the spirit of Garrison, Phillips and Douglass wholly die out in America; may the conscience of a great Nation rise and rebuke all dishonesty and unrighteous oppression toward the American Negro, and grant to him the right of franchise, security of person and property, and generous recognition of the great work he has accomplished in a generation toward raising nine millions of human beings from slavery to manhood.[27]

This was mild Pan-Africanism; it was not race centered or chauvinistic. Similar in spirit was the Universal Races Conference that Du Bois attended in 1911. It was in the transcendental spirit of the Races Conference that Du Bois published his "Hymn to the Peoples."[28]

> Save us, World Spirit, from our Lesser Selves!
> Grant us that war and hatred cease,
> Reveal our souls in every race and hue!
> Help us, O Human God, in this Thy Truce
> To make Humanity divine!

Du Bois buttressed his enthusiastic interracialism with sociological studies, for these were the years during which he "followed sociology as the path to social uplift as a result of scientific investigation."[29] Du Bois's sociology was never free of ideological influences; sociology never is. Unobtrusive elements of classical black nationalism were present even in the meticulous five-hundred page demographic masterpiece that he produced single-handedly in 1896, *The Philadelphia Negro.* Self-help,

Talented Tenth elitism, and the philosophy of domestic feminism had left their distinctive impressions upon him. He encouraged the "better classes" of blacks to undertake "preventive and rescue work," such as "keeping little girls off the street at night, stopping the escorting of unchaperoned young ladies to church and elsewhere . . . , exposing the dangers of gambling and policy playing, and inculcating respect for women. . . . Above all, the better classes of Negroes should recognize their duty toward the masses."[30]

From 1897 to 1911, Du Bois was editor of the *Atlanta University Studies*. With a series of substantial little books issued under these auspices, Du Bois once again proved himself a scientist of prideful craftsmanship and prodigious seriousness. Typically grounded in a careful study of scholarship on African as well as American societies, the *Atlanta University Studies* showed a concern for the processes of social change whereby groups evolve culturally in response to both external and internal pressures. *The Negro American Family* (1908), anticipated the work of Frazier. Familial institutions had been efficient and orderly in West Africa. Upon transplantation to America, said Du Bois, "the first instinctive effort of the transplanted group was to restore the ancestral *Mores* . . . " Even under such catastrophic conditions as slavery presented, traces of African institutions persisted. "They would, however, be traces only, for the effectiveness of the slave system meant the practically complete crushing out of the African clan and family life."[31] Black Americans were engaged in the process of rebuilding such institutions as the family after the American pattern. In other studies, *The Negro Chruch*, for example, and *The Black Artisan*, Du Bois again revealed his concern for the relative importance of African survivals and European influences on black community organization. This appreciation for the duality in black American culture, the dialogue between Africa and America, permeated Du Bois's work on all levels—scientific and literary.

Because of his leadership in the Pan-African Conferences of 1900, 1919, 1923, 1927, and 1945, Du Bois has been called the "Father of Modern Pan-Africanism," a title he shares with numerous other individuals. The conferences which he helped to organize have been hailed by such leaders as Jomo Kenyatta, Kwame Nkrumah, and Nnamdi Azikiwe as a source of inspiration in the struggle for African independence. Du Bois's conception of Pan-Africanism was broader and more democratic than Marcus Garvey's, whose concept of African nationalism, obviously modeled on European nationalism, led Garvey to affect the airs of an Austrian archduke. Du Bois's African nationalism was to be democratic and socialistic. More importantly, it was to be based on African patterns. The structure of the family among certain West Coast tribes, and the position of women within that structure were hailed as possible patterns for a modern African state. The native African village was to be the model for the neo-African culture, and in his essay, "What is Civilization? Africa's Answer," he calls the native village "a perfect human thing." It was Du Bois's philosophy, and not Garvey's, which was ultimately to form the basis for twentieth century Pan-Africanism. The statement on Pan-Africanism from *The Crisis* of February 1919 would be acceptable to many Pan-Africanists in the United States today:

> The African movement means to us what the Zionist movement must mean to the Jews, the centralization of race effort and the recognition of a racial front. To help bear the burden of Africa does not mean any lessening of effort in our own problem at home. Rather it means increased interest. For any ebullition of action and feeling that results in an amelioration of the lot of Africa tends to ameliorate the condition of colored peoples throughout the world.

Du Bois became a citizen of Ghana in 1963. He explained his emigration in one of his later poems, employing a classical Crummellian rhetoric. Crummell had said in 1848, "amid the decay of nations, a rekindled light starts up in us." Du Bois published the following in *Freedomways*, (Winter, 1962):

> I lifted my last voice and cried
> I cried to heaven as I died
> O turn me to the Golden Horde
> Summon all western nations
> Toward the Rising Sun.
> From reeking West whose day is done,

Who stink and stagger in their dung
Toward Africa, China, India's strand
Where Kenya and Himalaya stand
And Nile and Yang-tze roll:

. . . .

Awake, awake, O sleeping world
Honor the sun
Worship the stars, those vaster suns
Who rule the night
Where black is bright
And all unselfish work is right
And Greed is sin.
And Africa leads on
Pan Africa.

Du Bois is remembered as a radical liberal; he possessed certain traits of mind and character which make it reasonable to place him within this tradition. Such traits were his life-long commitment to free thought and common sense, his hatred of military "tinsil and braggadocio," his reverence for life. Du Bois campaigned for open housing while editor of *The Crisis* and he believed in the right of every man to choose his own friends. He defended the right to interracial marriage, although he personally possessed racial conservationist instincts. Du Bois supported the white working class in their quest for labor reform in spite of the racism endemic to American unionism. Like his predecessor, Alexander Crummell, he was an early fighter for women's rights. And although he became an atheist in his later years, he was always capable of genuine religious tolerance.

But Du Bois had his darker side, a mystical ethnocentric, formal authoritarian one. These tendencies were partially inherited from Alexander Crummell, the "born autocrat,"[32] and the American Negro Academy, which existed in order to dictate literary and artistic standards to black America, as well as manners and morals, and "to do for the Negro race what the French Academy did for France."[33] Du Bois was as much a "racial chauvinist" as Marcus Garvey. At times he became involved in a black "aryanism," tracing every civilized worldly thing to an African origin.

The primitive religion of Africa, as developed by the African village, underlies the religions of the world. Egyptian religion was in its beginning and later development of purely Negro character, and mulatto Egyptian priests on the stones of Egypt continually receive their symbols of authority from the black priests of Ethiopa. . . .
The religion of the black man spread among all the Mediterranean races. Shango, god of the West Coast, hurler of thunderbolts and lord of the storms, render of trees and slayer of men, cruel and savage and yet beneficent, was the prototype of Zeus and Jupiter and Thor.[34]

Du Bois often argued that all the culture of the Western world had originated in the region of the Nile-Congo watershed, because all Egyptian civilization was black in origin and all Western civilization originated in Egypt.

Like most black nationalists, Du Bois desired that America evolve into a truly pluralistic society, but, like the majority of black nationalists, he was reluctant to allow pluralism within the black community. He apologized for Stalinist totalitarianism and he came to reject utterly the concept of individual freedom:

But what is Socialism? It is disciplined economy and political organization in which the first duty of a citizen is to serve the state . . . the African tribe, whence all of you sprung, was communistic in its very beginnings. No tribesman was free. All were servants of the tribe of whom the chief was father and voice.[35]

Because Du Bois's life spanned almost a century, he was able to experience growth that few of his contemporaries were to realize. He escaped to some extent from the Protestant biases of most English-speaking blacks, and came by stages to accept the emerging ideal of a black nationalism that blended African and cosmopolitan values, as the following chapters will illustrate.

PART THREE

The Political Tradition
in Literature

The Negro race must come to a consciousness of itself before it can produce great literature. It must come to a consicousness of its aims and powers, to a self-realization of its ideals and talents, before it can produce great literature. The civilization of a people is reflected in its literature. Literature is something that wells up spontaneously from the soul-depths of the race. It is the expression, in artistic form, of the deep-seated thought and feelings, dreams and longings of the race.

WILLIAM H. FERRIS
The African Abroad, 1913

Chapter Seven

The Roots
of Literary Black
Nationalism
Delany's Blake

Martin Delany's *Blake* (1859) is the earliest known example of a black nationalist novel in the United States. Dominated by a Pan-Africanist plot and a tone of Christian racialism, it is a fictional statement of themes that were prominent in all black nationalist writing of the ninteenth century. Four observations may be made concerning *Blake* that will help to place the novel within the context of Afro-American literary tradition. First, *Blake* was Delany's substitute for a slave narrative. Second, it was inspired by the slave revolutionary tradition, which was sometimes nationalistic. Third, the novel is intimately tied to the religious racialism that is such an important factor in nineteenth century writing. Finally, *Blake* is an expression of the Pan-African strivings of Delany and his circle.

The most important variety of black writing in America before the Civil War was neither poetry, fiction, or drama, but autobiography in the form of slave narratives.[1] Accounts by ex-slaves of their bondage and quest for freedom were a popular literary form before the Civil War. Two of the most widely read varieties of this genre were the accounts of whites who had been enslaved by Indians, and the accounts of blacks and mulattoes who had been enslaved by whites. Black American slave narratives were usually sensationalistic and brutal, yet widely appealing in an age when genteel readers could accept stark realism only if they were convinced that it was truth and not fiction. Slave narratives appealed to nineteenth century audiences in much the same way that Nazi horror stories appeal to present day audiences: they were a form of pious titillation of the baser passions.

Slave narratives were successful popular art and effective antislavery propaganda. Those that survive are valuable historical documents and some of them are serious literature of high quality. The narratives of J.W.C. Pennington, William Wells Brown, Frederick Douglass, and Samuel Ringgold Ward were all products of talented literary minds. Slave narratives were usually written with a purpose. Their vivid, melodramatic descriptions of floggings, blasphemies, murders, rapes, and the splitting up of families were not framed for the sole purpose of gratifying pious Victorian prurience. The slave narrative combined sentimentality, sex, and sadism to attract an audience for its message: that slavery was a great social evil that eroded public morality in many indirect ways. The crux of the argument in slave narratives was that slavery was uncivilized and un-Christian. Where slavery existed, there one found fornication, adultery, intemperance, gambling, bull-baiting, murder, and a host of other abominations in both the white and the black populations. The slave narrative supplied its genteel reader with vivid descriptions of the seamier side of life. The reader could justify his or her morbid curiosity with the rationalizations that the narratives always had a strong Christian moral, and that they were not mere idle fictions, but descriptions of fertile fields for Christian activism.

Martin Delany was barred from writing a slave narrative and exploiting this medium of publicity because he had never been a slave, although he had traveled extensively in the South during 1839.[2] He therefore did the next best thing and wrote a slave novel. In this fashion did *Blake* allow Delany to participate in the most important of nineteenth century black literary accomplishments. Unlike the slave narratives, Delany's novel never achieved wide popularity. It was serialized in *The Anglo-African Magazine* and *The Weekly Anglo-African* (1859-62), but a complete edition in book form has never been published.[3] While the novel was neither a financial nor an artistic success, it did contain elements of strength and it captured successfully the spirit of the slave narratives as well as demonstrating its author's complete empathy with the slave's experience.[4] At the same time, the novel attains the status of myth: it is an encyclopedic, heroic, and therefore, epic statement of Pan-African ideals. To understand *Blake* is to understand a good deal about literary black nationalism.

Blake is the story of Henry Holland, a free Negro, who attempts to organize a revolt among all the slaves of the Western Hemisphere. The plot describes the travels of Holland throughout the South and to Cuba as he plans his conspiracy. The idea of a hemispheric slave revolt was not a fantasy of Delany's, but a notion that was popular among the slaves. This does not mean that every act of resistance by a slave may be interpreted as an expression of Pan-African nationalism, but there is evidence that at least two black conspiracies of the early nineteenth century had a Pan-African rhetoric. These were the plots of Gabrial in 1800 and of Denmark Vesey in 1820, both of which were inspired by revolutionary blacks outside the United States.[5] The latter of these conspirators, Denmark Vesey, was, like Delany, a free black entrepreneur. Delany mentions the conspiracies of Gabrial and Vesey in his novel, as well as the rebellion of Nat Turner.[6] Delany's Turner is a mythical creation, a sort of Robin Hood similar to the fictional Nat Turner in William Wells Brown's *Clotel*. Delany also mentions the possibility of unity with the Indians and reminds his readers of the alliance between rebellious maroons and the Seminole nation in Florida.

Blake is a typical exhortation to revolt by a free black pamphleteer. It may be compared to *Walker's Appeal*, and the *Ethiopian Manifesto* because of its apocalyptic tone and its promise of a great black messiah. Like his friend, Henry Highland Garnet, Delany was enraged by the claim that servility was a natural trait of the African personality. He believed that the spirit of revolt was a universal human trait and therefore a proof of the black man's humanity. The spirit of revolt was thus to be encouraged among the slaves by such pamphlets as Garnet's *An Address to the Slaves of the United States of America*. Delany may indeed have intended his novel as a blueprint for revolt. It is known that Delany became involved in conspiratorial meetings with John Brown in 1858. The idea of promoting a general revolt among the slaves had been widely discussed at the black convention of 1843. In *Blake*, Delany steered a middle course between those who encouraged unplanned opportunistic rebellions and those who, like Frederick Douglass and John S. Rock, argued against the wisdom of encouraging slave revolts.

Delany's *Blake* is a typical expression of the religious racialism that characterized black nationalist writing. Delany was critical of black religion, which is not to say that he was antireligious or that he was hostile to religious leadership. Delany in fact was given to exploiting religious rhetoric as he did when he quoted the prophecy that Ethiopia would "soon stretch forth her hands unto God," and courted the friendship of mystical Ethiopianists like Henry Highland Garnet.[7] Delany was also given to comparing the plight of American slaves to that of the Hebrews in their Egyptian bondage. This was a tendency present in the religion of the slave masses, as expressed in the so-called "Negro Spirituals." Delany sketches black religion as a potentially revolutionary force in *Blake*. He sees it as a mechanism for day-to-day resistance, a means of working out fears and frustrations. When Mammy Judy is brought before her white master for questioning after the disappearance of a valued slave, she goes into religious hysterics:

> "Come, come, Judy! what are you crying about! let us hear quickly what you've got to say. Don't be frightened!"
> "No maus Stephen, I's not feahed; ah could run tru troop a hosses an' face de debil! My soul's happy, my soul's on fiah! Whoo! Blessed Jesus! Ride on, King!" when the old woman tossed and tumbled about so dexterously, that the master and mistress considered themselves lucky in getting out of the way.[8]

Of course, Mammy Judy is only buying time and withholding the desired information so as to aid in the escape. The rapid movement of the plot is often interrupted by the noisy religious enthusiasm of the slaves that erupts without warning.

In *The Condition of the Colored People*, Delany had criticized black Christians for being too passive, for waiting too patiently for God to send them deliverance rather than working to free themselves. At the same time, Delany felt that Christian religion, like other elements of slave culture including heathen conjuring, could be utilized as forms of social control and community organization. Delany's ambivalence is reflected in his character Henry Holland, who vacillates between agnosticism and states of profound, almost ecstatic, religiosity. Delany does not portray his protagonist as a holy man, or a prophet, or an instrument of God. Henry Holland is a Christian hero, who finds strength in his faith, but does not use it as a crutch. He must live by his wits and solve his own problems. Delany once said that Christians must be self-reliant and not depend upon God's divine providence to punish the evil and reward the good in this world.[9]

If Delany did not subscribe to the millenial belief in divine deliverance from slavery as did his contemporaries, Blyden and Crummell, he certainly shared with them their beliefs concerning the God-given attributes and destinies of races. He saw black people as an artistic race and he saw whites as a hard, cold, warrior race. Black writers like Du Bois and Sutton Griggs would continue to employ stereotypes of blacks as an emotional, naturally religious race of people, with a sense of divine mission and an ever-present, although sometimes covert racial chauvinism. Delany once asserted, in a vein similar to the romantic racialism of Harriet Beecher Stowe, that blacks were naturally endowed with the highest traits of civilization:

> They are civil, peaceable, and religious to a fault. In mathematics, sculpture and arcitecture, as arts and sciences, commerce and internal improvements as enterprises, the white race may probably excel; but in languages, oratory, poetry, music, and painting, as arts and sciences, and in ethics, metaphysics, theology, and legal jurisprudence—in plain language, in the true principles of morals, correctness of thought, religion, and law or civil government, there is no doubt but the black race will yet instruct the world.[10]

Such an approach to the concept of the "Negro Genius" would thrive until well into the twentieth century to be codified by Benjamin Brawley in 1915.[11] Whether or not he actually believed in divinely ordained racial genius, Delany certainly argued very strongly for it in *The Political Destiny of the Colored Race*. And in *Blake* he asserted that "some of the proudest American statesmen in either House of the Capitol, receive their poetic vigor of imagination from the current of Negro blood flowing in their veins."

Delany's *Blake* combined the slave narrative tradition with religious racialism and the Pan-African nationalist tradition. It was not the first piece of writing to do so. In 1789 Olaudah Equiano's authentic *Narrative* had contained a plea for the redemption of Africa and for the uplifting of black humanity through the collateral agencies of Christianity and civilization. Equiano had proposed that through commercial development, Africa could soon eradicate the slave trade, thereby raising the status of blacks all over the world. Delany, too, favored economic development of the continent as a means to universal elevation of the Negro's status, but he also advocated armed resistance among the blacks of the New World. The slave revolts of the late nineteenth and early twentieth centuries had occasionally revealed Pan-African aspirations. Henry Holland's conspiracy was to be, like the conspiracy of Denmark Vesey, international. Vesey had hoped to establish ties with revolutionary Haiti; Henry Holland sought to bring off simultaneous revolutions in Cuba and the southern states by combining the slave revolt tradition, the slave narrative tradition, ideological Pan-Africanism, and religious racialism in the United States.

While *Blake* was clearly the product of well-established literary and intellectual traditions, it did not make an immediate or direct contribution to these traditions. Although it was the second black novel published in the United States, *Blake* never attained any popularity and consequently had no influence. *Blake* was, however, the first novel written as a deliberate expression of black nationalist ideals. We should also remember that Martin Delany expressed his ideas elsewhere more successfully than in *Blake*. Other writers expressed similar ideas not because they were influenced by Delany or *Blake*, but because they confronted the same environment that Delany confronted, and their reactions to it were similar. The most important promoter of continuity in a literary tradition is neither conscious imitation nor unconscious influences of past authors, but the power of social environments to cause successive generations to repeat certain types of literary behavior.

Delany's *Blake* was traditional without being influential. The following chapters deal with W.E.B. Du Bois, who was both traditional and influential, and with Sutton Griggs, whose novels were traditional but had little influence. The writings of both these authors contain elements that were present in earlier Afro-American authors, like Delany. The reason for the persistence of themes and myths present in Delany's work in authors as recent as Du Bois and Griggs is less likely due to influences than to the persistence of hostile race relations in the society in which the writing was produced. Ethiopian mysticism was never more than a literary device for Delany or Du Bois; neither had much faith in divine intervention on the black man's behalf. Pan-Africanism was likewise for Delany, Du Bois and Griggs, as much a literary as a practical experience. The purpose of this and of the following two chapters is to illustrate some of the ways in which black nationalism affected the poetry and fiction of three Afro-American authors.

Chapter Eight

The Poetics of
Ethiopianism
W.E.B. Du Bois
and Literary Black
Nationalism

Du Bois's position with respect to black nationalism has been described as ambivalent, reflecting his admitted double-consciousness as both a black man and an American, his "two souls, two thoughts, two unreconciled strivings; two warring ideals in one dark body."[1] This often-quoted line registers the double-consciousness manifested in the thought of many Afro-Americans, and, indeed, many Western intellectuals who have attempted to be at once culturally nationalist, and yet loyal to a more broadly conceived "western Civilization." Du Bois's early work struggles to fuse two complementary but substantially different mythological traditions. The first of these is "Ethiopianism," a literary-religious tradition common to English-speaking Africans, regardless of nationality.[2] The other is the European tradition of interpretive mythology, transplanted to America by its European colonizers.

The Ethiopian tradition sprang, as we have seen, from certain shared political and religious experiences of English-speaking Africans during the late eighteenth and early nineteenth centuries. It found expression in the slave narratives, in the exhortations of conspiratorial slave preachers, and in the songs and folklore of the slaves of the Old and the peasants of the New South.[3] On a more literary level, it appeared in the sermons and political tracts of the sophisticated urban elite. The name Ethiopianism is assigned to this tradition because early black writers and even some of their white allies often referred to an inspiring Biblical passage: "Princes shall come out of Egypt; Ethiopia shall soon stretch out her hands unto God" (Psalms 68:31). The verse was seen by some as a prophecy that Africa would "soon" be saved from the darkness of heathenism, and it came to be interpreted as a promise that Africa would "soon" experience a dramatic political, industrial, and economic renaissance. Others have insisted that the real meaning of the scripture is that some day the black man will rule the world. Such a belief is still common among older black folk today.

The Ethiopian prophecy seems to have been commonly known among free black people before the Civil War. In 1858, the African Civilization Society quoted the full verse in its contitution, along with an interpretation by Henry Highland Garnet. According to Garnet, Ethiopia would "soon stretch forth her hands"—"soon" meaning shortly after the work was taken up. The responsibility for seeing to it that the prophecy was fulfilled rested upon the Africans themselves. The signers of the constitution included the leading black nationalists of the day, among them, Daniel Alexander Payne, a bishop of the African Methodist Episcopal Church and Robert Hamilton, who was later to found *The Anglo-African Magazine*.[4] The quotation appeared in any number of documents published by free Africans in the northern states, and it seems unlikely that many literate free Africans were unfamiliar with it.[5]

At times the verse was directly quoted; at times it was referred to thematically. An early eloquent articulation of the Ethiopian theme was made by Alexander Crummell, who, as we have seen, eventually inspired Du Bois.[6] Crummell often used the direct quotation in sermons; but sometimes, as in his 1846 *Eulogium on the Life and Character of Thomas Clarkson*, the reference was indirect:

> Amid the decay of nations a rekindled light starts up in us. Burdens under which others expire, seem to have lost their influence upon us; and while *they* are "driven to the wall" destruction keeps far from us its blasting hand. We live in the region of death, yet seem hardly mortal. We cling to life in the midst of all reverses; and our nerveful grasp thereon cannot easily be relaxed. History reverses its mandates in our behalf—our dotage is in the past. "Time writes not its wrinkles on our brow."[7]

Another example of this indirect Ethiopianism was Daniel Alexander Payne's oration "To the Colored People of the United States," delivered in 1862 as the Civil War approached what seemed to Payne a climax of apocalyptic proportions:

> It is said that he is the God of the white man, and not of the black. This is horrible blasphemy—a *lie* from the pit that is bottomless—believe it not—no—never. Murmur not against the Lord on account of the cruelty and injustice of man. His almighty arm is already stretched out against slavery— against every man, every constitution, and every union that upholds it. His avenging chariot is now moving over the bloody fields of the doomed south, crushing beneath its massive wheels the very foundations of the blasphemous systems. Soon slavery shall sink like Pharaoh—even like the brazen-hearted tyrant, it shall sink to rise no more forever.[8]

The theme also appeared in verse, as in Frances Ellen Watkins Harper's "Ethiopia":

> Yes, Ethiopia yet shall stretch
> Her bleeding hands abroad;
> Her cry of agony shall reach
> Up to the throne of God.[9]

Paul Laurence Dunbar's "Ode to Ethiopia," addressed not to Ethiopia the nation but to the "Mother Race," recounted the past and present struggles of the Afro-Americans and predicted their future triumph:

> Go on and up! Our souls and eyes
> Shall follow thy continuous rise;
> Our ears shall list thy story
> From bards who from the root shall spring
> And proudly tune their lyres to sing
> Of Ethiopia's glory.[10]

Thus the theme of the rise of Africa became a tradition of reinterpreting the Biblical passage to speak to the experiences of the Anglo-African peoples. But rising Africa is only one aspect of Ethiopianism, the balancing theme looks to the decline of the West. The rise in the fortunes of Africa and all her scattered children would be accompanied by God's judgment upon the Europeans. A powerful expression of this belief occurred in *David Walker's Appeal*, published in 1829. In this volume, one of those forgotten American classics nonetheless well known in its time, and a book of importance to the legal and intellectual history of the United States, Walker warned of the impending doom of Western civilization. It would come as a judgment upon Christian sin in enslaving the Africans.[11] "I tell you Americans! that unless you speedily alter your course, *you* and your Country are gone!!!"[12]

Ethiopianism, with its two thematic components, rising Africa and decline of the West, provided one element of Anglo-African literary tradition on which Du Bois's mythmaking is based. Here is a typical example of a poem in the Ethiopian tradition. It was published in the tenth Atlanta University Publication in 1905, with the pseudonym, "The Moon."[13] Probably Du Bois, who edited the Atlanta publications and also edited a periodical called *The Moon*, was the author:

Ethiopia, my little daughter, why hast thou lingered and loitered in the Sun? See thy tall sisters, pale and blue of eye— see thy strong brothers, shrewd and slippery haired—see what they have done! Behold their gardens and their magic, their halls and wonder wheels! Behold their Gold, Gold, Gold!

Flowers, O Mother Earth, I bring flowers, and the echo of a Song's song. Aye and the blue violet Humility, the mystic image flower of Heaven. And Mother, sweet Mother, in these great and misty years, I have seen Sights and heard Voices; Stories and Songs are quick within me—If I have loitered, sun-kissed, O forgive me, Mother yet chide me not bitterly—I too have lived.

The typically Ethiopian element of this poem is its assumption that Caucasians and Ethiopians are separate varieties of humanity with distinct destinies competing for honor in the eyes of history and the world. The characters of this poem represent historical forces, not real human beings. The argument is that Africans are a special people with special gifts and that blacks are in some ways superior to whites. To the African genius are attributed such traits as tropical dreaminess, feminine aestheticism, and a childlike love of nature. The Europeans of the first stanza are assigned their own traditional qualities by the use of such words as "pale," "strong," "shrewd," and "slippery."

The dreamy little Ethiopia is a minor avatar of the sleeping titaness who looms in "The Riddle of the Sphinx":[14]

> Dark Daughter of the lotus leaves that watch the Southern Sea!
> Wan spirit of a prisoned soul a-panting to be free!
> The muttered music of thy streams, the whisper of the deep,
> Have kissed each other in God's name and kissed a world to sleep.

This woman is a personification of Africa, a sleeping world, a giantess, raped by pygmies while she sleeps. "The burden of white men bore her back and the white world stifled her sighs." The poet describes the ascendency of the West, based upon Mediterranean culture, and predicts its eventual going under:

> down
> down
> deep down,
> Till the devil's strength be shorn,
> Till some dim, darker David, a-hoeing of his corn,
> And married maiden, mother of God,
> Bid the black Christ be born!

In summary, Ethiopianism may be defined as the effort of the English-speaking black or African person to view his past enslavement and present cultural dependency in terms of the broader history of civilization. It serves to remind him that this present scientific technological civilization, dominated by Western Europe for a scant four hundred years, will go under certainly—like all the empires of the past. It expresses the belief that the tragic racial experience has profound historical value, that it has endowed the African with moral superiority and made him a seer. Du Bois's poetry, while highly original, is nonetheless a product of this tradition, and therefore traditional. T.S. Eliot's poetry, by way of comparison, works within the European tradition of interpretive mythology although it is clearly innovative.

European interpretive mythology is the second of the two traditions basic to Du Bois's mythmaking. In *The Survival of the Pagan Gods*, a study of classical mythology in the Renaissance, Jean Seznec discusses the medieval practice of examining Greco-Roman mythology with the intention of either discovering within it, or assigning to it, Christian meaning.[15] He discusses the ancient origins of this practice among the pre-Christian Greeks and Romans, who, attempting to understand the meanings of stories that were already very old, developed theories of interpretation in order to render myths intelligible. This tradition, once revived in the Middle Ages, endured throughout the Renaissance, and as Douglas Bush has shown, became a mode functional to English and American poetry.[16]

How can it be known that Du Bois was aware of the tradition of interpretive mythology and that he consciously wrote in this tradition? In Chapter VIII of *The Souls of Black Folk*, in the section titled "Of the Quest of the Golden Fleece," Du Bois demonstrated his awareness of this kind of writing and his desire to experiment with it:

> Have you ever seen a cotton-field white with harvest,—its golden fleece hovering above the black earth like a silvery cloud edged with dark green, its bold white signals waving like foam of billows from Carolina to Texas across that Black and human Sea? I have sometimes half-suspected that here the winged ram Chrysomallus left that Fleece after which Jason and his Argonauts went vaguely wandering into the shadowy East three thousand years ago; and certainly one might frame a pretty and not far-fetched analogy of witchery and dragon's teeth, and blood and armed men, between the ancient and the modern Quest of the Golden Fleece in the Black Sea.[17]

In an earlier chapter of the same book, "Of the Wings of Atalanta," Du Bois had demonstrated his skill at updating mythology and adapting it to the needs of his times. *The Quest of the Silver Fleece,* in 1911, brought to maturity the ideas briefly - outlined in the parent essay.[18] In this novel he created a universe in which the ideology of progressive socialism and the traditionalism of Christian black nationalism work harmoniously within the framework of a Greek myth.

The Quest of the Silver Fleece is a story of witchcraft and voodoo magic. Zora, the heroine of the tale, makes her first appearance as an elfin child, personifying the supposedly preternatural traits of the primitive mind. "We black folks is got the *spirit,*" she says. White folk may think they rule, but, "We'se lighter and cunninger; we fly right through them; we go and come again just as we wants to."[19] Elspeth, the mother of Zora, is a malevolent black witch, who sows a wondrous cotton crop in a scene reminiscent of Cadmus's planting the dragon's teeth.[20] The cotton crop is first stolen by the aristocratic Cresswell family, then woven into a wedding dress, and perhaps it is the magic of Medea (Elspeth-Zora) that begins to eat away at the vitality of Cresswell's bride.[21] By the end of the story, Zora matures from elf-child to Ethiopian queen, who appears as a haunting "mirage of other days," ensconced in a "settling of rich, barbaric splendor."[22]

So typical of Du Bois's rhetoric was Ethiopianism that George Schuyler's satirization of his speaking style, while grotesque, was nonetheless apt. "I want to tell you that our destiny lies in the stars. Ethiopia's fate is in the balance. The Goddess of the Nile weeps bitter tears at the feet of the Sphinx. The lowering clouds gather over the Congo and the lightning flashes o'er Togoland. To your tents, O Israel! The hour is at hand."[23]

A good clue to the meaning of any obscure poetic system may sometimes be found by examining its employment of traditional devices, and this method is useful in dealing with a poet like Du Bois. Among Du Bois's longer and more difficult poems is "Children of the Moon," which blends Ethiopian and Western mythological traditions.[24] It tells the story of a despairing woman who finds a "highway to the moon," at the end of which lies

> a twilight land,
> Where, hardly-hid, the sun
> Sent softly-saddened rays of

Red and brown to burn the iron soil
And bathe the snow-white peaks
In mighty splendor.

There she discovers a race of black men but no women:

Black were the men,
Hard-haired and silent-slow,
Moving as shadows,
Bending with face of fear to earthward;
And women there were none.

Under her guidance the men build a tower which she climbs to "stand beneath the burning shadow of [a] peak, Beneath the whirring of almighty wings," where she hears a voice from "near-far" saying:

"I am Freedom—
Who sees my face is free—
He and his."

The god reveals his name, but "who shall look and live?" Not daring, at first, to look, the goddess is persuaded in the end by "the sobbing of small voices—down, down far into the night," to climb:

Up! Up! to the blazing blackness
Of one veiled face.
And endless folding and unfolding,
Rolling and unrolling of almighty wings.

And then the poem moves to its climax:

I rose upon the Mountain of the Moon
I felt the blazing glory of the Sun;
I heard the Song of Children crying, "Free!"

I saw the face of Freedom—
And I died.

The poem calls to mind the Egyptian myth in which Isis, the Nile goddess, ascends the heavens to do battle with Ra, the sun god, to force him to reveal his name.[25]

In order to create the world of "Children of the Moon," Du Bois drew not only upon his knowledge of black Christian nationalism but also upon Greek and Egyptian mythology. The narrator is reminiscent of Isis, the moon goddess, patroness and teacher, Magna Mater of ancient Egypt, and Isis represents the Nilotic Africans whom Du Bois believed to have brought the Egyptians the civilizing arts. She was conceived by Du Bois as a black woman.[26] Born a woman, Isis was later elevated, according to the mythographers, to divine status. The goddess is an appropriate symbol of the spirit of black civilization within Du Bois's poetic system. She becomes the Great Mother of Men in the Moon—black people—as Isis was the nourishing mother of ancient Egypt. "Isis, the mother," said Du Bois, "is still titular goddess, in thought if not in name, of the dark continent."[27]

Du Bois provided one clue to the mythology of "Children of the Moon" when he spoke in a later essay of Ethiopian history as "the main current of Negro culture, from the Mountains of the Moon to the Great Lakes of Inner Africa." The Children of the Moon are described "moving as shadows." They live in a "twilight land," and they labor beneath the "burning shadow" of a peak. One suspects that this land in which they live is to be associated with Ethiopia, the land of shadows, mentioned in Isaiah and referred to as "Ethiopia, the shadowy" in *The Souls of Black Folk*.[28] Throughout the tradition references to Ethiopia were meant to include all African peoples, of course.

Du Bois's interest in Ethiopian rhetoric made itself felt in much of his writing, as for example, in the herald's oration in the pageant, *Star of Ethiopia*:

> Hear ye, hear ye! All them that come to know the truth and listen to the tale of the Wisest and Gentlest of the Races of Men whose faces be Black. Hear ye, hear ye! And learn the ancient Glory of Ethiopia, All-Mother of men, whose wonders men forgot. See how beneath the Mountains of the Moon, alike in the Valley of Father Nile and in ancient Negro-land and Atlantis the Black Race ruled and strove and fought and

sought the Star of Faith and Freedom even as other races did and do. Fathers of Men and Sires of Children golden, black and brown, keep silence and hear this mighty word.[29]

The Mountains of the Moon referred to in the above passage and in "Children of the Moon" are a semi-fictitious range, first mentioned in Ptolemy's *Geographica*. Recent scholarship associates them with the Ruwenzori Range. The Children of the Moon are blacks from central Africa, the area of the Nile-Congo watershed. They can be seen either as Congolese or Nilotics, therefore, which makes them symbolic of two of the great branches of African people; not only those who went down the Nile to Egypt but also those who followed the Congo, which "passed and rose red and reeking in the sunlight—thundered to the sea— thundered through the sea in one long line of blood, with tossing limbs and echoing cries of pain."[30] The Children of the Moon symbolized not only the ancient Ethiopians but twentieth-century Afro-Americans as well. And the moon goddess is no more Isis than she is the afflicted womanhood of Harlem.

The tedious tower building in "Children of the Moon" parallels the tower building in "Star of Ethiopia." Hear ye, hear ye! All them that dwell by the Rivers of Waters and in the beautiful, the Valley of Shadows, and listen to the ending of this tale. Learn Sisters and Brothers, how above the Fear of God, Labor doth build on Knowledge; how Justice tempers Science and how Beauty shall be crowned in Love beneath the Cross. Listen, O Isles, for all the pageant returns in dance and song to build this Tower of Eternal Light beneath the Star."[31] The Tower of Eternal Light, built in "Star of Ethiopia," like the tower that the Children of the Moon build is reminiscent of the Obelisk, which the Egyptians saw as representing a petrified sun's ray. It leads upwards towards the sun, for which the Egyptians used the symbol of a winged disk. In 1911, an adaption of the symbol, in which the solar disk is replaced by the face of a black man, was printed on the cover of *Crisis*, the official organ of the National Association for the Advancement of Colored People, edited by Du Bois. The black face surrounded by wings is, of course, the terrible vision that the goddess finally approaches in "Children of the Moon."[32] The wings are the wings of Ethiopia, mentioned by Isaiah in one of Du Bois's favorite Biblical passages:

> Ah! Land of the buzzing wings
> Which lies beyond the rivers of Ethiopia,
> That sends ambassadors by sea,
> In papyrus vessels on the face of the waters:
> To a nation tall and sleek,
> To a nation dreaded near and far,
> To a nation strong and triumphant.[33]

The narrator climbs the Tower up to the sun in much the same way that Isis, when only a woman, asccended the heavens to force the Sun God to unveil his secrets. To lift the veil of Isis is to read the meaning of some obscure riddle. Proclus, the Greek Neoplatonic philosopher, describes a statue of Isis bearing the following inscription: "I am that which is, has been, and shall be. My veil no one has lifted. The fruit I bore was the Sun."[34] What lies behind the veil of this poem? What does the woman see when the wings unveil the face? Perhaps she sees the face of blazing blackness, the eclipse of the West. Perhaps she sees her own reflection, the face of Isis, the African, "Star of Ethiopia, All-Mother of Men, who gave the world the Iron Gift and Gift of Faith, the Pain of Humility and Sorrow Song of Pain, and Freedom, Eternal Freedom, underneath the Star."[35] Du Bois's poetry often unveils the face of a black god as in the story of the King in the land of the Heavy Laden, who summons his only loyal servant, a woman, to go forth in battle against "the heathen." Smiling, the King commands:

> "Go smite me mine enemies, that they cease to do evil in my sight . . ."
> "Oh King, she cried, "I am but a woman."
> And the King answered: "Go, then, Mother of Men."
> And the woman said, "Nay, King, but I am still a maid."
> Whereat the King cried: "O maid, made Man, thou shalt be Bride of God."
> And yet the third time the woman shrank at the thunder in her ears and whispered: "Dear God, I am black!"
> The King spake not, but swept the veiling of his face aside and lifted up the light of his countenance upon her and lo! it was black.

So the woman went forth on the hills of God to do battle for
the King, on that drear day in the land of the Heavy Laden,
when the heathen raged and imagined a vain thing.[36]

The King is a personification of God, it seems clear; like the
"Things of Wings," he is veiled godhead. The "Thing of Wings,"
finally seen as "the blazing blackness / Of one veiled Face," is also
a black God.[37] The veil is not only a barrier it is a symbol of the
challenge that this barrier provides. Blackness, or the veil, stands
between black folk and the full promise of America, but the veil
will be put aside for those who are brave enough to see what lies
beyond it. In the words of Ralph Ellison, "Black will make you, or
black will un-make you."[38]

The veil is often but not always symbolic of black skin. It
represents the limits within which the souls of black folk are
confined, but veils also represent the limitations that white folk
have placed upon their own vision. Possibly Du Bois borrowed the
image from Thomas Jefferson, who spoke of "that immovable veil
of black which covers all the emotions of the [black] race." But Du
Bois gives things an ironic twist by persistently insisting that the
veil is a gift that, like an infant's caul, endows its bearer with
second sight.[39]

Du Bois was fascinated by mystic symbolism. As Kelly Miller
observed, he was poetic, "his mind being cast in a weird and
fantastic mold." He enjoyed ritual, as he tells us himself, in
describing his solitary twenty-fifth birthday celebration: "the
night before I had heard Schubert's beautiful *Unfinished Sym-
phony*, planned my little ceremony with candles, Greek wine, oil,
and song and prayer."[40] The mysticism of the Sphinx seems to
have had real meaning for him as it has had, not only for
Garveyites, but for the middle-class Africans and Afro-Americans
who have pledged secret societies. Charles Wesley's official
History of Alpha Phi Alpha recognizes the tendency of middle-
class blacks to experiment with the Ethiopian tradition in poetry:

Ask not culture for self alone;
Let thy brother share thy gain.
Perfect self is not our aim, but

Homage to God, love for brother
And high o'er all, the Ethiopian.

                    J.H. Boags and R.H. Ogle, 1909

Mighty Sphinx in Egypt standing
Facing Eastward toward the sun.
Glorified and e'er commanding
Your children bravely on.
Be to us a bond of union
Held fast by Peace and Right.

. . . .

Ethiopia Home of Sages
Thou art still our noblest pride
We, thy sons, through future ages
Will take thee for our guide
Trusting through thy boundless wisdom
To reach virtue's supernal heights.

                    W.A. Scott, 1915

Such poetry allows an identification with symbols of stability, permanency, and high culture. English-speaking, middle-class Afro-Americans during the late Victorian and Edwardian periods needed an opportunity to be proud of their Africanness, just as Garveyites would a decade later.[41]

Du Bois's Ethiopianism typified the nationalistic thinking of black middle-class intellectuals during the first two decades of the twentieth century. Of course, Du Bois was in a position to encourage Ethiopianism by publishing the verse of young poets who were interested in the tradition. Langston Hughes's poem, "The Negro Speaks of Rivers," often reprinted with the dedication, "To W.E.B. Du Bois," first appeared in the *Crisis* of June, 1921, and was possibly inspired by Du Bois's "The Story of Africa," which appeared in that same journal some seven years earlier. The similarities are, in any case, striking.[42]

Thus is it possible to speak of at least one black literary tradition, the Ethiopian, borrowing a term from Afro-Atlantic political studies and adding it to American literary history. This tradition is manifested in the work of major poets, minor poets, and unsophisticated versifiers. It rests upon a view of history outlined in Walker's *Appeal* and stated more calmly in such essays as Alexander Crummell's "The Destined Superiority of the Negro." W.E.B. Du Bois is the central figure in the tradition. The most traditional of Afro-American poets, he was yet the most innovative within the tradition. There is a difference in degree of sophistication—but not in sentiment expressed—between Du Bois's "Riddle of the Sphinx" and the following lines by Marcus Garvey:

> Out of cold old Europe these white men came,
> From caves, dens and holes, without any fame,
> Eating their dead's flesh and sucking their blood,
> Relics of the Mediterranean flood.[43]

Whether there are other Afro-American literary traditions and what, if any, effects the content of Afro-American literature may have had upon the forms employed must be the subject of future studies.[44]

Can Du Bois the social scientist be reconciled with Du Bois the poet and prophet of race? How could a man so well trained in social science have allowed the Ethiopian tradition, rooted in nineteenth-century *Volksgeist* mythologies, to dominate his thought?[45]

As a youth Du Bois was romantically involved with the idea of social science, which he naively believed might yield a science of racial advancement. He was infatuated, like many other young men of his generation, with the notion of a "science of man." But Du Bois's theories of social change were not always consistent. Sociology became relatively less important with the passage of years until by 1910 it was no longer Du Bois's chief concern. Though he was capable of writing perfectly good sociology, it does not appear that he wanted to. He turned—and it would seem with more satisfactory results—to the power of imagination as his chief instrument for changing public morality. He became a crusading journalist, a novelist, and a poet of Ethiopianism, dedicated to embodying his view of history in mythical form.

Chapter Nine

The Novels
of Sutton Griggs
and Literary Black
Nationalism

In Sutton Griggs's novels, black nationalist writing of the Golden Age reached a high level. His philosophy of art was notably nationalistic. Literature was to be functional, and he thought of the development of literary habits as social activity, bringing one into cooperation with fellow men who would not otherwise be available:

> There may be living in the same age, or country or village with a person an individual with great moral and spiritual strength that is far removed, for one reason or another, from the possibliity of direct personal contact, yet through what may be written of or by the individual who cannot be reached personally, the life and mind of this individual may be utilized as an aid through the habit of reading.[1]

He realized that black people were a people limited by illiteracy to oral communication. Since black people were more easily moved by verbal than by written appeals, they were, in his view, inefficient and disunited.

> To succeed as a race we must move up out of the age of the voice, the age of the direct personal appeal, and live in an age where an idea can influence to action by whatever route it drifts one's way.

When the time arrives that the Negroes are capable of being moved to action on a large scale by what they read, a marked change in the condition of the race will begin instantly and will be marvelous in its proportions.²

It was for such reasons that Griggs saw the need to produce a racial literature, and in rather gloomy Egyptian metaphor, he called for the development of such a literature:

> Not a single race that has no literature is classified as great in the eyes of the world. Here then is the situation: They who would foster the patriotic spirit so needful for the advancement of mankind must have a way of embalming the memories of those who thus serve their fellows, and the races that have no literature are devoid of a method of embalming.³

With the possible exception of Du Bois, Griggs was the only black novelist of his period who deliberately undertook the writing of novels as part of a definite plan to create a national Negro literature.

Sutton Griggs was born in 1872. Like his father before him, he was a graduate of Richmond Theological Seminary and a Baptist minister. The greater part of his education was acquired through individual diligence. He possessed that most important of scholarly attributes, curiousity. When he died impoverished in 1933, his library numbered two-thousand volumes. During his lifetime, Griggs produced more than a dozen books, including five novels, five social tracts, his own autobiography, a short biography of John L. Webb, and the *Kingdom Builder's Manual*. This last was a booklet of Biblical quotations, ostensibly selected for their pertinence to the predicament of black people of the United States. The social tracts represented his developing "science of collective efficiency"— a response to the rugged individualism of Spencerian Darwinists. In his studies Griggs had come across the works of Benjamin Kidd and Prince Peter Alexeyevich Kropotkin, both popular in the United States at the turn of the century, with their arguments that the progress of society was more dependent upon cooperation than upon competition. Griggs spent the most significant years of his career in Memphis, Tennessee, where he was able to maintain credibility of a sort as a black leader. Although he was involved in the Niagara movement, he was endorsed by many southern whites as a reasonable leader of the Negro community. He was the recipient of some financial support from white Baptists, through whose generousity some of his publishing ventures were funded. Griggs's books did not sell well in those days of black illiteracy, but his inability to make financial success of his literary career does not, of itself, constitute proof of irrelevancy. Certainly, like many sincere black nationalists, he was potentially a tool of white separatists but this does not prove that he was an Uncle Tom. The militant Henry McNeal Turner, and later Marcus Garvey, were successful speakers before white racist, segregationist audiences in the South, because they said the sorts of things that such audiences wanted to hear. Du Bois's assessment of Griggs as a serious author, sincerely concerned with speaking to his people seems accurate.[4]

The first of Griggs's novels was *Imperium in Imperio* (1899), the story of black Belton Piedmont and mulatto Bernard Belgrave, who conspire within a national Negro government to establish a nation within a nation with designs on the state of Texas as a last battleground for a soil-searing racial Armageddon. *Over-shadowed* (1901), describes the attempt of a white man to seduce Erma Wysong, a beautiful quadroon, and chronicles his undoing. The bloody drama that unfolds litters the stage with corpses long before the final curtain. Upon the death of Erma, her husband, Astral Herndon, leaves the United States to become a wandering "citizen of the ocean." In *Unfettered* (1902), Morlene, another of Griggs's ravishing colored heroines, marries Harry Dalton, a broken man, out of pity. But Morlene is "unfettered" when Harry redeems himself by a suicidal act of bravery. Morlene's lost love, Dorlan Warthall, is able to win her hand only by formulating a detailed plan for the solution of the race problem. *The Hindered Hand* (1905), which takes its name from the prophecy, "Ethiopia shall soon stretch forth her hand unto God," is another novel of conspiracy, like *Imperium in Imperio*. Ensal Ellwood, a black man, and Earl Bluefield, a mulatto, are close friends, who are, after many adventures, married, to sisters. Eunice, who is the wife of Earl, "passes for white" and goes mad when her racial identity is discovered. The two heroes of the novel debate a number of stratagems for solving the Negro's problems, including migration to Africa, general insurrection of the masses, and cooperation with a spectral Pan-Slavist, in a plot to overthrow the United States government. Griggs's last novel, *Pointing the Way* (1908), is the story of two couples: Baug Peppers and Eina Rapona, who are mulattoes indistinguishable from whites: and their darker friends, Conroe Driscoll and Clotille Strange. The most memorable of Griggs's creations is Uncle Jack, who appears in this book, an heroic combination of Uncle Remus and Uncle Tom, who dies defending his right to vote.[5]

In the novels of Griggs, we observe many of the themes that characterized black bourgeois nationalism during the nineteenth century: for example, the usual authoritarian conception of black leadership. This is in spite of his admission that "there seems to be a feeling in the Negro race to keep all upon a level and to resent anything that savors of superiority of one Negro over another." Anti-individualism accompanies authoritarianism, and is apparent both in Griggs's rhetoric and in certain idiosyncracies of his writing.

Griggs's writing style is an example of American primitivism—picturesque and decorative, but simple and economical. His genteel characters move with stylized grace over brilliantly colored landscapes. They are somewhat stiff and formal, not truly lifelike, and they resemble the people in those anonymous early American paintings who cast no shadows and whose feet never seem really to touch the ground. Ralph Ellison and Edward Bland provided an interesting framework for viewing such characterization, speaking of the "pre-individualistic" phase in Afro-American thought—a useful concept:

> In the pre-individualistic thinking of the Negro, the stress is on the group. Instead of seeing in terms of the individual, the Negro sees in terms of "races," masses of peoples separated from other masses according to color. Hence, an act rarely bears intent against him as a Negro individual. He is singled out not as a person but as a specimen of an ostracized group. He knows that he never exists in his own right but only to the extent that others hope to make the race suffer vicariously through him.[6]

All of Griggs's novels are set in the pre-individualistic South, during the period with which the present study is concerned. Griggs's characters represent types, not persons. Belton Piedmont speaks, in a sense, for all blacks who have accepted the accomodationist racialism of the late nineteenth century:

> The Negro is the latest comer upon the scene of modern civilization. It would be the crowning glory of even this marvelous age; it would be the grandest contribution ever made to the cause of human civilization; it would be a worthy theme for the songs of the Holy Angels, if every Negro, away from the land of his nativity, can by means of the pen, force an acknowledgement of equality from the proud lips of the fierce, all-conquering Anglo-Saxon, thus eclipsing the record of all other races of men, who without exception have had to wade through blood to achieve their freedom.[7]

And Bernard Belgrave represents the impatient, frustrated militant. Emotionally and intellectually, he is more white than black. More important than the fact that he is a mulatto is the fact that he is a disfranchised *assimilado,* always a threat to public tranquility. Belgrave's speeches show that Griggs knew that the black man who acquires the tastes and the habits of a white man is going to be very dissatisfied with his status in America:

> Float on proud flag, while yet you may. Rejoice, oh! ye Anglo-Saxons, yet a little while. Make my father ashamed to own me his lawful son; call me a bastard child; look upon my pure mother as a harlot; laugh at Viola in the grave of a self-murderer; exhume Belton's body if you like and tear your flag from around him to keep him from polluting it! Yes, stuff your vile stomachs full of all these horrors. You shall be richer food for the buzzards to whom I have solemnly vowed to give your flesh.[8]

Not only black characters, but whites as well are preindividualistic in their thinking. In *The Hindered Hand,* we are introduced to Mr. A. Hostility, "a cadaverous looking white man, wearing a much worn suit of clothes," who is really not a person at all, but an allegorical figure:

The A stands for Anglo-Saxon, the God-commissioned or self-appointed world conqueror. I am the incarnation of hostility to that race, or to that branch of the human family claiming the dominance of that strain of blood . . . .

The world, you see, will soon contain but two colossal figures, the Anglo-Saxon and the Slav. The inevitable battle for world supremacy will be between these giants. Without going into the question as to why I am a Pro-Slav in this matter, I hereby declare unto you that it is the one dream of my life to so weaken the Anglo-Saxon that he will be easy prey for the Slav in the coming momentous world struggle.[9]

In *Unfettered* (Nashville, 1902), a white man, Lemuel Dalton, and a black man, Harry Dalton, become involved in a fist fight, which is a fair tie until Lemuel draws a pistol and shoots Harry, severely wounding him. When word spreads to the white community, a meeting of the town fathers is called and a number of speeches are recited. Lemuel is mildly chided for having fought with a Negro "man to man," but his response is, "when I was a lad that Negro insulted and then beat me. No doubt he carried with him for years the thought that he was physically my superior. I was determined to wrest from him this conception. Had I proceeded against him on terms which he regarded as unfair, he would not have inwardly restored to me the palm which he wrested from me years ago . . . . I am in favor of the doctrine of Anglo-Saxon superiority in all realms, even the physical." But, of course, the fight has not been fair—a point lost on the senior Anglo-Saxons, who, impressed by these sentiments, advance to clasp his hand. Their spokesman says:

We understand you better now, sir. We are proud of you, sir. Lads hear what he says. In developing brain don't forget brawn. The darkey now has brawn. His strong physique and reproductive powers, show that he is in the world to stay to the end of time. If, in the years to come, he adds mental to physical endowment, we may be in the lurch unless we take care of the physical side of our endowment. Give me your hand again, sir," said Squire Mullen, once more shaking hands with Lemuel Dalton.[10]

But they do not relent in their determination to punish Harry for daring to defend himself against a white:

> It was decided that Harry had been punished equitably for his offense against Lemuel Dalton as an *individual*. They held that something must be done however, to avenge the insult to the white *race*, perpetrated when one of their number was assailed . . . . The practically unanimous verdict was that . . . Harry should have avoided the conflict . . . . In the dead of night, the whites rode up to the house and tacked thereon a notice, warning Harry . . . to remove from the settlement forever before the dawn of day on the first of January of the incoming year.[11]

The italics are Griggs's and he seems to be emphasizing his belief that the whites, too, are collectivistic in their thinking. They may interact with blacks as abstract racial entities, but individual contacts are forbidden by the etiquette of the South because they are potentially destructive to the myth of white superiority. Such contacts are uncommon, therefore, in the novels of Sutton Griggs, which tend to be in this respect at least, true to life. The rigid exclusiveness of the southern code is explained to Eina Rapona by Seth Molair, a young lawyer, in *Pointing the Way:*

> "Miss Rapona," began he, "the white people of the South are not individualists. With the possibility of racial antagonisms on the one hand and social commingling on the other always confronting us, we are more or less in a chronic state of spiritual war, and, just as in time of war you do not allow the individual soldiers personal liberty, we withhold a great measure of personal liberty from all Southern people, white and colored, and maintain certain well-defined customs."[12]

Griggs was decidely opposed to the extremes of anti-individualism that he described. A race-consciousness that would not allow for contacts among the better classes of both races, and that would not allow individuals to select their own friends, was not congenial to his spirit. Griggs believed in organized black community life—"collective efficiency," he called it—because he believed that racial cooperation was essential to racial greatness. At the same time his novels reveal a violent hatred of those who indiscriminately lumped all blacks together. In *Overshadowed,* Horace Christian, the despoiler of a black woman and the lyncher of a black man, embarks upon a night of debauchery "among the darky belles," and awakens in a jail cell. His head has been shaven, and his skin blackened with chemicals. It dawns upon Christian, too late, that he has been substituted, by means of a cruelly just hoax, for a condemned Negro who is to be hanged that very morning. Why is it possible for Christian to be mistaken so? Griggs explains that the political corruption of the South allowed the architect of Christian's downfall to carry out the substitution. Another factor in the success of the substitution plot was that "inasmuch as that the white people generally were indisposed to give close scrutiny to Negro countenances and were consequently deficient in ability to readily distinguish them, Lanier, knowing these things, felt confident of carrying out his plan of substituting Horace Christian for John Wysong." Griggs observed in passing that "the white woman who coined the phrase, 'All niggers look alike to me,'" was an illustration of the failure of the white world to treat Negroes as individuals.[13]

The pre-individualistic tendency witnessed in the novels of Griggs is a variety of thinking commonly expressed by many blacks at the turn of the century, as, for example, by W.E.B. Du Bois in *The Conservation of Races,* with its attack on individualism and exaltation of the race ideal as "the vastest and most ingenious invention for human progress." It is the attitude of collectivism that dominated the thinking of Alexander Crummell, William Hooper Councill, John Edward Bruce, and Henry McNeal Turner. Griggs made his own view clear in *Life's Demands:*

> Every man in the world is affected not only by his own reputation, but by that of the race to which he belongs. If a race has an evil name, each member of that race becomes an heir to his portion of this disfavor, which is handed out to him before he gets a hearing on his own individual score. Thus his individual case is handicapped by the evil name of his race, and the rising above this evil name is an additional obstacle that must be overcome.[14]

Collectivism is linked with authoritarianism, which Griggs inadvertently admitted to in his autobiography, *The Story of My Struggles* (1916). In this slim volume, Griggs seemed somewhat petulant. He felt unappreciated. Black people were to blame for the economic failures of his publishing ventures. Black people had failed to recognize the value of his contributions. In tones similar to those to be employed by Garvey a decade later, he called into question the racial pride of those who did not support him personally. He accused those who did not approve of and aid his efforts of a noncooperative spirit, implying that they lacked a sense of enlightened self-interest. And like Garvey, he boasted of his attunement to the life pulse of the masses, who he claimed had been a source of support:

> I went from door to door, visited, at dinner hours, places where plain workmen toiled. I went to schools where poor Negro boys and girls were struggling for an education. These humble people of the race came to me with their dimes, and I was thus able to at least hold my head above the threatening financial flood.[15]

Black uplift, or the civilizationist theme, is strong in Griggs's novels as it is in other documents of bourgeois nationalism. Middle-class and working-class blacks during the nadir were concerned with achieving the bourgeois respectability that was denied them by the larger society.[16] Writing in 1913, William H. Ferris, a black graduate of Yale and Harvard voiced the civilizationist attitude of the Talented Tenth:

> There are thousands of Negroes in the South, and scores in the North, who have practically been untouched by the civilizing forces of the modern age, and who are ignorant, illiterate, superstitious and poverty-stricken. The Negro is not an inferior being; but the race is a crude and undeveloped race. It is not a backward or child race; but it is an unpolished diamond, a diamond in the rough.[17]

Such an uncut jewel is Hannah Piedmont, the mother of Belton in *Imperium in Imperio*, who very quickly becomes a sympathetic character in spite of Griggs's heavy-handed employment of dialect:

Cum er long hunny an' let yer mammy fix yer 'spectable, so yer ken go to skule. Yer mammy is 'tarmined ter gib yer all de book larning dar is ter be had eben ef she has ter lib on bred an' herrin's, an' die en de a'ms house.[18]

But clearly the best illustration of the homey virtues of the black underclass is Uncle Jack in *Pointing the Way*. Uncle Jack tells Eina Rapona of his experiences as a slave during the Civil War, of how he cried when "ole massa rode erway," and of how he "stayed behin' an looked atter der wimmin wid er eagle eye."

Ole missus b'lieved in Jack, b'lieved in him wid all her soul. I slep' at her do' w'en eber de Yankees wuz er round. Yes, dey b'lieved in Jack. An fore God, I'd er died lak a cur dog fo'e I'd er let any scoundrel tech er stran' uv hair on enny uv 'um's head.[19]

Jack is no racial traitor; he is an archetype of the Old Negro, "the faithful, courteous slave of other days," over whose passing Du Bois, like Griggs, was ambivalent. This does not make him a fool; Uncle Jack has sufficient intelligence to recognize his political self-interest. He can also follow responsible leadership as he reveals to one of his aging contemporaries:

Yer see, Aunt Merlissa, my way and yer way uv managin' wid de white folks wuz to act kin' an' make out wid de bes' dat dey seed fit ter do. I hez fell in wid some youngsters in Belrose dat wants ter move 'cordin ter some principull, an' not jes' es er notion stracks de white people. Dey says dat de white people hez done gone an' disfrankshied ill-littered cullud folks 'thout disfranshieng ill-littered white folks. Dese cullud young uns says dat ain't right. Dey says dat ill-littered white folks an' ill-littered cullud folks ought ter hab one law 'cordin ter de constertution . . . .[20]

Jack is a teller of tall tales and a goldmine of slave folklore. His speciality is the tale of the "Old Marster and John" motif. This is the trickster tale, representing the antebellum slave's "puttin' on of ole massa," matching him in a battle of wits. As a boy Uncle

Jack learned "dat dare warn't nevah no harm in er white man ef you could jes' git him ter laf' right good' an hard." Jack realizes that times have changed, however, and that the "cullud race . . . mus' stan' up now an meet de diffunt qusshuns face ter face." So he attempts to exercise the franchise in Alabama, for which effrontry he is brutally struck down at the voting poll. Carried to the prison hospital with a fractured skull, he breathes his last words:

> Tell de white folks dat ez er slave I done my bes'. Tell 'um how I keered fur my missus an' her dorters in de war times. Tell 'um dat I nevah done er crimial ack in my life, an' dat I died tryin ter keep frum bein' blamed fur whut my grandaddy coulden't do, 'cause he wuz er slave. Tell 'um dat I died in jail. I wuz tryin' ter git my case ter de S'preme Coat uv de United States, but frum whut dey ells me my case is goin' even higher dan dat, goin ter de S'preme Coat erbove.[21]

Griggs's mythologizing of the black masses did not lead him to see only the diamonds in the rough; he was, like most preachers, also aware of the buffoon and the villain. The ridiculous hack preacher, Rev. Josiah Nerve, D.D.S. applies in *Overshadowed* to Erma Wysong for aid in acquiring the trappings of an education saying in his bizarre, distracting, and affected style:

> You-can-teach-me-English-grammar,-geography,-and-the-alphabets-of-the-Greek,-Latin,-and-Hebrew-languages. -With-these-things, I-can-wear-my-degree-with-dignity-when-it-comes. -I-have-got-my-plan-laid-to-bring-it-. -You-see,-I-know-what-it-takes-to-scoop-a-D.D.-from-the-very-best-nigger-colleges. -I-know-one-preacher-who-got-his-degree-by-buying-a-barrel-of-salt-herrings-for-a-nigger-college,-and-sat-on-the-barrel-in-the-front-yard,-threatening-to-take-the-barrel-of-herrings-home-in-case-the-trustees-did-not-give-him-the-degree. -My plans-are-more-dignified-than-that.[22]

But villains and fools are always foiled in Griggs's novels, where the mills of the gods grind small indeed. Rev. Nerve is later viewed making a hasty exit from town after bungling the arson of his own church.

A more vicious character in the same novel is the procuress, Dolly Marston, who plots the ruin of Elbridge Norval, whose father was the seducer of Dolly's sister and Erma Wysong's mother. Upon devising a plot for the white man's destruction, she experiences devilish ecstacy:

> "I might have known it! I might have known it! Have I struck the right trail at last? If I have, oh Satan, prince of Evil, I crave your help." Knitting her brows she shook her clinched fist in rage at the house into which the young man had gone. Having done this to her satisfaction, she started home at a rapid pace arriving there in an exhausted condition. As soon as she was sufficiently recovered from her exhaustion to permit it, she danced a wild, joyous sort of dance, uttering a succession of savage shrieks of delight.[23]

Griggs often attributes the folly or viciousness of his characters to their injudicious imitation of whites. The officious Rev. Josiah Nerve is described as a "poor deluded soul, contented to grasp with a death clutch at the *shadow* of Anglo-Saxon civilization." "His brethren," Griggs adds, "are many." Dolly Marston and her sister are victims of the desire to dress as stylishly as white Southern belles. Erma Wysong's salvation is her Tuskegee-acquired work ethic. Griggs did not advocate the unequivocal acceptance of all Anglo-Saxon values. He did wish to see blacks acquire some of the legendary gentility of the Old South, which with the leavening agent of the puritanical work ethic would surely produce racial greatness.[24]

Griggs's novels reflect the civilizationist aspirations of the black workers and middle class to live lives of genteel respectability in the face of almost overwhelming opposition. In *Imperium in Imperio*, Belton Piedmont secures a job as a postal clerk, but is soon dismissed for political reasons. At this low point in Belton's fortunes, Griggs cannot resist drawing out the allegorical significance of Belton's search for work:

> Belton began to cast around for another occupation, but, in whatever direction he looked, he saw no hope. He possessed a first class college education, but that was all. He knew no

trade nor was he equipped to enter any of the professions. It is true that there were positions around by the thousands which he could fill, but his color debarred him. He would have made an excellent drummer, salesman, clerk, cashier, government official (county, city, state, or national) telegraph operator, conductor, or anything of such a nature. But the color of his skin shut the doors so tight that he could not even peep in . . . . It is true that such positions as street laborer, hod-carrier, cart driver, factory hand, railroad hand, were open to him; but such menial tasks were uncongenial to a man of his education and polish.[25]

Here Griggs is turning his attention to the facts of not only employment problems for black males, but also to peculiar forms of discrimination practiced especially against middle-class blacks. Particularly, Griggs was interested in describing the ruthless stripping from the black middle class the marks of bourgeois respectability towards which working-class people usually strive. Parodied in the popular press, humiliated by social scientists, jeered at by small children in the streets, middle-class blacks were plainly discouraged from pretensions to gentility.

A study of Boston Negroes published in 1914 characterized the middle class as confused, pitiable, and bumptious. Rayford Logan has commented on the tendency to ridicule attempts by black Americans to achieve middle-class respectability. The tendency was especially strong at the turn of the century when the Currier and Ives prints and the *Darktown Comics* of Thomas Worth attempted to make ludicrous the activities of the black bourgeoisie and its voluntary organizations. These depictions, as Logan observed, "stood out in sharp contrast to the romantic joys of courtship, marriage and family life of genteel people." Self-assertiveness in the area of social equality was parodied in a popular jingle of the Gilded Age.[26]

In de by laws of dis lodge
You'll find dis rule right dere
Don't you stand on de platform
Of de one-horse bob-tailed car.
Get in and grab a seat;

Make white folks give you room
Or—excommunication
From de Third Degree Full Moon.

Such attempts to ignore or to ridicule black pretensions to respectability were offensive to the middle class Afro-American. As we have seen, Mrs. Booker T. Washington and others protested the fact that middle-class black women were forced to share railroad accomodations with the vicious and crude of their own and other races. In *The Marrow of Tradition,* Charles Chesnutt describes the disgust of a black doctor forced to share a railroad car with a white ruffian who spits on the floor and smokes an evil-smelling cigar. In *The Hindered Hand,* Griggs describes the customary attempt of white men to turn the Jim Crow car into a saloon, until Ensal Ellwood protests:

> Gentlemen, the law prescribes that this coach shall be used exclusively by Negro passengers and we must ask that you do not make our first class apartment a drinking room for the whites.[27]

Masculine self-assertiveness is a common trait among Griggs's characters, as it was a chief concern among the turn-of-the-century's great black leaders. One Baptist preacher addressed the National Baptist Convention (Colored) of 1889 with words to the effect that the surest guarantee of respectability for Negroes was for every black man to purchase a gun and use it at the slightest provocation.[28] Theophilus G. Stewart, an army chaplain and a member of the American Negro Academy, encouraged "the production of a robust and chivalric manhood, the only proper shelter for a pure and glorious womanhood," and proclaimed that "noble women are the crown of heroic men. None but the brave deserve the fair, and none but the brave can have them." Such ideals were difficult for black Americans to achieve, however, as the National Association of Colored Women maintained. One of Griggs's minor characters in *Pointing the Way* reveals that "the colored women protect the men. Knowing the menace that confronts their men, colored women swallow insults."[29]

In *Imperium in Imperio* Belton Piedmont disdains such craven comfort. Discovering to his embarrassment that he does not have sufficient funds to fully compensate the hack driver who has just transported his female friend to the railroad station, Belton remonstrates with the hackman to trust him for the remainder of the fee. But the hackman refuses and threatens to pursue the girl and obtain the money from her. This Belton cannot permit, so he wrestles the driver to the ground and restrains him until his girl friend's train leaves the station. Although Belton is later arrested and fined, he is nonetheless spared the mortification of seeing the lady disrespectfully accosted. His reaction is extreme, perhaps, by our standards, but his is the reaction of a callow black youth, who fully accepts the Victorian *ideals* of Anglo-Saxon manhood and womanhood:

> At Stowe University, Belton had learned to respect woman. It was in these schools that the work of slavery in robbing the colored woman of respect, was undone. Woman now occupied the same position in Belton's eye as she did in the eye of the Anglo-Saxon.
>
> There is hope for that race or nation that respects its women. It was for the smile of a woman that the armored knight of old rode forth to deeds of daring. It was for the smile of women that the soldier of to-day endures the hardships of the camp and braves the dangers of the field of battle.
>
> The heart of man will joyfully consent to be torn to pieces if the lovely hand of woman will only agree to bind the parts together again and heal the painful wounds.
>
> The Negro Race had left the last relic of barbarism behind, and this young negro, fighting to keep that cab driver from approaching the girl for a fee, was but the forerunner of the negro, who, at the voice of a woman, will fight for freedom until he dies, fully satisfied if the hand that he worships will only drop a flower on his grave.[30]

Instances of compulsive heroism, or pseudoheroic acts abound in the novels of Griggs. In *Unfettered*, Dorlan Warthell visits a medicine show and writhes in agony at the spectacle of Negro minstrelsy:

Dorlan's veins began to pulsate with indignation as he reflected on the fact that the ludicrous in the race was the only feature that had free access to the public gaze. He was longing for an opportunity to show to the audience that there was something in the Negro that could make their bosoms thrill with admiration. . . .[31]

In an attempt to vindicate his race in the eyes of the assembled whites, Dorlan volunteers to participate in a daredevil act in which a man is dropped by parachute from a gas balloon. After performing the feat, Dorlan goes home, fully relieved, having proven his manhood to himself. Conroe Driscoll, in *Pointing the Way*, a college student despondent because the intramural color prejudice of the black/mulatto community denies him the woman he loves, attempts a suicide of sorts during a football game:

"Two ribs broken, it seems," one doctor murmered to another.

"Oh, is he dead? Is he dead?" cried Clotille, dropping to her knees, clasping her hands, her heart the home of agony.

When Conroe regained consciousness he sprang to his feet and said: "I am all right... Get to your places, boys.. go away lady doctor. . . ."

The mighty throng held its breath.

Slowly, doggedly, with grim determination, Conroe, backed by his resolute team, continued to push his way until, across the goal line, he fell to the ground, clutching the ball as with hooks of steel.

A mighty shout broke out upon the air and men wild with enthusiasm rushed to the scene intending to carry Conroe on their shoulders around the grounds.

But when the struggling players had disentangled themselves it was found that Conroe did not rise.[32]

Manliness is often suppressed, however, and sometimes lost entirely in Griggs's novels. In *Imperium in Imperio*, Belton Piedmont is forced to assume the attire of a woman to engage in a private program of espionage. If we are to guess why Griggs would introduce such a bizarre and surrealistic incident into the novel, we may suppose that he is symbolically hinting at the fact that some black men have allowed themselves to be emasculated by racism. In *The Hindered Hand,* Percy G. Marshall, a young man who lets his mother persuade him to pass for white, loses all sense of resolution and impresses one as a weakling. The theme of identity loss is available as well in the novels of Charles Chesnutt, and in *The Marrow of Tradition,* the self-hating Uncle Tom is a disgusting parody of a human being.[33]

Self-hatred is not a common trait among Griggs's characters, but self-deprecation is. As Sterling Stuckey has observed, a common trait among black nationalists is the "tendency to exaggerate the degree of acquiescence to oppression by the masses of black people." "Where else," asks Stuckey, "among black people can one find such gloomy and devasting, such stereotypical portraits of black humanity as among nationalists?" Turn-of-the-century black nationalists demonstrated a surprising inability to question stereotypes concerning the Anglo-Saxon and the Negro characters. W.E.B. Du Bois may have thanked God that he had no Anglo-Sazon blood, but he was no rejector of Victorian cultural values which tended to portray Anglo-Saxons as a cold, hard, and masculine race, and blacks as soft, warm and feminine. Griggs, like most of his contemporaries, contrasted Afro-Americans with Anglo-Saxons, seeing in each group certain inherent racial vices and virtues. In *Imperium in Imperio,* whites are described as possessing the trait of "hardness" which has manifested itself sometimes as an honorable and sometimes as a dishonorable characteristic:

> That same hammer and anvil that forged the steel sword of the Anglo-Saxon, with which he fought for freedom from England's yoke, also forged the chain the Anglo-Saxon used to bind the negro more securely in the thralldom of slavery.[34]

Again, in *The Hindered Hand,* the technically competent and strong-willed Anglo-Saxon is described as a man of iron by Eunice, in her climactic courtroom scene.

> Remember what your blood has done. It hammered out on the fields of blood the Magna Charta; it took the head of

Charles I; it shattered the sceptre of George III; it now circles the globe in an iron grasp.[35]

But not all Anglo-Saxons are entitled to such positive portrayals, for in *Overshadowed*, this same Anglo-Saxon hardness is the cause of much grief, both for the whites, its original possessers, and for the black who imitates the trait. John Wysong, a menial worker who has been driven from the practice of his skilled trade by a racist labor union, overhears a conversation in which the head of that same union expresses the following sentiments:

> Now, our Union wants it distinctly understood that what we labor for WE MUST HAVE. We shall have it if we ignore all laws, defy all constituted authority, overthrow all government, violate all tradition. Our end MUST be attained, at whatever cost. If a foe stands in our way, and nothing will dislodge him but death, then he must die. That is the dictum of the Anglo-Saxon. The Negro, lacking this spirit, has no place in our ranks.[36]

Overhearing these sentiments leads John Wysong, desperate and demoralized, to murder the master workman in a mad attempt to be more like the indomitable whites.

Griggs took delight in occasionally portraying the white southern male as emasculate and effete, the loss of manly birthright being an important theme in Griggs's fiction. For example, in *Unfettered*, one white repressionist is portrayed as "a feeble-voiced young man, rising in a most timid manner, rubbing his hands together nervously.[37] There is a tendency as old as black writing to associate the slavery system with a heritage of moral decay, a tendency present in American literature long before Faulkner. In *The Hindered Hand*, Ensal borrows from Benjamin Kidd to describe the Anglo-Saxon race as

> a race of the colder regions and there evolved those qualities, physical, mental and temperamental, which constitute its greatness. A large section of the race has left the habitat and environments in which and because of which it grew to greatness, and in the southern part of the United States finds

itself confronted with the problem of maintaining in warmer climes those elements of a greatness hitherto found only in the colder regions.

The race in these warmer regions took firm hold of the doctrine of a foil, a something thrust between itself and the sapping influences of weather, sun and soil. The Negro was pressed into service as that foil. He was to stand in the open and bear the brunt of nature's hammering while the Anglo-Saxon, under the shade of tree or on cool veranda, sought to keep pace with his brother of the more invigorating clime, counting immunity from the assaults of nature and superior opportunities for reflection as factors vital to him in the unequal race that he was to run.[38]

Booker T. Washington put things somewhat more simply and accurately when he too noticed the same tendency of a loss of Protestant virtue among the southern whites. "My old master," said Washington, "had many boys and girls, but not one, so far as I know, ever mastered a single trade or single line of productive industry." This state of affairs was ascribed to the system of slavery in which all the gainful labor was performed by a class of people who had no fair share of the results of their labor. "As a result of the system, fences were out of repair, gates were hanging half off the hinges, doors creaked, window-panes were out, plastering had fallen but was not replaced, weeds grew in the yard."[39] In *The Quest of the Silver Fleece* (Chicago, 1911), Du Bois describes Harry and Helen Creswell, the children of a rich landowner, as spoiled, lazy, and valueless, totally lacking in the drive and aggressiveness of a young enterprising northerner who seeks the hand of Helen.[40]

As one can see, Griggs, like such contemporaries as Washington and Du Bois, held fast to images of the white South that are still a part of the mythological heritage of America. Blacks, too, were viewed in mythic terms. In *The Hindered Hand*, the "passing" mulatto Eunice describes her fellow blacks as "a race cursed with petty jealousies, the burden bearers of the world," shrieking hysterically, "My God! the thought of being called a Negro is awful, awful!"[41]

Mulattoes in the novels of Griggs are usually seen as vengeful and bitter. No doubt Griggs reacted in some degree to the opinions of such as Mrs. L.H. Harris, who observed that the mulatto had "enough white blood in him to replace the native humility and cowardice with Caucasian audacity." Griggs did believe that blacks were inherently tractable, and perhaps he also came to suspect that mulattoes were less docile than blacks because of their white blood. Griggs also hints that perhaps black people are less intelligent than other colored people. In *The Hindered Hand*, Gus Martin, a man of Negro-Indian mixture is described as more agressive than his pure black brothers:

> Ordinarily the well-known tractability of the Negro seemed uppermost in him, but this evening all of his Indian hot blood seemed to come to the fore. His voice was husky with passion and his black eyes flashed defiance.[42]

It should be observed, in this connection, that the mulattoes in Griggs's novels are usually more restless and discontented—ultimately more diabolically dangerous than are the blacks, usually portrayed as tender-hearted and long-suffering.

Black nationalism, as we have seen, is like the nationalism of most colonial peoples, profoundly influenced by the culture of the dominant civilization. A recurrent pattern of adaptation in the elitist black national tradition is the rejection of political control without any accompanying rejection of cultural values. The pattern is visible in the Garvey movement and in most African nationalisms until very recently. At the turn of the century, most black nationalists were very much under European influences. They often tended to see their captivity if not as a blessing, then certainly as an evil from which some good had come. Booker T. Washington was not atypically servile or accommodating when he said, "we went into slavery in this country pagans; we came out Christians. . . . We went into slavery without a language; we came out speaking the proud Anglo-Saxon tongue." Such sentiments show the tendencies to assimilationism, even within the philosophies of notable separatists.[43]

The theme of separatism dominates *Imperium in Imperio* more than any other of Griggs's novels. It is encountered among the articles of the plans that Belton and Bernard present to the leaders of the Imperium.[44] Belton's resolution reads:

> Resolved: that we spend four years in endeavors to impress the Anglo-Saxon that he has a New Negro on his hands and must surrender what belongs to him. In case we fail by these means to secure our rights and privileges we shall all, at once, abandon our several homes in the various other states and emigrate in a body to the State of Texas, broad in domain, rich in soil and salubrious in climate. Having an unquestioned majority of votes we shall secure possession of the State government.

Once the blacks have taken over the mechanism of government, they are, in Belton's plan, to establish themselves as a black state, but firmly within the American Union. But this plan is not radical enough for the vengeful mulatto, Bernard, who proposes the following alternative:

> Encourage all Negroes who can possibly do so to enter the United States Navy. . . .
> Enter into secret negotiations with all the foreign enemies of the United States, acquainting them with all of our military strength and men aboard the United States war ships.
> . . .
> We can then, if need be, wreck the entire navy of the United States in a night; the United States will then be prostrate before us and our allies. . . .
> We will demand the surrender of Texas and Louisiana to the Imperium. Texas, we well retain. Louisiana, we will cede to our foreign allies in return for their aid. Thus will the Negro have an empire of his own, fertile in soil, capable of sustaining a population of fifty million people.

Griggs's appreciation for the spirit of Pan-Africanism led him to create spokesmen for the movement among his characters. Such a spokesman flashes unexpectedly upon the scene in *Unfettered*, as Dorlan Warthell pauses to view a parade of Negro street musicians, followed by an exuberant black throng:

> There was a great concourse of Negro boys and girls, men and women, following the band of musicians. Their clothes were

unclean, ragged and ill-fitting. Their faces and hands were soiled and seemed not to have been washed for many a day. The motley throng seemed to be utterly oblivious of its gruesome appearance, and all were walking along in boldness and with good cheer.

"Now those Negroes are moulding sentiment against the entire race," thought Dorlan, as his eye scanned the unsightly mass.[45]

In the midst of the musicians was "a cart pulled by five dogs hitched abreast. In the cart stood a man holding aloft a banner which bore a peculiar inscription", which Griggs cannily does not reveal, but Dorlan, at length, feeling that its message is directed at him, cries out:

"Here," said Dorlan. The man looked at Dorlan, jumped from his cart and rushed through the crowd and ran to Dorlan's side. Taking a knife from his pocket he quickly made a slit in Dorlan's clothes just over the muscular part of his left arm. The purposes of the man were so evidently amicable that Dorlan interposed no objection. The man seemed to be satisfied with what he saw. He now threw himself at Dorlan's feet and uttered loud exclamations of joy. Arising he turned to pay and dismiss the band.[46]

Dorlan and the stranger repair to the former's room where the stranger first examines certain markings on the skin of Dorlan's arm, then speaks to him in a foreign language. Dorlan calls upon childhood recollections to respond in the same tongue:

The stranger now felt safe in beginning his narrative. Said he, in English, "My name is Ulbah Kumi. I hail from Africa. I am one of an army of commissioners sent out by our kingdom into all parts of the world where Negroes have been held in modern times as slaves. We are hunting for the descendants of a lost prince. This prince was the oldest son of our reigning king, and was taken captive in a battle fought with a rival kingdom. He was sold into slavery. The royal family had a motto and a family mark. You recognized the motto on the

192 / The Political Tradition in Literature

banner; you have the royal mark. You also look to be a prince.
Tell me your family history and I will make to you further
disclosures."[7]

This surrealistic interlude reveals that Griggs's heart vibrated to
the iron string of Pan-African brotherhood. An appendix to the
novel, entitled "Dorlan's plan," is in reality Griggs's plan. It
mentions the importance of maintaining ties with Africa, as
migration may some day become a viable option for blacks to
exercise. In *The Hindered Hand*, Ensal Ellwood and Tiara
Merlow climax their eventful courtship by becoming "joyfully
married" on one evening and sailing for Africa on the next day, to
provide a home for the American Negro.

Since the early years of this century, one of the more interesting
literary debates in the Western world has been the dialogue
between proponents of cultural, religious, and political responsibility on one hand, and the prophets of personalism on the other.
Some artists deliberately concern themselves with "cultural tradition" in the sense that T.S. Eliot employed the term; others
concern themselves with the more subjective expression of their
struggle against the restraints which the national group inevitably
imposes, as in the case of James Joyce. In Afro-American fiction,
the concern with individuality is most prominently represented by
Richard Wright, James Baldwin, and—if we are to believe his
literary polemic, as distinct from his actual practice—Ralph
Ellison. The concern with the national culture is represented by
Sutton Griggs and W.E.B. Du Bois, and in more recent years, by
Amiri Baraka and the ironic Ishmael Reed, all of whom consciously occupy themselves with the creation of a black literature.
Du Bois, defining literature broadly enough to include the
sermons of Daniel Payne and the historical essays of William
Wells Brown, was convinced of the existence of a black literary
tradition. Within this tradition he included Sutton Griggs, who,
in his estimation, "spoke primarily to the Negro," while
Chesnutt's and Dunbar's works "spoke to the whole nation."[48]

Most black nationalists writing between 1890 and World War I,
like Booker T. Washington, William H. Ferris, W.E.B. Du Bois,
and that throwback to the nineteenth century, Marcus Garvey,
were committed to the Victorian sentimental racialism that

Griggs exemplified. There are self-accusatory tendencies in black nationalism and Griggs's thinking was like that of many black nationalists when he accused blacks of being too submissive and accommodating. He was more influenced by white racialism than he knew, for he tended to employ in his rhetoric many of the same degrading stereotypes that his white contemporaries were inventing. In *Pointing the Way,* Uncle Jack says:

> I allus jes' nachally laked white folks. I laked de gran' way dey walked an' talked. I laked de way dey wern't skeert uv no botty. I laked 'um fur feelin' lak purtectin' de wimmin folks. Ter make er long story short I jes' nachally laked white folks.[49]

This is reminiscent of Ferris's statement that the Anglo-Saxon ideal of manhood and womanhood are the highest the world has ever seen.[50] Such sentiments were never too remote from the consciousness of the Talented Tenth.

PART FOUR

Shifting Sands

The civilization by which America insists on measuring us and to which we must conform our natural tastes and inclinations is the daughter of that European civilization which is now rushing furiously to its doom. This civilization with its aeroplanes and submarines, its wireless and its "big business" is no more static than that of those other civilizations in the rarest days of Greece and Rome. Behind all this gloss of culture and wealth and religion has been lurking the world-old lust for bloodshed and power gained at the cost of honor.

W.E.B. Du Bois
Crisis, 1916

Chapter Ten

Pan-Africanism
at the Turn of the Century
Background to Patterns
of the Garvey Movement

We have seen in earlier chapters how patterns of authoritarian collectivism, separatism, mysticism, and civilizationism appeared in black bourgeois cultural and institutional life during the nineteenth century. These traditions were revitalized at the end of reconstruction, nurtured during the decades before World War I, and returned with a flourish, which Marcus Garvey symbolized, but did not create. The present chapter is not concerned specifically with the rise of Marcus Garvey, who did not arrive in the United States until 1916, but with those expressions of bourgeois nationalism that anticipated the thrust of his movement. Whatever may be said of Garvey and his movement, favorable or unfavorable, the idea that he introduced radically new ideas is debatable.

Most scholars concerned with proto-Garveyism have focused their attention on the spectacular back-to-Africa movements of Bishop Henry McNeal Turner, and Chief Alfred C. Sam. Precursors of the Garvey movement may also be observed elsewhere, however; for example, in the pseudomilitarism of the Hampton-Tuskegee traditions, where uniforms and drill practice re-emphasized the importance of a New Negro who would repudiate the legendary cultural softness of an excessively languid and aesthetic people. Fraternal institutions, such as the Masons and the racially exclusive Greek letter societies provided the patterns of lodge hall

gentility and self-conferred importance that would later characterize Garveyism. The entrepreneurial spirit of the National Negro
Business League encouraged the same spirit of economic independence and energetic self-sufficiency as Garveyism. Garvey's Ethiopian metareligiosity was inherited from Crummell, Turner,
Walters, and the nominally atheistic W.E.B. Du Bois, all of whom
were committed to Pan-African unity and liberation. Achievements of journalistic respectability, not only in T. Thomas
Fortune's New York *Age*, but also in the middle-brow literary
magazines of the day, illustrated the sense of racial pride and
independent mental effort that would later characterize Garvey's
journalistic success, *Negro World*.

There were three principal means whereby the ordinary black
American received information about Africa and sometimes even
Pan-Africanist political indoctrination. These were the literary
societies, the missionary societies, and the literary magazines. The
literary societies had their origins in the early nineteenth century
for the expressed purpose of encouraging an interest in letters and
ideas. Dorothy Porter has shown that these societies existed not
only because blacks were barred from the white literary societies,
but because they were a means of organizing and educating black
communities with respect to their peculiar needs. Porter has
observed that "in many instances members of the literary societies
were officers and members of the anti-slavery societies." After the
Civil War, such "literary societies" continued to exist, sometimes
indistinguishable from women's social clubs and Bible study
groups.[1]

Probably the most important of the literary societies by the 1890s
was the Bethel Literary and Historical Association founded in 1881
by Bishop Daniel A. Payne. At its meetings, papers were read on
such subjects as the identity of the ancient Egyptians and their
relationship to modern brown-skinned peoples; and "The Ethiopians—Who Were They?" Various black men and women of
letters delivered papers on sundry racial themes, both African and
domestic. Militant spokesmen, like Frederick Douglass, Alexander Crummell, and Henry McNeal Turner were given princely
welcomes by the membership of this society which included
teachers in the public schools.[2]

Rev. Francis J. Grimke, brother of Archibald Grimke, was

involved in a group called the Saturday Circle. When Edward Wilmot Blyden, the Liberian nationalist, visited the States in 1889-90, he met with this group more than once. After his return to Africa, Blyden maintained a correspondence with Grimke, occasionally exchanging materials on Africa and Afro-America with him.[3] Alexander Crummell included members of both the Bethel group and the Saturday Circle among the membership of his American Negro Academy, whose younger members went on to disseminate Pan-Africanist ideals in various regions of the United States. The literary societies were not institutions for the promotion of racial separatism, but separatists did penetrate such circles, and black nationalistic ideas were occasionally aired.

Missionary activities were also a means by which black Americans learned something of African brothers and sisters. Church magazines, such as the *Baptist Missionary Magazine* and the A.M.E. Church *Review* carried messages from Africa to America that were both educational and edifying. *The Missionary Review of the World* (June, 1904) carried an article on "The Ethiopian Movement in South Africa," exploring the relationships between independent African Churches and "South Africa's Race Problem:"

> . . . Ethiopianism is nothing if it is not anti-white. In one aspect, it is the reply of the native to the unfriendly attitude of the colonist. Furthermore, the appearance of the American negro from the bitter scenes enacted in the Southern States will hardly help to allay the racial antagonism. . . . Too often trusted converts woefully confuse the things of Caesar and the things of God. . . . It is feared that the native possessed of this genius [for intrigue] and already estranged from the European in religion, is but a step removed from organized resistance in matters social and political.[4]

Such thought-provoking material was hardly inaccessible to Sunday school classes and "Saturday Circles," and for those whose consciousness had been raised by the likes of Blyden and Turner, it must have been enthusiastically received.

In 1895, the Stewart Missionary Foundation sponsored a Congress on Africa in connection with the Atlanta Exposition. This provided a context in which black and white friends of the Negro and of African regeneration could exchange ideas and inspiration. T. Thomas Fortune, Henry McNeal Turner and Alexander Crummell gave addresses in connection with the biracial event, and Edward Wilmot Blyden sent his blessings by mail.[5] The missionary Pan-Africanism that can be witnessed at the Atlanta Congress and at the Columbian Exposition two years earlier, represents a phase during which whites were still prominent participants in Pan-Africanist activity.

The literary magazines were by no means strident in their nationalism, but their pages did contain a rhetoric and a message that was Ethiopianistic in no uncertain terms. This message was not limited to the political essays of the intellectual leadership, who contributed to such journals as *The Colored American, Voice of the Negro,* and *Alexander's Magazine.*[6] It appeared even in the genteel serialized fiction of Louise Burgess-Ware and Pauline Hopkins. The works of both these women contain inspiring messages of racial uplift, but Hopkin's writing was particularly traditional, set in a surrealistic world similar to that of Sutton Griggs. Pauline Hopkins carries her readers away to a hidden city, discovered beneath a pyramid and inhabited by "descendants of the ancient Ethiopians, who await the return of their king." They claim the hero of the novel as their lost monarch "because of the royal birthmark on his breast—a lotus lily." The spokesman of the Ethiopians addresses the hero in stately tones:

> You are in the hidden city Telasar. In my people you will behold the direct descendants of the inhabitants of Meroe. We are but a remnant and here we wait behind the protection of our mountains and swamps, secure from the intrusion of a world that has forgotten, for the coming of our king who shall restore to the Ethiopian race its ancient glory.[7]

Certainly, no one was converted to black nationalism as a result of this, but Pan-Africanism was insinuating its way even into sentimental magazine serials. This symbolizes the pervasiveness of Pan-African ideals, whose contact was unavoidable if one happened to be a literate urban black during the early 1900s.

The A.M.E. Bishop, Henry McNeal Turner, represents a trend

that revived in 1878, when a group of 206 emigrants sailed from Charleston, South Carolina for Liberia. Turner is significant because he was the most articulate African repatriationist in post-Reconstruction America.[8] He visited Africa in 1891, 1893, 1895, and 1898, and Like Crummell and Blyden, was anxious over the threat of black extermination. Turner, unlike his two fellow nationalists, was a shining yellow mulatto, and was certainly defensive about it.[9] Perhaps he found it necessary to "out-black" his brothers for this reason. Born to free but poor parents in South Carolina in 1834, he seems to have inherited the fiery spirit of his paternal grandmother, "a woman of fearful resources. . . [although] not so notable for goodness and female modesty."[10] During his early twenties Turner became an itinerant preacher to both black and white audiences, and throughout his career he maintained an ability to speak to both races. Du Bois eulogized him as "a man of tremendous force and indomitable courage," but also commented that he lacked "the education and the stern moral balance of Bishop Payne."[11]

Turner was a direct man, whose personal likes and dislikes were clearly revealed in his writing. He held traditional Pan African beliefs, such as the idea that "Africa will be the thermometer that will determine the status of the Negro the world over. . . . The Negro will never be anything here while Africa is shrouded in heathen darkness."[12] This rhetoric was as blunt as any that Crummell or Delany had employed in the 1850s, but hardly different in its general tenor. Turner was aware that a semiseparatist destiny was unworkable. Blacks would not be able to survive in the United States without participating in social institutions, just as all ethnic communities aspired to do. "Whoever this white race does not consort with, they will crush out," said Turner. "Social equality is as necessary to our existence in this land as air to breathe and water to drink."[13] When he became convinced that social equality was not forthcoming, Turner's rhetoric became more inflamed. He confessed in 1893 that he did not see "any manhood future in this country for the Negro." He was vitriolic in his attack on those with whom he disagreed, calling them "cowardly coons" and "braying Jackasses."[14] Turner was an emotional man, but perhaps a man of his temperament was needed for the times. A brilliant demagogue, Turner is sometimes credited with having contributed to the political development known as Ethiopianism in South Africa, which led to native uprisings. Be that as it may, Turner certainly worked for the establishment of the underground intellectual movement that pervaded all of Africa by the beginning of World War II. He was a fearless confrontationist in an age of compromise, and his heritage is the freedom movement that shakes the world today.[15]

Another A.M.E. bishop involved with the African movement was William H. Heard (1850-1937), who from 1895 to 1899 was United States Minister Resident and Consul General to Liberia. Heard was accompanied on his journey to this Liberian post by Bishop Turner, who was then embarking on his third African tour. Heard's amusing description of their voyage to the Gold Coast and Liberia provides a view of the hardships involved in traveling to Africa:

> After six days we were in the Bay of Biscay, called the "Ocean Graveyard." It was very rough and Bishop Turner was very much afraid. The boat was a cargo boat and the front was very low, so we shipped thousands of tons of water.
>
> Bishop Turner became very much excited and said: "Heard this ship is liable to sink at any minute." He went on the bridge and asked the captain. The captain told him yes, it was liable to sink at any minute. He came back and informed me of the condition. I went to my room and went to bed. He remained on deck tramping water knee deep part of the time.[16]

In due course, however, the two bishops safely arrived in the Land of the Blacks, where they were feted by the natives as "American Daddies." Heard returned to American church work after his term as consul. He retained a positive opinion of the tenacious little republic, but offered a word of caution to the potential immigrant: "he must be a man; boys cannot stand the hardships of pioneer life."[17]

A movement to repatriate Negroes in West Africa was undertaken by Chief Alfred C. Sam, a representative of the chiefs of the tribes of the Akim.[18] He made his appearance in Okfuskee County, Oklahoma during the summer of 1913, organizing among the

Negroes of Oklahoma's all-black towns. One newspaper alleged that Sam's activities were no more than "a slick confidence game."[19] The chief was selling stocks in a migration company, as Marcus Garvey would begin to do within the same decade. Sam claimed to be the grandson of the Chief of Obosse and Appasu, and, as such, legitimate heir to the throne. He was able to speak Twi, his native tongue, well enough to convince Liberian audiences that he was a real African, and he repatriated sixty black Americans in 1914, despite protests of *The Crisis*. When Chief Sam's S.S. Liberia arrived in the Gold Coast, its passengers were joyously welcomed by Orishatukeh Fadumah, who wrote a report for the Gold Coast *Leader* describing the colorfully costumed and jubilant throng that waited at the docks. "The ringing of church bells gave an air of sanctity to the gathering and was in keeping with the idea of the West African Movement, mainly that it is a Divine and therefore Sacred Movement."[20]

Fadumah was a West African patriot with affinities to the American Negro Academy. He had found a forum for his literary productions in black periodicals since the late 1880s. Born W.J. Davis, he adopted his African name by combining the names of Orisha and Tukeh, two Yoruba divinities. Fadumah attended London University a generation before Garvey appeared at that institution, and upon graduation, served as senior master of Wesleyan High School. During the early 1890s, Fadumah attended Yale University on a scholarship awarded for excellence in Hebrew, and later served a pastorate in the all black town of Boley, Oklahoma. Fadumah wrote passable if undistinguished verse in the Ethiopian tradition, which he published in the AME Church *Review:*

> A hundred years with howling beasts of prey,
> And numerous foes to intercept our way;
> Through customs strange destructive to the race,
> And dire doctrine launched at our face:
> That Afric's land is doomed by iron fate
> And hoary Noah's unrelenting hate.
> Besotted men and blind who do declare
> That our sad state to mend we cannot dare.
> With trembling eyes we read thy will, O Lord,
> And see the rise of Ethiop in thy word.[21]

Fadumah displayed the dreamy idealistic qualities common to American Negro Academy associates. He was an advocate of liberal philosophical education, who interestingly defended the concept of black individualism, almost as if he anticipated the excesses to which the Garveyites would carry the Pan-Africanist philosophy that he was helping to develop:

> In the education of a race, *unselfish* individuality in action should not be discouraged. Every successful attempt to deindividualize a man makes him lose whatever virtue there is in him, it makes him a chameleon-like man—a mere reflection of a man, a stage-player versed in the art of personifying. . . . The *unselfish* living "I" is of more worth than a selfish, inactive, dead "we." The first and last influence upon which both God and man have to act is your inmost self, your special character or individuality—don't trifle with it, don't sell it for a mess of pottage, for peace, for quiet.[22]

Fadumah was also the author of the tenth American Negro Academy Occasional Paper, "The Defects of the Negro Church." In this paper, Fadumah revealed a trait that was recurrent in the writings of such contemporary nationalists as Crummell and Payne. He was suspicious of black folk culture, especially as it appeared in the religious practices of the illiterate black poor. There was one significant difference, however, for Fadumah was a participant in the cultural nationalist movements burgeoning in West African nations. Perhaps it was for this reason that he wrote of the emotionalism in black American religion with sensitivity and understanding. "In [the black's] worship we may see things which are found in the heathen rites of the native African, in the Bacchanalia of the Greeks, among the Sali or dancing priests of the Romans, and among the Corybantes."[23]

Black nationalism was not limited to a lunatic fringe at the turn of the century, nor was the back-to-Africa movement. By 1900, most people would have acknowledged the sound sense of Josephine Ruffin's judgment that repatriation of all black Americans was a mechanical impossibility.[24] Repatriationists traveled in the most respectable circles, nonetheless. Bishops of the church and members of the American Negro Academy were emigrationists, consorting freely with colleagues who were less extreme.

Black nationalist and emigrationist influences passed from the intelligentsia to the stable working class through the popular and literary magazines.

Boston's Charles Alexander was the third president of the American Negro Academy and the editor of *Alexander's Magazine,* which some scholars have recently associated with Booker T. Washington's Tuskegee Machine.[25] Of his admiration for the Tuskegee philosophy, Alexander made no secret. Over certain aspects of Washington's program, he was sincerely enthusiastic. Alexander was "a teacher of the Printing Art and the author of a text book on printing, which was written while he was teaching at the Tuskegee Institute." Alexander allowed a wide variety of opinion to find its way into his magazine, however, some of it critical of Washington's policies. On September 15, 1905, Alexander published an editorial entitled "Dr. Booker T. Washington's Mistake," in which he frankly stated his disapproval of Washington's having apologized to the South for dining with John Wanamaker, saying, "he has lost thousands of staunch friends both among the white and black people in this country by his attitude." But this same issue of the magazine devoted many pages to publicizing Washington's National Negro Business League.[26]

Among the many interesting aspects of *Alexander's Magazine,* was its focus on African regeneration and other aspects of black nationalism. On the first page of the first issue of *Alexander's* was a full-page portrait of Samuel Coleridge-Taylor, the Afro-English composer who wrote "serious" music on African themes—a hero of the bourgeois cultural nationalists.[27] On the opposite page was a reprint of an editorial from the *Baptist Missionary Magazine.* It was a rather bland article, a general description of conditions of the continent and limited to two slender columns, but its placement at the beginning of volume one showed significant commitment to publicizing facts about Africa. And facts about Africa have always been difficult to obtain by blacks in the United States. *Alexander's* was more concerned with assuming a militant stance on Africa than were either of its two Tuskegee-supported rivals, *Voice of the Negro* and *Colored American Magazine.* In April of 1906, Alexander himself wrote a lengthy and interesting article, "As to the Congo Free State." A few blunt photographs showing natives with severed hands and feet—the result of Belgian atrocities—illustrated the reasons for Alexander's hostility to the Belgians, should anyone neglect to read his steaming prose:

> A striking picture appears in "King Leopold's Soliloquoy" by Mark Twain, of a camera suspended in the air over the king and under the picture appears the words "The only witness I couldn't bribe." Pictures play an important part in the education of mankind and especially are photographs valuable—they do not tell falsehoods—they cannot be bribed. The pictures we exhibit in this connection are taken from photographs—they are the tangible indictments against the king's misrule and slaughter of the poor, ignorant natives of the Congo Free State.[28]

The primary responsibility for reporting on African affairs in *Alexander's* was assigned to Walter F. Walker, whose saga is one of the most interesting examples of back-to-Africa idealism among bourgeois blacks. Walker was like the personification of one of Sutton Griggs other-worldly heroes; his idealism was to be rudely battered. Walker's good intentions were not supported by any sophisticated knowledge on his part of conditions in Africa, and he therefore reiterated the outmoded redemptionist schemes of the antebellum decades. The somewhat prim and proper Walker contributed an article on "The Young Man and the Church" to *Alexander's* in the September issue of 1906. Walker boasted of the fact that his church,-the Columbus Avenue A.M.E. Zion Church of Boston, had a class of 130 young men organized "with the express purpose of Bible study in view." Walker was apparently quite a social being who enjoyed voluntary associations and group activities. He also wrote musical reviews and reports on women's clubs events for *Alexander's* in addition to his duties as editor of the African department.[29]

In August of 1905, an article in Walker's department described the accomplishments of Professor John Wesley Hoffman, D. Sc. A Charleston, South Carolina-born, and Tuskegee-experienced agriculturalist, Hoffman worked for the British government in the Colony of Lagos, West Africa as an expert in the cultivation of cotton. Hoffman collected information on the Yoruba tribe, and certainly such descriptions as he provided must have been inspiring to Walker and his friends at the Young Men's Bible Study Group in Boston. Lagos, he reported, was a modern city of 50,000, with less than 500 white men among its inhabitants. "Four fifths of the government officials are native Africans." A railroad 200 miles long was "operated by natives in every position except that of engineer." Hoffman, as one of Walker's sources of information on West African peoples and customs, apparently provided the description from which the following was adapted. It provided a better and more accurate picture of native life than is generally assumed to have been available to black Americans:

Oyo, the capital of the colony, and the home of King Alafin, is a walled city of 150,000 inhabitants. The houses are large and substantial, though built of clay, dried in sun. They have thatched roofs so perfectly constructed as to defy tropical rains. They are usually circular in form and have porches all around, with a court in the center.

Both women and men are very skillful in the art of weaving, and the walls and floors of their houses are decorated with beautiful mats woven of palm leaves or of cotton, linen or silk thread. They also make many beautiful ornaments in leather, which they dress, tan and dye.[30]

Walker also admired Hoffman's plan for African regeneration through economic development. Interestingly, this idea was in no significant respect different from that proposed by Delany a half century earlier. West Africa was to grow cotton for British mills and compete with the American market, producing a superior article through the use of inexpensive native labor.

Walker published a defense of Liberia in August of 1907. By that time, he had announced his editorial purpose was "to give reliable information about Africa in general and Liberia in particular." Walker proposed to defend the little West African nation from her detractors, arguing that the widespread disaffection among repatriates with conditions there, was due to the personal failings of many of the repatriates, themselves.

In every case where large parties have gone to Liberia, they have suffered from this one delusion: that a livelihood could be got without work. Such a delusion could attract only ignorant individuals; the wise man realizes that underlying all success in life in any spot on the globe, is this one thing—hard, persistent work. Anyone going to Liberia to escape work will come to a miserable and regrettable end.[31]

In August of 1907, the African section of *Alexander's* carried an autobiographical statement by A.B.C. Merriam-Labor, who was the founder of the African General Agency. The story of his experiences will have a familiar ring to students of Marcus Garvey and his movement. Merriam-Labor was born in Freetown, Sierra Leone in 1878. He began his studies in the Sierra Leone grammar school, where he remained until age sixteen, around which time he began teaching at St. Mary's School, Gambia. He was a self-trained scholar of some formidability, passing the Sierra Leone civil service examination of November, 1895 with flying colors. His greatest accomplishment in the civil service was, according to his own statement, the organizing of 100 government officers and the presentation of ten demands for reform in the civil service, as a result of which his salary was doubled. After ten years in the civil service, Merriam-Labor resigned, "having entered Lincoln's Inn, a few months earlier. My first three bar examinations were passed within four months of each other." In 1905, he began to study commerce, embarked upon a tour of the United Kingdom, and passed his final bar examination with distinction. Merriam-Labor told of how he gave up the study of law on discovering that "no one, not even a lawyer could be an effective champion without wealth behind him. Nobody respects a nation that is poor. The Negro race is powerless and despised chiefly because as a whole it is poor."He rejected the idea that either book learning, or a distinctive African lifestyle, or even the force of arms and national independence would make Africa powerful. Economic development was his panacea, and "wealth will come soonest to us when we have one of our own to watch our financial interests on this side; when we dismiss the middleman . . ." For the purpose of keeping African wealth in African coffers, Merriam-Labor founded the African General Agency in 1905. "Our duty," he said, "is to find out for the African merchant the cheapest warehousemen and manufacturers and for the exporter, the best market for his products."

Walker too was interested in economic ventures. He established ties with Francis H. Warren, of Detroit, who in turn had ties to Bishop Turner and to the American Colonization Society. William H. Heard, who by 1907 was declaring his intention of becoming a Liberian citizen, joined forces with them to form the Liberian Development Association. Heard, who was incidentally contending for the African Bishopric of the A.M.E. Church, claimed that a failure to win that honor would not dissuade him from migrating.[32] The association hoped to settle 1000 people "in Liberia's hinterland," after securing a grant of 2000 acres of land as a site for Turner City. "Our association," announced Walker, "is already in touch with persons in every part of North and Central America." On September 15, 1907, Walker had quoted the Rev. Dr. R.A.M. Deputie as saying "I wish that 100,000 Africans in America would come to Liberia within the next five years and develop that great country. We need farmers, carpenters, builders and experienced men along all these lines." Beneath this, Walker had a laconic little poem published which presented "the humorous aspect the Negro's oppression presents to the Free Liberian."

> Liberia's bridges, mills, and dams,
> Need many thousand Afro-Ams.
> Liberia's ewes, Liberia's lambs,
> Like black sheep, baa for Afro-Ams.
> Liberia's roads, Liberia's trams
> For steady jobs want Afro-Ams.
> To handle nuts and cogs and cams,
> There's much demand for Afro-Ams.
> The barber shops, like Uncle Sam's
> Give hope to myriad Afro-Ams.
> There's bacon, hominy, yes hams,
> For all industrious Afro-Ams.
> With faintest praise Liberia damns
> The slow arrivng Afro-Ams.
> Unless their woes at home are shams
> Why don't they go, the Afro-Ams.[33]

Also in a humorous vein, that same issue of *Alexander's* contained a note on "The Christianity of King Menelik," of Ethiopia.

Walker, revealing a degree of admiration for the Christian Soldier-King, reported that "His Majesty is so desirous of promoting the study of the Bible among his soldiers that he will not hesitate . . . to fell an officer with a blow of his fist for any deficiencies in Scriptural knowledge."[34]

Walker turned to more serious subjects in October, reporting on an uprising among the Belgian Congolese, who revolted against the system of forced labor in lieu of the payment of taxes. He also voiced his hostility to French expansionism in Morocco, warning Europeans that after the yellow peril would come the black peril. He spoke of the Senussia, "a Mohammedan religious organization founded in Africa in 1835 by a lineal descendant of Mohammed, with the main purpose of freeing all Muslim countries from infidel rule by a universal Jehad or holy war." Constantly, he was a booster of Liberia and he continued to point out the hopeful prospects for any blacks willing to settle there.[35]

In February and March of 1908, *Alexander's Magazine* had a more strongly Pan-Africanist character than at any other point in its five-year history. Alexander reprinted a snatch of bitter doggerel by W.E.B. Du Bois:

> My country 'tis of thee
> Late land of slavery,
> Of thee I sing
> Land where my father's pride
> Slept where my mother died,
> From every mountain side
> Let Freedom ring![36]

J.J. Dossin's brief historical sketch of Liberia was reprinted in both of the aforementioned issues, and in both issues appeared full page portraits of Warren, Alexander, and Walker, identified as officers of the Liberian Development Association.

During the months from April through July of 1908, the African emphasis disappeared from *Alexander's*. Then in August a lengthy epistle from Walter F. Walker mailed from Monrovia, Liberia furnished an anticlimactic coda for the enthusiastically proclaimed migration scheme of a few months earlier. Walker, as we have seen, was not totally ignorant about conditions in West

Africa, although he was inclined to view the situation optimistically. He was apparently unprepared for what he found in Liberia, however. He told a tale of widespread disappointment among the immigrants surviving from earlier migrations, many of whom reported that if they had known what lay in store for them they would never have relocated. "The lack of means alone keeps many a restless and disappointed soul in this land." The motto of the Republic, "the love of liberty brought us here," had been vulgarly expanded into:

> The love of liberty brought us here. And the want of money keeps us here.

The shock of actually being in an underveloped country was overwhelming. There were no roads into the hinterland. Beasts of burden were rare, because of the climate and the tsetse fly. Walker described the climate as "enervating" and warned that "The Negro cannot judge his labors here by what he can do in the states."

> One must necessarily suffer the fever on coming to this country, which in the case of immigrants proves alarmingly fatal. To maintain life even the healthiest foreigner must make of his body a miniature apothecary's shop for a long time, if not forever. You cannot revolutionize affairs here. The obstacles cannot be removed or conquered at will.

Walker is reported to have remained in Liberia as a missionary, despite the fact that his advice to prospective immigrants was not encouraging.[37]

One of the most interesting of American Pan-Africanists during the early teens was William H. Ferris, a member of the American Negro Academy and later Vice President of the Universal Negro Improvement Association (UNIA). In 1913, Ferris published his two volumes of philosophical meanderings, *The African Abroad.* "All I am, or ever hope to be is expressed in this volume," admitted Ferris.[38] *The African Abroad* was the embarrassingly earnest confession of Ferris's heartfelt admiration for Anglo-American civilization:

Our God is a man of War. He reigns to human history at the same time. He speaks in no uncertain tones in the common sense and conscience of mankind. He manifests himself in the laws of reason. He utters his voice in the moral laws that have held such a mighty sway in human history. God has given the Anglo-Saxon the dominion of the earth, only because he has obeyed His moral laws, Only because he has reverenced and held sacred the purity and virtue of woman, and has respected the sanctity of the marriage tie. So we pray to a God who can melt the Anglo-Saxon's race prejudice just as the rays of the rising sun dissolve the mists.[39]

Ferris was an admirer of Alexander Crummell and seems to have been acquainted with almost every black leader of note among his contemporaries. He agreed with Crummell, who was "always saying to me, 'We need an educated gentry.'"[40] Ferris was hostile to the idea that "all the Negro needs is a bank account, a block in a city square, and stock in a railroad to win the respect of mankind." A graduate of Yale, with M.A. degrees from both Yale and Harvard, Ferris was interested in literature, philosophy, and the social sciences, but in nothing that Booker T. Washington would have considered practical. He was hostile to Tuskegee, which represented to him the essence of crass materialism and mundane commercialism. He agreed with Washington that it is "up to the Negro to do something and work out his own salvation."[41] But while he acknowledged Washington's "genius as an organizer, excutive, moneyraiser and orator," he viewed him as "a follower rather than a leader of public opinion. . . . He has a following among the Negroes; but that following is largely made up of men and women of imitative minds and flexible disposition."[42]

Ferris was also representative of that class of black Americans who kept abreast of events in Africa. Like several other figures discussed in this chapter, he too maintained ties with African intellectuals. Orishatukeh Fadumah was an acquaintance and Ferris noted with enthusiasm the achievements of P. Ka Isaka Seme, "a young Zulu" student at Columbia University and an eloquent speaker who had won a medal in oratory, saying:

The regeneration of Africa means that a new and unique civilization is soon to be added to the world. The African has precious creations of his own, of ivory, of copper and of gold, fine, plated willow-ware and weapons of superior workmanship. Civilization resembles an organic being in its development—it is born, it perishes, and it can propogate itself. More particularly, it resembles a plant, it takes root in the teeming earth, and when the seeds fall in other soils new varieties sprout up. The most essential departure of this new civilization is that it shall be thoroughly spiritual and humanistic— indeed a regeneration moral and eternal!

O Africa!
Like some great century plant that shall bloom
In ages hence, we watch thee; in our dream
See in thy swamps the Prospero of our stream
Thy doors unlocked, where knowledge in her tomb
Hath lain innumerable years in gloom.
Then shalt thou, waking with that morning gleam,
Shine as thy sister lands with equal beam.[43]

Ferris and his African contemporaries, like their nineteenth-century predecessors, had only the faintest appreciation for tribal cultures. They were still Anglo-Africans, still Victorians, still *assimilados,* and like most men, they found it difficult to view the world except through their own cultural spectacles. Life was not easy for such men as Ferris, Fadumah, and Seme. The eastern institutions at the turn of the century were centers of snobbery. Worst of all was West Point where a black cadet's ears were slit. Close behind came Princeton, where blacks were for the most part denied admission. At Rutgers, Paul Robeson had his fingernails torn off when he tried out for the football team. William Ashby, a student at Yale, recalls a class on Shakespeare in which the professor embarrassed him during a class on *Othello* by asking the students how they would feel if Moors were to ask for their daughters in marriage. "I am Senator of Venice. This Moor seeks social equality with me. I call upon my friends, my attendants to "lynch this nigger." A few students in the classroom took this occasion to stare and snicker.[44] Ridiculed by Tuskegee, and jeered at in the popular literature of the day, black intellectuals of the middle rank, like Ferris, were obviously motivated by a sincere love of knowledge, for they received little compensation, either social or financial, for their efforts at living the life of the mind. William H. Ferris did not like to be called a Negro. He felt that the term was a misnomer, because it properly applied to the pure blacks of equatorial Africa, and not to the mongrelized coloreds of the United States. He felt that the term conjured up unpleasant images such as "low, receding forehead, knotty, kinky, wooly hair, broad, flat nose, enormous lips, a monkey grin that stretches from ear to ear, thick, coarse, heavy brutal features, guttural utterance, flat-footed and either bow-legged or knock-kneed and usually reeking with the malodor of perspiration."[45] The term could never be redeemed from such associations nor could any people ever hope to raise themselves with such a burdensom epithet hanging about their neck. "What causes more of a shudder of revulsion to run through the frame than the phrase, 'A big, burly Negro?'"[46] asked Ferris. "The term 'Negro' suggests physical and spiritual kinship to the ape, the monkey, the baboon, the chimpanzee, the orangoutan and gorilla."[47] Ferris was aware of Alexander Crummell's bitter observations on the aristocracy of color which based its superiority on bastardy. But Ferris felt that the name given to black Americans ought to be "ethnologically true," and so he hit upon the term "Negrosaxon" as the most accurate description available. Ferris warned that "unless the Negrosaxons or colored people stop blackguarding and libelling themselves and besmirching their reputations by calling themselves Negroes, the lynching, shooting down and stringing up of often innocent Negrosaxons by crazed mobs will continue to go on in the South." Obviously committed to the idea that the black American mission and destiny were to "absorb and assimilate the Anglo-Saxon civilization,"[48] Ferris planned to provide the race with a name prophetic of its destiny. In *The African Abroad*, Ferris impresses the reader as a man who feels very intensely the pain of social rejection by whites.[49] Nonetheless, Ferris felt that the Anglo-Saxon civilization was "the highest and the best yet evolved in the history of the human race."[50] He therefore sought to create a mythological linkage in terminology, which would work like a magical incantation to create the unity with the white world that he desired but could not hope to achieve.

It is well known that Marcus Garvey made a great commotion

about the importance of the name Negro, scoffing at the National Association for the Advancement of *Colored* People, and at the mulatto aristocracy that controlled it.[51] The sometimes bitter debate over what to call themselves, resurrected by blacks during the 1960s, is nothing new. William Cooper Nell anticipated Ferris in 1855 when he spoke of fugitive slaves, the maroons of the Great Dismal Swamp, as "Black Saxons" in the tradition of Robin Hood.[52] The term Anglo-African had commonly been used throughout the antebellum decades as indicative of the cultural and racial affinity of black Americans to the Anglo-Saxon tradition. We have seen in another chapter how the National Association of *Colored* Women wrangled with the question of whether they should identify themselves as Afro-American.[53] On October 15, 1905, *Alexander's Magazine* carried a poem called "The English Speaking Race" by someone writing under the alias Kelt-Nor. It was reprinted several times, and described by the editors as "a song of the 30th Century, to be sung by Uncle Sam in those days."[54] In Boston, where blacks sometimes openly spoke of the miscegenation in their family past, the term "Afro-American" was appropriated by the mulattos for a time. "Colored" was also acceptable, but "Negro" was considered a term of opprobrium.[55] Garvey's insistence on replacing "colored" with "Negro" was similar to the drive of the 1960s to replace "Negro" with "Black," and had clear associations with a spirit of class and color consciousness.

Charles Alexander went on record in 1906 as being in agreement with Booker T. Washington that "the proper name by which representatives of this race scattered throughout our country, should be designated, is Negroes." Said Alexander, "An attempt to discard this name on the part of members of the race is an evidence of inexcusable weakness."[56] James M. Boddy contributed an article to *The Colored American,* which was putatively under Tuskegee control, in which he used such words as "Euro-African" and "Afro-European" to describe the black American people.[57] T.N. Carver of Harvard University, a white man, gave the following advice to readers of *Alexander's Magazine*, in an article entitled, "Make the Name 'Nigger' Honorable."

What does a name signify anyway? I am not urging Colored men to adopt the name "Nigger," but I think it would be better to adopt it rather than to resent it. I would urge them at least to absolutely cease paying attention to names and devote their energies to the task of making whatever name is given them an honorable one.[58]

In 1906, T. Thomas Fortune was still holding out for "Afro-American," as the only proper race designation of the people of African origin in the United States. "An American recently returned from Abyssinia told me that if a person should call an Abyssinian a Negro he would fell him in his tracks. He would take it as a term of reproach, as an insult." The term "colored" was a "cowardly subterfuge." It had neither geographical nor political significance and was equally applicable to red, to white, and to black or brown-skinned people. The blacks of the United States were a new race, "much nearer the American than the African type." The term "Negro" could never be given dignity and honor, "because it is a common noun, defining physical qualities of a race; and we can never make it a proper noun in popular usage. . . . Until we get this race designation properly fixed in the language and literature of the country we shall be kicked and cuffed and sneered at as a common noun, sufficiently and contemptuously characterized by the vulgar term "Negro."[59]

J.W.E. Bowen, on the other hand, agreed with Washington and Du Bois, that there was nothing wrong with the term Negro which was simple, honest, and logical.

> This word, like the word "Black," is no more interchangeable with "Inferiority" than is the word "White" interchangeable with "Superiority." The word has become spotted by evil associations. It is true in even literature and history as well as in ethics that "Evil communications corrupt good manners."
> Let the Negroes instead of bemoaning their lot and fretting because they are Negroes and trying to escape themselves by questionable methods, to say the least, in some places, rise up and wipe away the stain from this word by glorious and resplendent achievements. Good names are not given, they are made.[60]

After the Great War, Fortune and Ferris were to become editors of Marcus Garvey's newspaper, *Negro World,* and fittingly so, for both were competent and experienced journalists. But it is interesting to notice that both betrayed an ambivalence with respect to their own blackness; neither wanted to be identified with "Negroes." At the same time, both were anxious to be associated with Africa and with the struggle for liberation of the continent.

Barred from social ties to the larger society, blacks continued the tradition of maintaining their own voluntary associations. The Prince Hall Masons were endowed with eminent respectability, by virtue of their long history of association with the struggle for civil rights.[61] Although never publicly taking sides on the nationalist/ assimilationist struggle within the black community, the Masons contained proto-Garveyists within their ranks. One writer asserted with typical Ethiopian enthusiasm that the first Mason was a black man:

> When the ancestors of the present haughty Saxons—the Gauls, the Normans, and the Celts, were naked barbarians, living in grottoes and dropping caves; slinging stones at wild animals for food, and eating that food uncooked, there was on Africa's soil, in Egypt, the land of the black man, a civilization resting on "the pinnacle of national splendor" far exceeding that of Greece or Rome today. On the great Oasis in the desert of antiquity blossomed the golden deeds of the world's first Masonry.[62]

A new development in black college life was the "Greek Letter Society." The first of these, organized in 1904, was Sigma Pi Phi, which was not a campus organization, but an association of college graduates.[63] Alpha Phi Alpha fraternity was founded at Cornell University in 1906. Chapters were soon established at Howard University, University of Toronto, University of Michigan and Yale University. The rhetoric of Alpha Phi Alpha was the usual Anglo-African nationalism, the civilizationistic Negro improvement philosophy of the Talented Tenth, as we saw in the chapter on Du Bois's poetry.[64] Henry Arthur Callis, one of the founders of the fraternity lends credence to Frazier's assertion that black fraternities have more extended community functions than do their white counterparts. Callis reports that he and his comrades were inspired by Du Bois and were eager to institutionalize the Talented Tenth in the form of a fraternity that would be committed to overcoming race prejudice.[65]

Black nationalist elements were clearly present in the Negro Business Movement of the early twentieth century, which seemed closer in spirit to black fraternalism than to mainstream American commerce. In 1911, Chief Alfred C. Sam founded the Akim Trading Company with $600,000 in capital.[66] A.B.C. Merriam-Labor's efforts to establish a Pan-African economy anticipated Garvey's economic policies, just as Chief Sam's did. A nationalistic approach to business, without Pan-African rhetoric was proposed by Booker T. Washington in 1900 in the form of the National Negro Business League. The idea of organizing Negro business men's leagues originated with Du Bois and was taken over by Washington with Du Bois's cooperation.[67] The league was not made up of black captains of industry; it was dominated by clergymen and professionals, who were only incidentally entrepreneurs. Alexander noted that "the actual business man must take a back seat when the big preacher or lawyer or physician or politician makes his appearance."[68] He had put his finger on a crucial point, although unwittingly. Business in the black community was an aesthetic, rather than a commerical matter. Black petty entrepreneurs met in annual meetings to delight in the patronizing sermons of white politicians and captains of industry.[69] But there was to be no real flourishing of black business during these years, or thereafter. Afro-Americans had no merchant tradition, and they were excluded from those social, political, and marital ties through which they might have gained commercial sophistication. Black business and black fraternalism were merged, and black businessmen had difficulty distinguishing business activity from fraternal activity, as the following advertisement from *Alexander's Magazine* shows:[70]

WANTED

A NEGRO ARMY

One hundred thousand (100,000) strong. A force five times as great could be used by THE

ETHIOPIAN PROGRESSIVE ASSOCIATION OF AMER-
ICA, at salaries ranging from $50 to $75 and more than $100 per
month. . . .

The Ethiopian Progressive Association billed itself as "a Fraternity" which would allow only black people to be admitted to
membership or purchase stock. The Association was to acquire
capital through the sale of stock and to use its economic weight to
influence legislation, national and international, for the advancement of the race. It was to maintain a real estate department to help
its members buy homes. It was also to establish stores where its
members could purchase household goods and clothing. The
pattern was clearly the same as that to be followed by Garvey and
later by the Nation of Islam in their programs for racial advancement within the United States.

The foregoing pages have shown that there was a thriving Pan-
African intellectual movement among English-speaking Africans
at the turn of the century. Missionary ties established during the
earlier nineteenth century were one means through which contact
was maintained between the African intelligentsia and black men
and women of letters in the United States. Middle class magazines
distributed through literary clubs, church groups, and lodge halls
carried the Pan-Africanist message to the ordinary blacks—the
bell hops, elevator boys, and drug store clerks who were the stable
working class.[71] Bible study groups were infiltrated by Pan-
Africanists. Bishops of the Church encouraged the movement
from the pulpit. Sentimental magazine fiction was filled with
Ethiopian rhetoric and imbued with black nationalistic ideals.

Back-to-Africa movements proliferated. Schemes for the economic improvement of blacks throughout the world were common. All of these were ingredients of Garveyism—traditions well-
established in the Afro-American community before World War I.
Aided by such experienced newspapermen as Ferris and Fortune,
Garvey, who was himself an experienced journalist, was more
successful at publicizing the nationalistic militancy of the stable
working class blacks than anyone else, even Du Bois. But it must
be admitted that Garvey stood on the shoulders of other men, the
"little Du Boises," who had created an audience capable of
understanding and supporting the goals of the Universal Negro
Improvement Association.

Chapter Eleven

World War I
The Decline of the West

When Chief Alfred C. Sam sailed for the Gold Coast in 1914, it was in disregard of the heated criticism of his scheme by the *Crisis,* which referred to the movement as "a poorly conceived idea." Accurate indeed was the dire prediction that "ordinary inexperienced farmers and laborers migrating from America to Africa would succumb to the trying climate in very short time." The *Crisis* urged Oklahomans to remain where they were and to fight out the battle in their own state, saying that Chief Sam was no more than a charlatan and a thief who belonged in jail. Migration, on the eve of the First World War was a serious matter, for as the *Crisis* editor knew, the European nations were maneuvering for position on the African continent. It had been possible, during the late eighteenth and early nineteenth centuries, to repatriate black people along the West Coast of Africa, as had happened in the cases of Liberia and Sierra Leone. But by the time of Sam's departure, European colonialism in Africa had become an issue of such economic importance that the European powers were inclined to view his black nationalism, feeble though it was, as a threat to their African empires.[1]

The Great War, as its contemporaries called it, was very much a black man's war; some historians have described it as a war over African policy. Early battles between England and Germany were fought in Togoland on the West Coast of Africa. Many

Africans fought and died for both the Allied and the German causes. West African perceptions provided cognates and analogues of Afro-American thought. From the European point of view, the First World War was an apocalyptic event. It signaled the beginning of the end for European civilization, and it was the fulfillment of prophecies by thinkers as remote from one another as David Walker and Oswald Spengler that Western culture had all along contained the seeds of its own destruction. For World War I marked the rising of that inexorable tide of events that was to sweep Europe from her preeminence and to erode the lofty confidence of the United States. It was the destruction of an old order, mourned by T.S. Eliot and Ezra Pound, bewailed by Ernest Hemingway and the bourgeois reactionaries for whom they spoke so well. For black people, the war was, in spite of its trauma, the confirmation of their own world view. It showed Western civilization at its worst and allowed black thinkers to view the white masters of the world in a moment of moral insecurity.

The cycle of events began with the Berlin Conference of 1884, the meaning of which has not ceased to puzzle historians, just as it perplexed its contemporaries. Its most puzzling features have to do with German colonial ambitions in Africa. It was presided over by the wily genius of Prince Bismarck, Iron Chancellor of the German empire, whose aims even in the light of recent scholarship remain mysterious. The importance of the congress with respect to the present study is that it was the event at which the Congo Free State was endorsed by all the Western powers. The Congo Free State—a misnomer if ever there was one—was not a typical European colony; it did not belong to Belgium proper, but rather it was a personal possession of Leopold, King of the Belgians. Leopold was able to gain control over the Congo as the result of several factors. He was apparently supported by Bismarck, who preferred to see the territory fall into his hands rather than those of France or Portugal. France, Portugal and England were eager to see the creation of a treaty that would frustrate what they believed to be German colonial aspirations in Africa. Leopold had insisted to the world since the Brussels conference of 1876 that his country was "small, happy and content with her lot," unmotivated by egotism and having no selfish ambitions as far as Africa was concerned.[2]

In 1884 Leopold had proclaimed the existence of the Congo Free State which was to occupy the entire Congo River Basin. Working through a skeleton crew of Belgian officers, a regular native army of 20,000 and an armed militia of 10,000 to 15,000, Leopold completely disrupted the human ecology of the region by flooding it with firearms. The system was aimed at forcing the Congolese to adopt Western patterns of wage labor, although the wages paid were in most cases mere token salaries of a few cents per month. The system of forced labor was exceedingly harsh. Methods were described in the secret diary of a Belgian government official:

> Each time the corporal goes out to get rubber, cartridges are given him. He must bring back all not used, and for every one used he must bring back a right hand. M.P. told me that sometimes they shot a cartridge at an animal in hunting; they then cut off a hand from a living man. As to the extent to which this is carried on, he informed me that in six months the State on the Mambogo River had used 6000 cartridges, which means that 6000 people are killed or mutilated. It means more than 6000 . . . for the people have told me repeatedly that the soldiers kill the children with the butts of their guns.[3]

It is within this context that we recognize the ambivalence of Afro-American intellectuals at the time of the German invasion in 1914. Du Bois wrote in November of 1914 that Belgium deserved "every pang she is suffering after her unspeakable attrocities in the Congo." And yet Du Bois recognized the ironic fact that the Congolese were fighting in Belgium, "fighting to protect the wives and daughters of the white Belgians, who have murdered and robbed his people, against 'Christian' Culture represented by [the Germans]." Even more bitter was Lester Granger who published his feelings concerning the rape of Belgium:[4]

> Today they tell us of a great fight
> In the land of the white men;
> They tell us of a curse, a curse fallen
> On Belgium, the land of our oppressors
> They tell us of invading armies, ruthless and cruel;

They cry of homes burned of men and women slaughtered;
Of women, hunted and ravished and killed.
So we look about us
At the blackened ruins of our huts;
At the thinned numbers of our tribe,
And at Shenzi Khanga;
And we hasten to him and gather about him and tell him
The news from the North.
Shenzi Khanga hears,
And raises his face with the useless eyes,
And lifts the useless stumps,
And Shenzi Khanga
Laughs!

This was a very dramatic statement. Certainly there is an element of metaphoric truth in its lines. But Granger was not a Congolese, not even an African, and his poem had conveniently avoided the paradox that Du Bois so wryly observed. "Black soldiers" read a *Crisis* headline, were "fighting to protect the civilization of Europe from itself." Troops from the Congo were fighting for Belgian freedom, and as a matter of fact, it is accurate to generalize that with a few exceptions Africans tended to be loyal to the Allied cause and fought gallantly for their colonial oppressors. The Kaiser too had loyal African subjects, and although Togoland was quickly defeated by British and Gold Coast troops before the end of August, 1914, black troops fought most gallantly for the Fatherland and against overwhelming odds in the Cameroons and in South West Africa. In East Africa, a force consisting of 300 Germans and 11,000 black men sustained terrible losses, but remained a functional army and did not surrender until after the armistice. With respect to the Congo, one reluctantly observes that the most dramatic instance in which Congo reform sentiment was transformed into active resistance to the Allied cause occurred not in Africa or America, but in Ireland.[5]

Sir Roger Casement, a militant Irish nationalist who collaborated with the Germans during World War I, was hanged in 1916 for conspiring to participate in the famed Dublin Easter Rising earlier that year. The Easter Rising resulted in the execution of fifteen revolutionary leaders in addition to Casement. The British army suffered 234 casualties. Casement had long tended to think of the colonial situations in Africa and Ireland as comparable. Once he had wistfully commented that the Congo would be free before Ireland; by sheer force of numbers, she would someday be able to expel her invaders. He was less certain of the future of Ireland. Casement had been one of the important figures in exposing conditions in the Congo. Black newspapers in British West Africa which reported his arrest showed no trace of sympathy, however. So fully committed to the war effort and the struggle with Germany were his majesty's Negro subjects, that Casement's well-known sympathies for the African peoples did not prevent his being roundly denounced. West Africans seemed to be completely blind to any similarities that may have existed between their own nationalistic aspirations and the Irish struggle for independence from England.[6]

Similarly, the West African press showed little sympathy for the views expressed by Edmund D. Morel, another opponent of European colonial policies in Africa. Morel had worked with Casement from 1904 to 1908 in the Congo Reform Association. Was it not ironic, Morel inquired, that Belgium, one of the most brutal of the colonial powers, whose king had been guilty of instituting slavery on the rubber plantations, whose government had maimed and raped and burnt in the name of Christianity and civilization, should now seek the sympathy of the civilized world, when victimized by Germany? West African leaders did not follow the logic of Morel. They sympathized with Belgium and pointed to the Huns as destroyers of civilization and ravagers of a noble and peaceful nation.[7]

Sir Harry Johnston observed in a pamphlet published in Britain in 1915 that the Germans had hoped for widespread revolt among Africans and other colored races but had been disappointed. His observations seem to be accurate, certainly with respect to the Gold Coast and Nigeria. Loyal West Africans were not inclined to publicize an abortive revolt in Nyassaland, led by the American-educated John Chilembwe. Occasionally a West African newspaper would bitterly remark to the effect that Africans were only pawns in the struggle between the European titans, and that conditions were not perfect in the British colonies. Generally, however, the support of the black British for the war effort, like that of their black American cousins, was heartfelt and steadfast. Needless to say, I do not mean to suggest that Africans should have exchanged British masters for Germans. Du Bois was certainly correct when he said that for all her sins "England as compared with Germany is an angel of light." Still, it is not easy to explain the loyalty of the German West Africans who fought against the British Empire. If the Germans made mistakes in Africa, they apparently had some successes in winning loyalty as well. And I, for one, am dismayed by the failure of West Africans to draw the parallel between their own condition and that of the Irish, a failing of which Du Bois, to his credit, was not guilty.[8]

In August of 1916, the same month in which Casement went to the gallows, Du Bois wrote in the *Crisis* of the sufferings of the Irish people at the hands of England, which he felt few colored people were aware of or cared about. He recognized the reasons for Afro-American apathy with respect to Irish sufferings. In America, the two ethnic groups had been bitter competitors on the bottom rung of the social ladder. He recalled the Civil War draft riots where the Irish had protested against a war which—as they saw it—was being fought to free the slaves. But like Frederick Douglass before him, Du Bois was keenly aware of the similarities between the Irish and the Afro-American situations. "We must remember," he wrote, "that the white slums of Dublin represent more bitter depths of human degradation than the black slums of Charleston and New Orleans, and where human oppression exists, there the sympathy of all black hearts must go. The recent Irish revolt may have been foolish, but would to God some of us had sense enough to be fools."[9]

Du Bois's perceptions of the First World War were extraordinarily complex because he viewed the war not only from an American perspective, but from an African one as well. It is easy to oversimplify Du Dois's reactions to the war, to accuse him of accommodationism, to compare his cooperation with the war effort to the conscientious pacifism of other reputed radicals. Of course the comparison is not a fair one, because Du Bois carried the weight of moral responsibility for all black people, at least in his own mind. His attitude towards the war could not be simply an expression of his own values; it had to be an articulation of the position he felt would be most beneficial to his people. In any case

Du Bois was only one of many American progressives who rushed to their tents as the war spirit burgeoned.[10]

Du Bois first began to cover war stories in 1914, in contrast to some other journals which showed no similar concerns so early. His editorial policies had never been isolationist. He was consistently given to viewing the black American struggle in world perspective. Like colored races in other parts of the world, Afro-Americans would soon witness an erosion of the color line resulting from the European conflict. He immediately saw that an opportunity would present itself for black people to demonstrate their loyalty to America, and anticipated from the beginning the possibility that black troops would be called on to fight. Were not the British, French, and even the German colonials already involved in the struggle? He quoted the *Northern Budget* of Troy, New York, which reported that "the German ambassador has announced to the United States that he is 'unconditionally opposed' to the use of colored troops" on the European fronts. Du Bois agreed with the reply of the *New York World* which read:

> When Germany went to war with the British Empire she must have expected to fight the British Empire, and not merely a selected part of the population the color of whose skin happened to meet the approval of Berlin.
>
> If Germany were at war with the United States her troops would have to meet our Negro cavalry, than whom there are no better soldiers in uniform.
>
> German denunciation of the Indian troops is futile as German denunciation of the Japanese as "yellow bellies." It is too late to draw the color line in the war. That line was erased more than fifty years ago by Abraham Lincoln in that noble letter to the Springfield Convention: "And there will be some black men who can remember that with silent tongue and clenched teeth and steady eye and well-poised bayonet, they have helped mankind on to this great consummation."[11]

Du Bois's chief concern in 1914 when these observations were made was not, however, with the utilization of black troops, for America was not yet at war. His concern was rather with the comparison between atrocities in Europe and lynchings in the

United States—a comparison that was often made in other quarters. Rustem Bey, the Turkish Ambassador, made a cutting criticism of American domestic policy by comparing his country's military atrocities to lynchings in the United States. The *Crisis* continued to publicize such criticisms and comparisons throughout the war, especially in the summer of 1917 when a riot in East St. Louis destroyed half a million dollars in property, drove 6000 black people from their homes, and left 40 dead.[12]

Du Bois's war years have been described as a period of "accommodationism." Accommodationism is a loaded word, conjuring up images of Booker T. Washington at Atlanta, and when used as Professor Rudwick uses it, connoting an ironic and dramatic reversal in Du Bois's public stance. It is clear when one looks at the *Crisis* editorials of 1914 that Du Bois's siding with England against the Germans was more than an accommodation to American war hysteria. It was, on the contrary, the result of a heartfelt opinion based on what he knew about German history and economics. Du Bois was no subscriber to racist theories of German moral inferiority. If a martial spirit was capturing the German mentality, this was due to the suffering of the German people during the eighteenth and nineteenth centuries and not to some genetic predeliction for authoritarianism. Du Bois had been critical of German colonial policy at a time when the British Foreign Office, the United States State Department, and the Tuskegee Machine were praising it to the skies. Du Bois, perhaps with the wisdom of hindsight, claimed to have noticed that Germany was drifting in the direction of global aggression as early as his years in Berlin, when he studied under the "fire-eating pan Germanist," von Treitschke, who had "stood for the imperialist doctrine in its fullest extent, and taught that Germany's most pressing need was the acquisition of colonies." Von Treitschke's philosophy was the repudiation of the old liberal theme of the preceding century, articulated by Johann Fichte, who in 1808 had encouraged the German people to rely upon their own labor and ingenuity, "instead of wishing to draw a profit from the sweat and blood of a poor slave across the seas!" While in attendance at the First Races Conference in London, 1911, Du Bois and the other participants had been shocked when the German delegate, Professor Felix von Luschan ended an otherwise commendable paper with the following statement:

The brotherhood of man is a good thing, but the struggle for life is a far better one. Athens would never have become what it was, without Sparta, and national jealousies and differences and even the most cruel wars, have been the real causes of progress and mental freedom.

Nations will come and go, but racial and national antagonism will remain; and this is well, for mankind would become like a herd of sheep, if we were to lose our national ambition and cease to look with pride and delight, not only on our industries and science, but also on our splendid soldiers and our glorious ironclads. Let smallminded people whine about the horrid cost of Dreadnoughts; as long as every nation in Europe spends, year after year, much more money on wine, beer, and brandy than on her army and navy, there is no reason to dread our impoverishment by militarism.[13]

Because he could remember such a manifesto, Du Bois had a more sophisticated appreciation of German colonial ambitions than did most other black American leaders. To accuse him of opportunism, as Hubert Harrison did, or to suggest that he "sold out" and became a war hawk simply because the bait of a military commission was dangled before him is unfair.[14]

Du Bois's concerns were international and related intimately to his concern for African affairs, but they were also related to domestic considerations. In every war since the American Revolution, black people and their leaders have been beguiled by the idea that fighting the nation's battles would inevitably lead to an improvement in the status of black Americans. The idea contains elements of truth and falsehood. Du Bois's arguments were not far removed from the arguments of Frederick Douglass during the Civil War. Douglass had felt, and rightly so, that black people should assume a part of the burden of their own emancipation, so that after the war they could demand, rather than request, the rights of citizens. Willard Gatewood and George P. Marks have argued convincingly that black opinion during the Spanish American War was hawkish. Once again during World War I black people hoped to make the argument that staunch defenders of the nation should be entitled to all the privileges of citizens. There was, however, considerable public grumbling—more than had occurred during the Civil War, for as American black people continued to fight the nation's wars, they became increasingly cynical. If black Americans have become increasingly sophisticated with the passage of time, they have also become less unified in times of war. World War I marked the first instance in which responsible and intelligent leadership in the black community seriously questioned the value of fighting. The young E. Franklin Frazier published at his own expense a pamphlet called "God and the War." He opposed the draft because of his feeling that the war was being fought over questions related to economics and imperialism and had nothing whatsoever to do with democracy. A. Philip Randolph and Chandler Owen went to jail. Ida B. Wells refused, as usual, to stay in line with other black leaders, preferring to crusade against injustice, rather than to give patriotic speeches, build myths and bolster morale. Naturally she was accused of creating disunity, branded a traitor, rebuffed by black leaders, and harrassed by police.[5]

But Du Bois felt that it was once again time to close ranks and to prove worthiness of full citizenship. Besides, the question in 1917 was not only one of whether or not black men would be willing to fight, but the more basic question of whether or not they would be allowed to fight. And so Du Bois, far from passively accommodating to a warlike spirit and pressure, actively carried the war fever into the black community:

> These Bourbons and Copperheads know that if Negroes fight well in this war they will get credit for it. They cannot "Carrizal" the news and boost the white putty-head who blundered, forgetting the very name of the brave black subalterns. No! those fool French will tell the truth and the Associated Press will not be able to edit "Niggers"; so the Copperheads and Bourbons do not want Negro soldiers. They think they can trust Southern State officers to juggle that little "agricultural laborer joker" and keep us out of the ranks.[16]

Well, if black soldiers were not to be allowed to fight, then perhaps they would find opportunities for other kinds of struggle long denied on the home front. Like it or not, America would have to accept the fact that there were forces at work far beyond the control of her provincial domestic politics.

If they do not want us to fight, we will work. We will walk into the industrial shoes of a few million whites who go to the front. We will get higher wages and we cannot be stopped from migrating by all the deviltry of the Slave South; particularly with the white lynchers and mob leaders away at war.

Will we be ousted when the white soldiers come back?

THEY WONT COME BACK!

So there you are, gentlemen and take your choice,—

We'll fight or work.

We'll fight and work.

If we fight we'll learn the fighting game and cease to be so "easily lynched."

If we don't fight we'll learn the more lucrative trades and cease to be so easily robbed and exploited.[17]

As the war slowly progressed, Du Bois's emphases in the *Crisis* changed. At the commencement of European hostilities, he had been concerned with the larger questions—German colonial ambitions, the balance of power in Africa, the question of whether this war could be misinterpreted as only a white man's war. He believed—and in a sense he was correct—that the war would lead to the independence of Africa and Asia. Indirectly it did, and still does. As the war progressed and the United States made her entry, he focused on the specific concerns of black Americans. This is our country, he said, and since this was true, black people should not only obey the call of duty, but demand the right to fight in her defense. The nation was far from perfect in her treatment of black people, but conditions could hardly be expected to improve if black people seemed to be unpatriotic. By September of 1918 he was able to answer critics of his war policies by listing a number of gains that had been made as a result of black America's war effort:

Recognition of our citizenship in the draft; One thousand Negro officers; Special representation in the War and Labor departments; Higher wages and better employment; Abolition of the color line in railway wage; Recognition as Red Cross nurses; A strong word from the President against lynching.

Blessed saints! Is this nothing? Should it not discourage
slackers and fools? Come, fellow black man, fight for your
rights, but for God's sake have sense enough to know when
you are getting what you fight for.[18]

Du Bois was certainly not above accommodationism and
compromise. He was an idealist, but was nonetheless capable of
pragmatism. All leaders must be capable of compromise. To
criticize Du Bois's war efforts as particularly accommodationist or
singularly compromising, to suggest that he was selfishly motivated is to ignore the fact that Du Bois's attitudes on the war were
well-considered, long considered, and more systematically developed than those of most other Americans, black or white. But
those who are disturbed by any elements of accommodationism in
the writing of Du Bois during the war years will be interested in
the responses of West Africans which were even more complex
than those of Du Bois.

J. E. Casely-Hayford, 1866-1930, was a Gold Coast lawyer and
publisher of the *Gold Coast Leader*, whose social thought was a
significant influence on Du Bois, one which Du Bois himself
acknowledged.

Hayford was among the first rank of Pan-Africanists. In 1914,
when Alfred C. Sam and Orishatukeh Fadumah sought to resettle
migrants from some of Oklahoma's all-black towns in the Gold
Coast, his newspaper applauded their efforts while the *Crisis*
fulminated against them. Hayford was a critic of British colonial
policy and his journal was a forum for protest. On January 3, 1914,
readers of the *Gold Coast Leader* were treated to an attack on white
rule in British South Africa by Dr. Abdurahman:

> Instead of kindly, humane treatment, we find barbarous
> cruelty and inhumanity. Instead of ameliorating our lot they
> endeavor to accentuate its bitterness. The object of the white
> man's rule today is not to develop the faculties of the colored
> races so that they may live a full life, but to keep them forever
> in a servile position.

But later in that year, and for the duration of the war, there were to
be no sweeping indictments of white rule. Germans were to bear

the brunt of the attack. On August 29, 1914, shortly after the beginning of hostilities, an editorial expressed the opinion that while no European nation was blameless in its dealings with subject races, "unquestionably, the Germans take the cake." Speaking in defense of the conquest of Togoland by British and Gold Coast troops, the *Leader* reported that "the worst state of native governments, however steeped in barbarity, is in substance only a trifle worse than German administration in Africa." The editors went on to express hopes for continued British presence in Togoland and opined that while the British are not perfect, "to liken German rule to British rule is to perpetuate a gross and unmitigated slander on the latter." And yet the same issue of the journal carried ads from German firms and in the issue of December 12, that same year, an editorial attacked the idea of all German shops being closed. It argued in favor of Germans being allowed to preserve competition among foreign traders in fairness to native consumers.

But German brutalities were frequently reported, as, for example, when the Germans passed a law banning interracial marriage. "The natives of this colony are loathsome to the idea of marrying white men," argued a native of Aneho; "if they do now, it means they want to be free from persecution." The anonymous Togolander argued that certain advantages accrued to those native families whoe daughters married Europeans in German colonies. They became exempt from the system of forced labor used in the construction of public works. The correspondent argued that the purpose of the law was to prevent the diminution of its involuntary labor force. The native of Aneho reported that "the German administration is making itself very ridiculous by summoning the 240 half breeds which the colony boasts of to appear in the court house and to be forced by the judge in the name of the Governor to relinquish his or her father's name and assume his or her mother's or in default pay 7.10.0. with 6 months' imprisonment."[19]

The *Leader* early displayed hostility to the idea that this was to be a white man's war.

One of the areas of contention concerned the raising of war funds. A controversy arose on the question of whether or not blacks should organize efforts to support the war and whether or not blacks should work in biracial organizations to give economic support to the Imperial War Effort. Casely-Hayford, who was founder of the Imperial War Fund, argued that the war had been an African concern from the beginning. Indeed cocoa production, a matter entirely in the hands of native labor, was an important support of the war effort. The Aborigines Protection Society opposed the native Africans' attempts to establish their own war fund, said Hayford, because they wished to keep Africans in the status of a protected people and did not want to acknowledge them as fellow protectors of a common interest. But it was impossible, of course, to keep blacks out of the war, for not only had the invasion of Togoland made Gold Coasters the first British subjects to actually participate in battles, but in Rhodesia as well natives were involved before policy could be debated. Black Rhodesians made it clear that they feared attacks from pro-German peoples. When white colonials suggested to them that the conflict was none of their business, they shrewdly responded that they only wished to fight to keep the European missionaries from being massacred.[20]

The *Leader* consistently reminded its public that the realities of war were forcing the whites to acknowledge black equality. France was using Algerians and Senegambians. Britain, it was to be remembered, had used black troops as far back as the war against the thirteen colonies. A quotation appeared from an editorial in the *New York News* of August 6, 1914, which observed that "the result [of intra-European strife] will be that all will be set down at least a peg; all the subject domain of Africa will get at least less stern and repressive rules from the kingdoms of the continent." The *New York News* anticipated Du Bois's remarks of some years later when it predicted that black workers were going to get new labor opportunities as a result of the war and that "advantages will accrue to the African while Europe fights."

The *Leader* encouraged the closing of ranks in common cause against the Germans. It was not that the interests and concerns of West Africans in the Great War should blind them to the realities of political life, read an editorial; it was rather that Africans should be patient during a time of crisis.

> The West African native does not desire to add un-
> necessarily to the worry of his rulers at the present time, and
> our rulers, we are glad to note, have shown their appreciation

of this restraint by the relaxation of their censorship of local articles bearing upon the war.[21]

Criticism of colonial administration in the Gold Coast was thus treated in the most formal and guarded tones. British colonial policy in Nigeria, on the other hand, received more stringent criticism:

> The question of the recognition of our rights to better, more responsible and more lucrative appointments is as acute now as ever it was, and the gates of opportunity in the Public Service to our young men who have qualified as medical practitioners and engineers in British Universities are as shut now as ever they were before.
>
> In Nigeria where the experiment of governing natives on German lines was set in motion a few years back by the Germanised school of British officials, the rights of natives to fair and just government are being as ruthlessly trampled upon as ever before.[22]

The Great War was a great leveler, in the view of the *Gold Coast Leader*. It showed that Europeans could be every bit as "barbarous" as the so-called primitive races of Africa. The behavior of the German was, in the opinion of the editor, "enough to startle the ghosts of the ancient natives of Ashanti and Dahomey. It is true that these ancient savages indulged in human sacrifices as other nations before them . . . But to say that these ancient peoples wantonly burned houses, roasted the inmates alive or raped women and speared children when they invaded enemy country would be a highly coloured story."[23]

One of the most interesting features of the *Gold Coast Leader* during the war years was a column of correspondence from Togoland, beginning in 1913, contributed by an anonymous "Native of Aneho." Materials contributed by the Native of Aneho were intended to show German colonial policy in its worst light, but one does not gain an impression that conditions in Togoland under German control were any worse than conditions in Missippi or Alabama during the same years: in some respects they were better. Of course German administration in some areas of Africa was extremely harsh. The war against the Herero nation in Southwest Africa was comparable in its brutality to the reign of terror in the Congo. It would seem, then, that Du Bois and Casely-Hayford were correct, and that, viewed in continental perspective, British colonial policy was generally superior to German. Still, rule by any foreign power over Africans should have been seen as undesirable. Much of the West African loyalty during the war seems to have sprung from a stongly-held belief that British colonialism was a good thing. How else can we explain the prominence given to such editorial statements as the following, taken from a newspaper managed by a prominent African nationalist?

We know that even if British rule were to be voluntarily withdrawn from West Africa, we cannot at present rule ourselves. We know further, that every other race which found itself in the predicament in which we are to-day, has had to be under the tutelage of another nation more advanced in the Science of Government than they until such time as they were sufficiently advanced to manage their own affairs, and then the idea of their continued domination by an alien power had to be decided by an overruling Providence. Ancient History is full of instances of this nature, and we have sufficient faith in God to know that we are not going to be an exception to the general rule.[24]

I would not like to leave the impression that West African intellectuals were totally accommodationist during the war, or that they viewed it without a sense of bitter irony. Typically, they saw it as Europe's baptism by fire and hoped that it would raise the West to a higher plane of civilization. One writer asked, "is the world going mad?" for it seemed to him that the war was direct proof of "the madness of civilization, itself"; A madness demonstrated by "the white nations carrying war into realms of air and the under-seas where aeroplane and submarine contend in the new elements for the bloody country." Where would it all end?[25]

G.A. Williams was born in Sierra Leone around 1852 and died in Nigeria in 1919 after editing the *Lagos Standard* for twenty-four years. During the war, the *Standard* and its editors revealed the same contradictions witnessed in the *Crisis* and the *Gold Coast Leader*. There was a thinly veiled hostility to European colonialism and a critical approach to white power. This often found expression in editorials on the poetic justice of the Belgians' fate:

> Yesterday it was God's will that Congo natives should suffer destruction of their homes; loss of lives and barbarous treatment; today it is God's will that Belgium should share a similar fate. Perhaps it is for a Divine purpose. To teach the truthfulness of life's philosophy and give an example of its bitter realties. For there is always a reaction to every race and each country for a particular Fate.
>
> Western civilization, say what we like, has received a fatal blow from the hands of Germany and presented and given it to [the] less cultured as a thing of Scorn and hate . . .
>
> We want to ask Europe through [Belgium], to show greater consideration and sympathy for the failings of the African natives and to ask in the words of the Sixth article of the Berlin Congress of 1884 that "All the powers exercising Sovereign rights or influence in their respective territories . . . watch over the preservation of the Native tribes and . . . care for the improvement of their moral and mental well-being . . ." No power in Europe at the present moment is better fitted to do this than Belgium. For she has suffered in a manner similar to ours.[26]

Noting that Congolese soldiers were fighting in defense of Belgium, the *Standard* praised the reforms that had taken place in the Congo a few years before the war, attributing loyalty of the natives to the enactment of these reforms:

> We had just cause a few years ago to measure tongues with you Belgiums over what was then known as "Congo atrocities." England took the lead and we, as was only natural, followed our father's footsteps in crying down the horrible deeds of those days, in that part of Congo under Belgian rule.

Thanks to God to-day we hear tell of a Reformed Congo. Comparative peace reigns there and the natives have borne testimony to this, as there are in the battlefields of Europe to-day, African soldiers fighting to uphold the honour and dignity of Belgium and the Belgian flag. This we hope will prove to you [Belgium] particularly and Europe generally that the black man by nature knows and appreciates all who recognize and appreciate him.[27]

There are many ironies here, for black people, by their loyalty and forgivingness during the war proved themselves to be more Christian than their Christian teachers. Indeed, the war was proving to the English-speaking African elite that European Christianity was morally bankrupt. And yet—here is the central irony—despite their awareness of European moral collapse, British West Africans continued to profess that they believed "without the least hesitation, equivocation, or reservation . . . in God, in the British Empire and in Humanity."

Thus, the pattern of response that we see among Gold Coast and Nigerian leaders during the war was one of loyalty. However, loyalty did not mean the abandonment of criticism or agitation in subtle forms, nor by any means did it signify the loss of a sense of irony. The Afro-British were forced into the position of supporting British power in Africa, of supporting their colonial masters, at least for the time being until Germany was defeated. Of course, this meant ignoring the fact that Britain had historically done more to disrupt African cultures and to degrade black people than Germany had ever done. But Germany was a colonial power, which like Belgium had not entered Africa until the 1880s. Her colonies were less stable, and still undergoing the painful process of adapting to foreign domination, and consequently there was more bitterness among her subjects than among the Afro-British. There was no German speaking colonial elite to speak of, there were no large numbers of blacks living in Germany and asserting their loyalty to the empire. But the British Empire did have a large English-speaking elite, and they were not ready to exchange one set of masters and customs for another. In this respect they were similar to the Francophone African elite.

What we have seen of the opinions of leading Afro-British journalists provides the context for turning to Blaise Diagne. This Senegalese leader is still very much misunderstood by Americans who persist in viewing him through the eyes of Du Bois. Diagne was not peculiarly accommodationistic; his pattern of support for French colonial power was similar to the patterns of support for British colonial power among comparable English-speaking black elites. Diagne was responsible for bringing Africans into the regular French Army during the war. His motivations were similar to those of Du Bois, Hayford, and Williams. He was motivated, as they were, by the idea that Africans earn status in the white world by demonstrating loyalty in time of war. Like Casely-Hayford, he was not ready to see his country make the great leap to nationalism in the middle of the war. Furthermore, he could observe that even during the period of his lifetime, conditions for black Frenchmen had steadily improved. The war would provide Senegalese with needed leverage in their push towards full equality. Diagne realized that black troops were in demand and raised the threat that blacks would not fight unless given full rights and privileges. "This is a chance to prove to many Negrophobe functionaries in French West Africa that we are truly worthy of our status as voters and French citizens."[28]

If France had lost the war, and Senegal had become a German colony, the Senegalese would have lost their right to vote and to participate in government. Therefore, from the point of view of Senegalese leadership, at least, the question of loyalty never was seriously raised. It was so patently obvious that if France lost her colonies to Germany the Senegalese would lose everything.

By 1917, when the United States entered the war, colored people all over the world had demanded the right to fight. Even in the United States there was little sympathy for the idea that this was to be a white man's war. Afro-Americans wanted to fight for the same reason that Africans did—they felt that they could improve their status by demonstrating their loyalty. A number of fine studies have shed light on the odyssey of the black soldiers through the Great War. These have described the discrimination from which black soldiers suffered, the unfair treatment of Colonel Young, the rioting at Camp Logan in Houston, Texas, and the Jim Crowing of black men in uniform. The triumphs of the Ninety-second and

Ninety-third divisions can only be mentioned here. To the ushering in of the Jazz Age by the popular Noble Sissle, and James Reese Europe, who carried black music to France, we likewise give only passing acclaim. Black soldiers were hailed throughout Europe, not only as bold fighting men, but as one French official condescendingly put it, "wonderful children, with generous hearts, a spirit of good comradship, possessing also a French trait—that of loving and making themselves beloved." But the war did not bring equality; the words of A. Philip Randolph still ring true after fifty years:

> Since when has the subject race come out of a war with its rights and privileges accorded for such participation? ... Did not the Negro fight in the Revolutionary War, with Crispus Attucks dying first ... and come out to be a miserable chattel slave in this country for nearly one-hundred years after? ... And have not prejudice and race hate grown in this country since 1898?[29]

Although the war did not bring racial equality, ironically, it contributed evidence of equality in an unexpected way. During the war, the United States Army administered I.Q. tests to black and white soldiers alike, and even though the tests were culturally biased and unfairly administered, the results were most interesting. They smashed a number of dearly held myths concerning black intellectual inferiority. These tests did, and still do, provide some of the most straightforward data available for theorists on the question of mental equality. They show that in the United States during World War I, geography was far more important than race as a determinant of I.Q. scores. Black soldiers from the states of Ohio, Illinois, and Indiana achieved higher median scores than did whites from seven of the southern states. Subsequently it was shown that I.Q. scores are "highly correlated with the yearly educational expenditures of the states from which the testers were drawn." No studies have been able to refute the conclusions of Montagu, or Marcuse and Bitterman that the influence of environment on I.Q. scores is incalculably high. Still, the army tests proved nothing to those who did not wish to be convinced. What was true in the testing centers was true on the

battlefields and on the home front. Euro-Americans simply were
not ready to deal with black Americans either as a group, or as
individuals. The performance of the black man in the war was not
destined to endow him with his nation's gratitude.[30]

Not only did the war provide a chance for black men to prove
their manhood, Afro-American women as well viewed the war as
an opportunity to demonstrate their loyalty and willingness to
serve. Addie W. Hunton and Kathryn M. Johnson were two
colored women who traveled overseas as welfare workers with the
YMCA. Like most of their contemporaries, they worked to
encourage the spirit of wartime unity. These women, like most
people who had contact with black soldiers, told the familiar story
of segregation and discrimination. Recreation facilities in the
leave areas were in some cases rigidly segregated, and unpleasant
conditions prevailed in those facilities that were set aside for
blacks. Hunton and Johnson were concerned with providing a
decent Christian recreation center of the sort described in the
following report:

> Our building was opened each morning at 8:45. A twenty-
> minute religious service began at 9 A.M. and this was known
> as "Start the Day Right Service." Breakfast . . . was served till
> about noon. . . . Free refreshments were served three times a
> week at night and always to entertainers and educators, . . . A
> reception with free refreshments was always tendered outgo-
> ing troops. At many of these we served more than a hundred
> men. During each of these receptions a strong moral or
> patriotic talk was made by some of the secretaries, and I have
> seen men go away with tears in their eyes.[31]

French ladies of the villages sometimes volunteered their
services at the Sunday afternoon gatherings where tea and cake
were served and piano and violin music was provided. The
recreation centers also provided athletic and educational programs and worked to remove "immoral women" from the
environs to which soldiers came on leave.

A continuous theme throughout the Hunton-Johnson report
was the contrast between the treatment black troops received from
the French and that which they received from their fellow

countrymen. After the war they contemplated the cost and evaluated its rewards in a few thoughtful paragraphs:

> Some were not anxious for the colored soldier to take a part in the great World War. They felt that it would be a needless sacrifice for something that would bring no tangible results by way of alleviating his present condition; others felt that if he offered his life upon the altar for the principles of a new freedom, the remaining shackles that have so long bound him would be wholly broken.
> Neither were correct; for while the shackles have not been wholly removed from his body there have been wonderful results accomplished that have in some measure removed the fetters from his soul.[32]

The response of the Tuskegee machine to the war effort was totally loyalist. The machine did not demonstrate great concern over the complex array of issues that were involved. They were concerned with one very important issue, true—the issue of bolstering the black image and of demonstrating the unequivocal loyalty of the majority of blacks to the United States. The attitudes of Booker T. Washington himself can never be completely known, for he died in 1915, long before the United States entered the war. Washington had been involved for some time in African policy, however, and his African politics involved Germany. Louis Harlan has shown that Washington had agents in Togoland, the Sudan, South Africa, the Congo and Liberia. In 1910 he gave full endorsement to German colonial policy in a Berlin speech where he said:

> I have followed with great care the policies and the plans according to which the German officials have dealt with the natives of Africa. . . . Their work succeeds by these means in a wholesome and constructive manner. They do not seek to repress the Africans, but rather to help them that they may be more useful to themselves and to the German people. Their manner of handling Negroes in Africa might be taken as a pattern for other nations.[33]

This praise, totally out of line with what was being said by such legitimate spokesmen as Casely-Hayford and W.E.B. Du Bois, should be contrasted with the actuality of German colonial practice during the pre-war years when 14,000 Herero natives of South West Africa were driven into the desert to starve. At the time General Trotha, who was responsible for driving them off their land, made the following public statement, almost unbelievably cruel:

> Herero people must leave the land. If it refuses I shall compel it with the gun. I shall assume charge of no more women and children, but shall drive them back to their people or let them be shot at.[34]

There were ties between Casely-Hayford, his brother Mark, and Booker T. Washington, but it is unlikely that they would have agreed on the question of German benevolence. In fact Casely-Hayford felt that the work of both Washington *and* Du Bois was "exclusive and provincial" and that they were concerned primarily with the conditions of blacks in the United States. He was wrong about Du Bois and Washington, for both were concerned with the universal status of black people, although Du Bois's attitude was clearly more progressive in terms of the values that most African nationalists seemed to accept at the time.[35]

Washington was a devious man, subservient in the presence of superiors; ruthless in his dealings with subordinates. His ethics were determined purely by situations; he had little in the way of guiding principle. Publicly, he said that black people should be separate from whites in all things purely social; privately he assured Edna D. Cheney that nothing was purely social. Publicly, he advocated black unity; privately he carried on a campaign of back stabbing and subterfuge. Washington would have felt no compunctions whatsoever about completely reversing his position on German colonial policy, had he lived. He would have been committed, as were his surviving lieutenents, to the war against the Hun.

Washington's successor at Tuskegee was Robert Russa Moton, who wrote the President at the beginning of the war to assure him of the continuing loyalty of the Afro-American:

I have not acknowledged your very kind letter of some weeks ago. A number of people of prominence have approached me with reference to the attitude the Negroes would assume in case the country should go to war. I understand also that certain high officials of the Government have raised similar questions.

Notwithstanding the difficulties which my race faces in many parts of this country, some of which I called to your attention in my previous letter, I am writing to assure you that you and the nation can count absolutely on the loyalty of the mass of Negroes of our country; and its people, North and South, as in previous wars, will find the Negro people rallying almost to a man to our flag.

Whatever influence I may have personally, or whatever service I can render in or outside of the Tuskegee Institute, I shall be glad to put at your disposal for the service of our country.[36]

Moton felt that he could best "perpetuate the ideals of Doctor Washington" by dedicating the resources of Tuskegee to the service of the country. He saw his work as one of strengthening the government's faith in black people and "strengthening the confidence of the colored people throughout the country in the purpose of the Government." Under Moton, Tuskegee Institute was responsible for training 1229 draftees in needed technical skills. Moton was also responsible for the appointment of Emmett J. Scott, formerly Booker T. Washington's secretary, as Special Assistant to the Secretary of War. Scott produced two works in connection with the war, both of which still remain standard reference tools for research in the period. His *History of the American Negro in the World War*, profusely illustrated, provides the best introduction to the war years in a single volume, providing not only a quantity of factual material, but a primary source for cultural history. His sociological study, *Negro Migration During the War*, chronicles the great changes taking place among the black masses as a result of wartime disruption.

At the end of the war, Moton was sent by the President and the Secretary of War to France. Moton has been accused of going in order to quiet the angry black troops, resentful over the discrimination they were facing. He traveled on the same ship, the *Orizaba*, that carried Du Bois to his many and perhaps conflicting activities in Paris over the next two months. Du Bois said that "whenever possible," he and Dr. Moton "gladly cooperated, but our missions were distinct in every respect." Moton remembered that he and Du Bois had many frank and pleasant talks. Du Bois wrote that Moton brought a message that the black soldiers did not want to hear, "and again the wrath of black America descended on his head." What Moton actually said was this:

> You will go back to America heroes, as you really are. You will go back as you have carried yourselves over here—in a straightforward, manly, and modest way. If I were you, I would find a job as soon as possible and get to work. To those who have not already done so, I would suggest that you get hold of a piece of land and a home as soon as possible, marry and settle down. . . . Save your money, and put it into something tangible. I hope no one will do anything in peace to spoil the magnificent record you have made in war.[34]

But Moton also investigated "countless damaging rumours" as he called them, and secured interviews with high-ranking officials, both military and civilian, including General Pershing, who attested at least to the competency of black troops and officers. Moton was interested mainly in public relations and he carried out his program well to the extent that he managed to communicate the black point of view to racists like Wilson and to his conservative army officers. He was also successful in publicizing the black man's legitimate grievances with a larger public than the more radical black leaders were capable of reaching.

Spokesman for the radical wing of black leadership was A. Philip Randolph, a black socialist and editor of a monthly magazine, *The Messenger*. He was similar to Du Bois in that he saw the parallels between the Irish struggle and the Afro-American struggle:

> Here is a new problem that has come to the fore in our American life.
> The Irish in America are making a militant fight for the

freedom of Ireland. They are giving forceful and determined utterance to the ideals of Casement and O'Connell, those martyrs of the Sinn Fein revolution.

The Irish are calling for Great Britain to make good her claim of "fighting for the smaller nationalities" by lifting her imperial heel from off the tired neck of Ireland. For 800 years Great Britain has withheld "Home Rule" from Ireland. Irishmen remember the bitter days of the potato famine. And the Friends of Irish Freedom are calling for an accounting. They have Great Britain on the hip and they are going to feed fat the grudge they bear her.

The radicals must thank these brave souls for standing firm for free speech. They are doing their "bit" in keeping what democracy we have in the world.[38]

But agreement with Du Bois ended here; Randolph did not support the war effort. He protested almost everything about the war, from the maltreatment of black soldiers to the anti-German hysteria which demanded the suppression of German-American culture. When black dissidents were charged with being dupes of German propaganda, he responded, "the discontent among Negroes was not produced by propaganda, nor can it be removed by propaganda."[39] In August of 1918 he embarked with his partner, Chandler Owen, on a speaking tour to cover Cleveland, Chicago, Milwaukee, and Washington, D.C. They were arrested in Cleveland and served two days in jail. Upon their release, they continued their trip as planned, making a final stop in Boston, where, says Randolph, William Monroe Trotter "was the only Negro who had the guts to join us on the platform."[40]

Trotter, that fiery veteran of the Niagara Movement, and founder of the Boston *Guardian*, had long harbored cynical views concerning the war, although, according to Steve Fox, he campaigned to defend the Afro-American people from accusations of disloyalty. He accused Du Bois of betraying the cause, nonetheless, when the *Crisis* called upon its readers to close ranks and support the drive for a black officers' training camp at Fort Des Moines. Trotter characterized this as an accomodation to segregation.[41]

Trotter did not oppose the war effort, but he certainly felt that his efforts should be directed toward working to assure that blacks would reap the benefits of the war, rather than urging them to join the crusade with unquestioning loyalty. Apparently he felt that the crusade would take care of itself, but that reaping the rewards for supporting it would be a struggle. This led him to his famous journey to the Paris Peace Conference in 1918. He stowed away on the S.S. *Yarmouth* as a galley servant and made his way to Paris with only the clothes on his back and a small sum of money in his pockets. He managed to get a respectable amount of publicity in the French press, but was unable to force the conference to discuss the question of the color line.[42]

The effects of World War I were not immediately felt in the black world. Small victories had been achieved at the cost of many lives lost and disrupted. The real changes in black America's mentality as a result of the war had taken place as Alain Locke observed later, "beyond the watch and guard of statistics." The larger issues often went unobserved. Du Bois, as usual, attempted to focus attention upon the remote cosmopolitan goals. Along with Blaise Diagne, he organized the first Pan African Conference in Paris in 1919. Du Bois reminded readers of *The Crisis* of his 1914 essay, "The African Roots of War," which he offered as proof of his consistency. Now, in Paris, he would try to persuade the world of the need for justice in Africa, as a means of insuring continued peace. His attempts, he soon realized, would be unsuccessful. His chief goal, the reorganization of the former German colonies under a League of Nations protectorate, was not to be realized.

On the home front, too, there were disappointments. Even the usually conservative and accommodating Kelly Miller, who had successfully straddled issues during the heated Washington-Du Bois debate of twenty years earlier was moved to anger when he viewed the Great War in retrospect:

> During the war the nations relied upon the forgiving spirit and patriotic emotion of the Negro and that reliance was not in vain. Although he had just cause for deep dissatisfaction, he held his grievances in abeyance, but not in oblivion. He was a good American while the war was on and wishes to be considered as an American now that the war is over. His valor and courage contributed in full measure to the consumation of the struggle. The slogan of democracy was harmonious to his ear. It aroused in him hopes and ambitions that he would

enter as full participant in the fruition of that democracy which he was called on to sustain and perpetuate. He was given every assurance that the nation would no longer deny him a just share in the new democracy which his courage helped bring to the world. Andrew Jackson advised the Negro troops who won the belated victory behind the fleecy breastworks of New Orleans to return to their masters, and be loyal, obedient servants, but no one now expects the Negro soldiers of the World War to revert with satisfaction to the status they occupied before the war for the emancipation of mankind.[43]

"The Negro," said Miller, is "a natural conservative." The black man was not inclined towards the radicalism represented by the Bolsheviks or the Industrial Workers of the World, he argued. Circumstances, however, can alter racial character. Before the war, Booker T. Washington with his spirit of humility and foregiveness, had been the incarnate symbol of the black American, but perhaps in this new world order black people would develop a new character, born of the successive disillusionments experienced during and since the war. "It is too much," said Miller, "to hope that he [the black man] will forever requite cruelty with kindness and hatred with love and mercy."

Miller put his finger on a very important point, for the 1920s were to mark the growth of a spirit of radicalism in black America such as had not been seen since the Civil War. The age of Washington had marked not only a spirit of humility and forgiveness, but a spirit of black unity that was unhealthy and stagnating. Booker T. Washington had triumphed in a period when the greatest energies of the Afro-American people had been directed towards making blacks acceptable to the larger white society. His efforts had been directed toward the creation of a New Negro for a new century, a useful cog in the new industrial machinery.[44] Du Bois's early efforts were not dissimilar, for his energies had gone into a series of studies to demonstrate that this New Negro was rapidly evolving. But the Afro-American in the postwar world would be less concerned with assmilitaing white values. He would be a manipulator of his environment. If he did not find the world hospitable as it was, he would seek to change the world to suit himself, rather than keeping his peace and adjusting to conditions as he found them.

A new generation of leadership was on the rise; the new leaders would ignore the Tuskegee voices and denounce even Du Bois as an Uncle Tom. Representative of these was Hubert Harrison, who founded the Liberty League as the voice of a *new* New Negro. Harrison observed:

> Twenty years ago all Negroes known to the white publicists of America could be classed as conservatives on all the great questions on which thinkers differ. In matters of industry, commerce, politics, religion, they could be trusted to take the backward view. Only on the question of the Negro's "rights" could a small handful be found bold enough to be tagged as "radicals"—and they were howled down by both white and colored adherents of the conservative point of view. Today Negroes differ on all those great questions on which white thinkers differ, and there are Negro radicals of every imaginery stripe—agnostics, atheists, I.W.W.'s Socialists, Single Taxers and even Bolshevists.[45]

Harrison was guilty of exaggeration. There had been currents of black radicalism in America before the turn of the century. T. Thomas Fortune, for example, had supported the father of the single tax theory, Henry George. Henry Adams testified before a Senate committee in 1879 as to the existence of grass roots politics among the black masses of the South. Other names, like that of Jack Turner, continue to surface in recent scholarship as evidence that there were radical and progressive elements among black Americans during the dark ages. Still, there is an element of truth in what Harrison said, because certainly the 1920s did witness a growing diversity of opinion within the black community, and much of the opinion was radical.

Another new leader was Marcus Garvey, who denounced Du Bois as a color-conscious elitist. Garvey had his faults. He was a short-sighted separatist, and a racial chauvinist. But the appearance of Garvey signified a healthy development. Du Bois had become too secure and too powerful. He was becoming isolated from the masses of black people, especially after the rapid urbanization of the World War period. Du Bois's public exchanges with Garvey were healthy for the black community. They made it clear to white America that all black people are not stamped out of the same mold, that all do not have the same aspirations or the same values. A. Philip Randolph entered the lists and the debate became three-cornered. While some may wring their hands and lament the disunity that was publicly displayed, others may be inclined to argue that this was the essence of the Harlem Renaissance, an organic flourishing of emotion. How different it was from the dark mechanical unity, the industrial conformity, the sterile standardization symbolized by the age of the Tuskegee juggernaut.

The traditional authoritarian collectivism that had characterized Washington's age was rapidly eroded during the war. It did not disappear, as Ralph Ellison and E. Franklin Frazier have ably demonstrated, but it was decidedly weakened. Also on the decline was the spirit of black separatism. Marcus Garvey was in more than one way a throwback, but ultimately even he was forced to repudiate his doctrine of non-participation in U.S. politics by his endorsements of Calvin Coolidge and Royal Weller.[47] The tradition of Ethiopian mysticism was likewise weakened. Urbanization had produced a new secular leadership class no longer dependent upon the church pulpit for their livelihood, and no longer dependent upon the church-suported college. The new leaders symbolized by Randolph, Harrison, and Garvey, were given to social explanations for social problems. Although the old church-oriented patterns influenced their rhetoric, they were maverick social engineers.

The most important change brought about by the war, however, was the decline of the civilizationistic pattern in the thinking of black leaders. It has become trite to speak of the postwar disillusionment that settled like a black cloud over the Western world with the end of the Great War. Things fell apart, in the words of Yeats. Western civilization became a vast wasteland. The sun was setting on the British Empire. Black people had seen Western Europe at its ugliest. Garvey made an appropriate observation:

> For the Anglo-Saxon to say that he is superior because he introduced submarines to destroy life, or the Teuton because he compounded liquid gas to outdo in the art of killing and

250 / *Shifting Sands*

that the Negro is inferior because he is backward in that direction is to leave one's self open to the retort "Thou shalt not kill" as being the divine law that sets the moral standard of the real man.[48]

Black Americans, and black Africans as well, had gone into the war as civilizationists. It would be too much of an exaggeration to say that they emerged as cultural relativists. But surely the tendency of the Jazz Age to glorify the primitive, the emotionally exuberant stereotypical Harlem Renaissance Negro, must be attributed at least in part to a disillusionment with the standards of industrial civilization and the idea that black people should slavishly conform to them.

Chapter Twelve

The Rising Tide
of Color

"It was not Germany that lost the World War," wrote Oswald Spengler, "the West lost it when it lost the respect of the colored races."[1] Spengler was not the only prophet of doom to emerge in the age of anxiety following the First World War. On the American side of the ocean, Lothrop Stoddard noted with fear and trembling that white world supremacy was being threatened by forces from without and within. In a preface to his work, *The French Revolution in San Domingo*, Stoddard said:

> The world-wide struggle between the primary races of mankind—the 'conflict of color,' as it has been happily termed—bids fair to be the fundamental problem of the twentieth century, and great communities like the United States of America, the South African Confederation, and Australasia regard the "color question" as perhaps the gravest problem of the future.[2]

In 1920 Stoddard published *The Rising Tide of Color* with an introduction by Madison Grant, another white supremacist, and a social scientist of eminent respectability.[3] In this book Stoddard expressed his dread of the rising African and Asian nationalisms. In the dawn of the century, the Russo-Japanese War had "dramatized and clarified ideas which had been germinating half-unconsciously in the millions of colored minds, and both Asia and Africa thrilled with joy and hope. . . . The legend of white invincibility lay, a fallen idol, in the dust."[4] The Great War, Stoddard and Grant agreed, was a tragic internecine struggle, a civil war of the white world. And now, since the war, Bolshevik agitators had tramped across Africa and Asia, provoking dissatisfaction and proving that Bolshevism was "the renegade, the traitor within the gates, who would betray the citadel, degrade the very fibre of our being, and ultimately hurl a rebarbarized, racially impoverished world into the most debased and hopeless of mongrelizations."[5] Islam was appealing not only to Arabs, but also to the naturally militant instincts of Negroes south of the Sahara. Indications of hostility were to be seen in the militant Christianity of the Ethiopian Church movement, which united black fanatics in Africa with their counterparts in the New World. The Pan-African Congress, called by Du Bois in Paris in 1919, was "an interesting indication of the growing sense of negro race-solidarity."[6] While Stoddard did not believe that black nationalism was even potentially capable of mounting an independent threat to white power, he feared, nonetheless, that "Pan Islamism once possessed of the Dark Continent and fired by militant zealots, might forge black Africa into a sword of wrath, the executor of sinister adventures."[7]

"War did the white races tremendous harm in Africa as elsewhere," wrote the Frenchman Maurice Muret in *The Twilight of the White Races*.

> The Europeans prided themselves rightly on having put an end to the incessant wars among the sultans and the petty rival princes of the negro kingdoms, when suddenly the great powers of Europe dragged thousands of blacks into the most bloody massacres, and the negroes have not forgiven the whites for following so imperfectly the pious instructions of their missionaries.[8]

Muret also viewed with dismay the rise of Pan-Africanism, the growth of Pan-Islam and the rise of a new brand of militant black leadership. Unlike Stoddard, he took black nationalism seriously even when some francophone Africans apparently did not. Muret noticed, as did other observers, that military organization tends to influence all other aspects of life and culture. Even the native style of dancing had been changed by the war. "The dancers now wear a uniform, and their gestures show that they have been successfully drilled by European officers. . . . If all the negroes began to dance like those at Mombasa, would not the Europeans run the risk of being made to dance also?"[9] Not only the war, but the entire 400-year colonization process had brought unity to the formerly segmented and ethnically diverse local cultures of Africa. "The white domination has destroyed these local characteristics and developed a culture, or an effort at culture, superficial, but more advanced, and which tends to produce, among the black populations, a race consciousness dangerous to strangers."[10]

Although he knew little of either man, Muret was aware of the activities of Garvey and Du Bois in the United States. He saw Garvey as a conceited and impractical visionary. "Surrounded by twelve disciples, he proclaims the gospel of 'Africa for the African' on the model of Zionism, which preaches Palestine for the Jews."[11] Du Bois was, he admitted, "more learned than Garvey, whom he detests, but not less crammed with unsound ideas. . . . Du Bois struggles to extend the rights of the blacks in America, and believes in solving the problem by an amalgamation of the two races of which he is himself an example. . . . "[12] Clearly, Muret did not understand the mind of Du Bois, who was as much a racial chauvinist as Garvey, in his own way.

"The great victory won by little Japan over great Russia in 1904," wrote Basil Mathews in *The Clash of Color*, "was the end of an age and the beginning of a new era. It stopped the white man from carving up the Far East as he had partitioned Africa." The Great War, only ten years later, Mathews went on to observe, was viewed by the Asians as a "stupendous white civil war." It had demolished Europe's authority already undermined by the Japanese triumph. Not only were Asians affected, but the people of India, Turkey, China, Egypt, and Ireland took up the cry for self-determination. "Negroes in America and Africa felt for the first time in the story of their people a consciousness of race unity." Mathews was incorrect to suppose that this was the first time that a spirit of political unity had been present among the Negroes of the Old and the New World. But he was not mistaken in his belief that a new spirit was in the air.[13]

Like Stoddard and Muret, Mathews was aware of the Pan-African Congress in Paris in 1919, a symptom of the growing spirit of African unity. "In America, causes similar to those operating in Africa have been at work to create discontent and race feeling." American Negroes were making "common cause with every people in the world that is under white tutelage today in the cry for self-determination."[14] Able leadership had arisen in the United States, leading to three great schools of thought. The first of these, which, as Mathews observed had "gained strength enormously since the war," was led by W.E.B. Du Bois, "out for militant aggressive agitation—vehement, fiery propaganda that will even break out into the use of organized force if need be." The second great school was led by the "tremendous demagogue," Marcus Garvey, who harangued crowds with the cry, "the bloodiest war is yet to come, when Europe will match its strength against Asia, and that will be the Negroes' opportunity to draw the sword for Africa's redemption." Mathews saw Garveyism as a black counterpart of the Ku Klux Klan, "a melodramatic anarchic explosion of the more sulphurous volcanic fumes of the race movement." The third school was led by Robert Russa Moton, Booker T. Washington's successor at Tuskegee, who still counseled education, cooperation and patience. Mathews's sympathies were clearly with the latter school and he counseled support for them lest the opportunity to influence the black world should be lost entirely.[15]

The day for supporting the Tuskegee program of uplift and civilization for the masses was rapidly passing. The black world was in the process of discovering the virtues of the masses. The masses were beginning to be viewed as a mighty repository of strength, rather than as uncivilized heathens to be uplifted. "Sentimental interest in the Negro has ebbed," observed Alain Locke in his introduction to *The New Negro*. "It is a social disservice to blunt the fact that the Negro of the Northern centers has reached a stage where tutelage, even of the most interested and well-intentioned sort, must give place to new relationships, where positive self-direction must be reckoned with in ever increasing measure."[16] The New Negro Movement was a mass movement, in Locke's estimation. Demographically, but also ideologically, the move of black cultural leadership from rural South to urban North was a social movement headed by "the man farthest down."

"The clergyman following his errant flock, the physician or lawyer trailing his clients, supply the true clues," Locke hypothesized. "In a real sense it is the rank and file who are leading, and the leaders who are following. A transformed and transforming psychology permeates the masses."[17]

As Locke accurately noted, the race leaders of the nineteenth century had been concerned with lifting the masses from above. Before the Civil War it had been impossible to view the culture of the majority of black people as a repository of truth and virtue. The masses were slaves, the descendants of "savages," and even more degraded than their barbarous ancestors by virtue of their condition as victims of "the peculiar institution." After slavery, black leaders continued to base their policies with respect to race relations on their view of the black majority as victims of catastrophe. With the exception of Du Bois, there had been few to see the culture of the black belt as containing the higher spiritual strivings of the race-soul. And the urban ghetto culture had yet to evolve. But beyond the watch and guard of America, it was evolving. Post-war Americans, black and white alike, were abandoning the old Victorian myths and ideals that had been dealt their deathblows by the Great War. The Western world was attempting to rediscover the primal barbarian energy that had been long buried in the "metaphysically exhausted soil of Western Civilization." Not only in the black world, but in the white as well, there was an attempt to rediscover spiritual childhood. Black people, with what Vachel Lindsay had called "Their Basic Savagery . . . Their Irrepressible High Spirits," symbolized the "soul" which in the West had been triumphed over by intellect. The black masses became acceptable to the black world—more than incidentally—at the same time that they were becoming more acceptable to the white.

This new and limited acceptance by whites by no means amounted to an endorsement of social equality. The years immediately following the war can only retrospectively be viewed as a time of dramatic advancement in the history of black progress. The summer fo 1919, often referred to as the "Red Summer," witnessed twenty-five race riots, and some seventy-six lynchings occurred between December and June.[18] Even so, a new spirit of sympathy was awakening among white liberals and radicals in

America. "Until we have learned to house everybody, employ everybody at decent wages in a self-respecting status, guarantee his civil liberties, and bring education and play to him, the bulk of our talk about 'the race problem' will remain a sinister mythology," wrote Walter Lippmann in the wake of the terrorism of 1919. "In a dirty civilization the relation between black man and white will be a dirty one. In a clean civilization the two races can conduct their business together cleanly, not until then." Lippmann was joined in expressing such sentiments by Carl Sandburg, Joel Spingarn, and Geroid Tanquary Robinson.[19]

A new sociology tended to emphasize social, as opposed to racial, reasons for the existence of prejudice. Robert E. Park was in the vanguard of a new group of American sociologists who not only studied the American racial conflict, but actually encouraged sympathy for black people. Park, who had been an assistant to Booker T. Washington at Tuskegee, claimed in later years that he had "learned more about human nature and society, in the South under Booker Washington, than I had learned elsewhere in all my previous studies."[20] Perhaps this was sentimental, patronizing drivel; perhaps it was sincere, but it represented an attitude towards the black experience that was recurrent in the thinking of American social philosophers. It was the idea that profound social truths could be learned from life among the lowly. Howard Odum, another white sociologist who wrote in 1910 that the Negro is "as destitute of morals as any of the lower animals,"[21] would come to romanticize the black underclass by 1928 in his *Rainbow Round My Shoulder: The Blue Trail of Black Ulysses*. This novel was a sometimes sensitive discussion of black folkways, presented as the personal narrative of a black drifter, but a less than successful experiment in dialect writing:

> Like I said, I gits mighty tired stayin, in any one place. Likewise, I gits mighty tired being road hustler. Still, sometimes I tries out road again. But heap mo' fun and mo' successful being' hustlin' sport, if fellow can git 'way with it like me. Way it is, I works round three or four weeks maybe, saves up my money an' rides the cushions to some other place. Gits money gamblin' an' hustlin' jes' anywhere big jobs is. Maybe some town on boom with big buildin' jobs. So I comes

in, has two suits clothes, one blue, one with light trousers an' carryin' cane. So I gits good place to board and hustles up my money, gamblin' an' livin' on women like I told 'bout.[22]

This fascination with a fanciful African genius that had been expressed by Vachel Lindsay before the war, was echoed by such unlikely voices as that of Ezra Pound, thereafter. "I should also have more respect for the Afro-American intelligentzia [sic] and for the Negro millionaires...," said Pound, "that are rumoured to flourish in Harlem if they had shown more alacrity in hearing of an author Leo Frobenius, who has shown their race its true character of nobility and who has dug out of Africa tradition overlaid on tradition to set against the traditions of Europe and Asia."[23] This was nonsense, for Pound knew absolutely nothing about Harlem or the reading habits of its leadership. But if Pound may be suspected of insincerity, there were others who seemed deeply committed to black people. Nancy Cunard, daughter of the wealthy shipping family, identified herself with the black cultural renaissance of the twenties as did Carl Van Vechten, Iowa-born man of letters. In the scholarly world, Leo Wiener, who founded Slavic Studies at Harvard, argued that African civilizations had influenced the New World long before Columbus. Melville Herskovits, a young lecturer in anthroplogy at Columbia University, began to expose what he called "The Myth of the Negro Past."[24]

In contrast to those white supporters of the black revival who revelled in the African rhythms of the "Jazz Age" were Ernest Hemingway and T.S. Eliot, whose art bewailed the decline of the West, as had the pseudosociology of Stoddard and Grant. They seized upon the myth of the wounded Fisher-King to symbolize the wounded West, and white male supremacy—hurt in the war. They revealed a good deal of their own racial psyches with such creations as Prufrock and Jake Barnes, impotent heroes emasculated by the jaded heroines of the postwar novels. Indeed, it was Nancy Cunard—the incomprehensible—who served as the model for Aldous Huxley's Lucy Tantamount in *Point Counter Point*.[25] But Du Bois, Claude McKay, and Langston Hughes rejoiced in the world changes witnessed by the twenties. Their salvation was the white world's decline. The Ethiopian prophecy, as Garvey proclaimed, was on the verge of fulfillment. The culture of the black masses was coming into its own. These were heady times.

Claude McKay was the symbol incarnate of the rediscovery of the masses by the artists and intellectuals of the New Negro Movement. So passionate was McKay in romanticizing the free and easy lifestyle of the urban ghetto black that Du Bois was moved to denounce his *Home to Harlem* as "utter licentiousness"

> which conventional civilization holds white folk back from enjoying—if enjoyment it can be called. That which a certain decadent section of the white American world, centered particularly in New York, longs for with fierce unrestrained passions, it wants to see written out in black and white and saddled on black Harlem. . . . [McKay] has used every art and emphasis to paint drunkenness, fighting, lascivious sexual promiscuity and utter absence of restraint in as bold and as bright colors as he can. . . . As a picture of Harlem life or of Negro life anywhere, it is, of course, nonsense. Untrue not so much on account of its facts but on account of its emphasis and glaring colors.[26]

Such a reaction showed that Du Bois was still caught up in the old Victorian civilization myths—the Negro improvement rhetoric that sought to make the black masses more assimilable by emphasizing their acculturation to the moral values of the Anglo-American bourgeoisie.

Of course, neither *Home to Harlem,* nor its sequel, *Banjo,* attempted to describe the lives of the statistical majority of Afro-American people. They did attempt to validate in emotional terms an attitude to life shared by a minority of black men and women who, despite their ignorance and poverty, possessed nonetheless the vital power to force the world to take them seriously. McKay was, as Du Bois observed, portraying a lifestyle that Americans and Europeans—especially among the upper middle classes—were beginning to envy. Jake, the hero of *Home to Harlem,* is everything that Jake Barnes of *The Sun Also Rises* would like to be. He is a hard-drinking, fast-living, sexually emancipated army deserter; generous, good hearted, sensitive in his own way and, withall, wholesome. By contrast, Ray, his friend, is a Haitian intellectual, less spontaneous in his lust for life, a thinker and a reader. Although somewhat jaded, Ray is reminiscent of the old-school black nationalists of the nineteenth century. He is a writer, and entertains Jake with tales of African glories:

> He told Jake of the old destroyed cultures of West Africa and of their vestiges, of black kings who struggled stoutly for the independence of their kingdoms: Prempreh of Ashanti, Behanzin of Dahomey, Ewari of Benin, Cetawayo of Zulu-Land, Menelik of Abyssinia. . . .
>
> Had Jake ever heard of the little Republic of Liberia, founded by American Negroes? And Abyssinia, deep-set in the shoulder of Africa, besieged by the hungry wolves of Europe? The only nation that has existed free and independent from the earliest records of history until today! Abyssinia, oldest unconquered nation, ancient-strange as Egypt, persistent as Palestine, legendary as Greece, magical as Persia.[27]

Banjo is even more removed from statistical mundanities than *Home to Harlem*. McKay, like his creation, Ray, seems committed to the "principle of stressing the exception above the average." Set in Marseilles in the twenties, the novel takes its name from that of its hero, Banjo, the leader of a group of "beach boys." Pan-African in its composition, the group includes Afro-Americans, black Frenchmen, West Indians, and West Africans. It is a bilingual clique in which the English language is often seasoned with a French that varies widely in degrees of purity. Banjo is like Jake, a man who catches life as it flies and is reluctant to bind himself to any joy. Ray reappears in *Banjo* and we learn more about the thinking of this complex man who, one feels, is sometimes a mouthpiece for McKay's actual beliefs. Ray is more self-conscious than his friends of the New York black belt and the Marseilles docks. Two souls are at war within his breast, where a struggle is constantly waged between the proletarian Pan-Africanism that Ray is discovering and the prejudices of Western civilization. "Rather than lose his soul," Ray vows desperately that he will "let intellect go to hell and live by instinct."[28] He feels with a

Spenglerian sense of prophecy that the salvation of black people and of the entire universe is to be found in the philosophy of the Jakes and Banjos who live healthily within, but detached from civilization.

> Ray had felt buttressed by the boys with a rough strength and sureness that gave him spiritual passion and pride to be his human self in an inhumanly alien world. . . . From these boys he could learn how to live—how to exist as a black boy in a white world and rid his conscience of the used-up hussy of white morality. He could not scrap his intellectual life and be entirely like them. He did not want or feel any need to "go back" that way. . . . He was, of course, aware that whether the educated man be white or brown or black, he cannot, if he has more than animal desires, be irresponsibly happy like the ignorant man who lives simply by his instincts and appetites. Any man with an observant and contemplative mind must be aware of that. But a black man, even though educated, was in closer biological kinship to the swell of primitive earth life.[29]

The literary discovery of the black urban masses brought other names to the fore, notably Langston Hughes and Rudolph Fisher. These writers, like McKay, seemed to have abandoned the ideal of civilizing the masses and making them more like whites. They were inclined to romanticize the lower-class blacks of the city streets who, in their view, represented virility and vitality of which white American culture was almost devoid. Hughes found his subject matter in the lives of the urban blacks who had migrated north during the war; he took his rhythms from jazz, which was to him "one of the inherent expressions of Negro life in America: the eternal tom-tom beating in the Negro soul."[30]

> In a Harlem cabaret
> Six long-headed jazzers play.
> A dancing girl whose eyes are bold
> Lifts high a dress of silken gold.
>
> Oh singing tree!
> Oh' shining rivers of the soul![31]

He did not compose in the demiurgic mode that had dominated the writing of Delany, Griggs, and Du Bois, nor did he favor, as a rule, the quaint rusticity of Dunbar's dialect verse. He wrote of life as he found it on the streets of Harlem:

Droning a drowsy syncopated tune,
Rocking back and forth to a mellow croon,
I heard a Negro play
Down on Lenox Avenue the other night
By the pale dull pallor of an old gas light
He did a lazy sway. . . .
He did a lazy sway. . . .
To the tune of those Weary Blues.[32]

The romanticization of the black urban proletariat was in many ways a healthy thing. It was well that black artists and intellectuals and their white supporters were learning to appreciate the strength and beauty of black folkways and beginning to abandon the old civilizing formulae of the nineteenth century. But there were pitfalls along this pathway which many of the urban enthusiasts preferred not to notice. Du Bois noted some of these pitfalls in his scathing reviews of Claude McKay and Carl Van Vechten. The practice of the latter was especially reprehensible.

The author counts among his friends numbers of Negroes of all classes. He is an authority on dives and cabarets. But he masses this knowledge without rule or reason and seeks to express all of Harlem life in its cabarets. To him the black cabaret is Harlem; around it all his characters gravitate. Here is their stage of action. Such a theory of Harlem is nonsense. The overwhelming majority of black folk there never go to cabarets. The average colored man in Harlem is an everyday laborer, attending church, lodge and movie and is as conservative and as conventional as ordinary working folk everywhere.[33]

Not only was there a tendency toward stereotyping black life during the years of the Harlem Renaissance, but the stereotypes created tended to follow in the traditional patterns of antiblack prejudice. A consistency of attitude toward black people can be seen in the writings of Gobineau, Conrad, O'Neil and Lindsay. For all of these conceived of Africans as sensual and passionate, high-spirited and exotic. There is certainly a spiritual kinship between Lindsay's "The Congo" and Countee Cullen's "Heritage." The emphasis, in both cases, is upon the exotic, the colorful, the jungle dream of the Westerner, rather than the reality of African cultures. As Alain Locke protested ineffectually, obscured by the din of the cabaret:

> The characteristic African art expressions are rigid, controlled, disciplined, abstract, heavily conventionalized; those of the Aframerican, —free, exuberant, emotional, sentimental and human. Only by misrepresentation of the African spirit, can one claim any emotional kinship between them—for the spirit of the African expression, by and large, is disciplined, sophisticated, laconic and fatalistic. The emotional temper of the American Negro is exactly opposite. What we have thought primitive in the American Negro—his naivete, his sentimentalism, his exuberance and his improvizing spontaneity are then neither characteristically African nor to be explained by his ancestral heritage.[34]

Marcus Garvey successfully combined the energies of the new urban mass consciousness with those of traditional Pan-Africanism. He was one of those ungainly figures who stand with one foot planted firmly in the past while with the other hailing the dawn of a new day. He yoked together the conventional and the novel aspects of black nationalism. The traditional elitism and authoritarianism of the movement persisted in his ostensibly proletarian version of Pan-Africanism. The collectivist ideal led him to announce that his movement was the first expression of fascism, and that Mussolini had only stolen the idea from him.[35] The Ethiopian mysticism of the nineteenth century that had asserted that God was on the black man's side and that God was black, was resuscitated by his allies—the African Orthodox Church, the Moorish Temple of Holy Science, and the Falasha Jews.[36] But to recognize that Garvey was traditional is not to ignore that he was the first black leader to organize the amorphous enthusiasm for Pan-Africanism, latent in the mass consciousness.

Garvey was a native of St. Anns Bay, Jamaica. His father was a stonemason and the owner of several pieces of real estate. The senior Garvey was a stern and contentious man, who enjoyed literary pursuits, biblical debates, and litigation. The Garvey property adjoined that of a white Wesleyan minister, whose church they attended, and that of another white man, the father of three daughters, with whom Marcus played as a child. Between the ages of twelve and fifteen, Garvey was under the influence of a printer named Burrows, who eventually took him as an apprentice. Burrows kept a small library of books and magazines and his shop was a gathering place where black men exchanged opinions on history, politics and current events. Another influence on Garvey was the Jamaica *Advocate*, published by Dr. Robert Love, a well-traveled Pan-African nationalist, who had been ordained as an Episcopal priest.[37]

As a young man Garvey worked in a Kingston printery, where he gained experience as a union organizer—losing his job in the process. He then went to work in the government printing office, became involved in black politics and joined the National Club where he met W. A. Domingo, a socialist who would later number among his Harlem rivals. An uncle in Costa Rica secured him a position as timekeeper on a fruit farm and Garvey began his Latin American tour which eventually included Gautemala, Panama, Nicaragua, Ecuador, Chile, and Peru. Garvey then went to England, where he is believed to have attended Birkbeck College between 1912 and 1914. While in England, Garvey associated with the Egyptian nationalist, Duse Mohamed, and contributed to his *African Times and Orient Review*. It was during this period that Garvey began to read of conditions in America. He was particularly impressed by Booker T. Washington's *Up From Slavery*, which inspired him to become a "race leader." Garvey asked himself the following questions:

> "Where is the black man's Government?" "Where is his King and his kingdom?" "Where is his President, his country and his ambassador, his army, his navy, his men of big affairs?" I could not find them, and then I declared, "I will help to make them."[38]

Garvey was a black leader in the "civilizationist" tradition. He returned to Jamaica in July of 1914 and formed the Universal Negro Improvment and Conservation Association and African Communities League. The name implies an affinity to the old civilizing and uplifting ideals of the nineteenth century.[39] Garvey himself is responsible for the myth that middle class blacks, mulattoes, and conservative intellectuals wrecked his plans. Actually, all of these types were well-represented in his organization. Garvey attracted a circle of Pan-African intellectuals who were creative, well-trained and experienced in the Pan-African movement. Emmett J. Scott—former secretary to Booker T. Washington, who had died in 1915—was appointed a Knight Commander of the Sublime order of the Nile; T. Thomas Fortune, a mulatto, served as editor-in-chief of *Negro World,* the UNIA newspaper; William H. Ferris was its literary editor. Among the other men and women of letters attracted to the Garvey movement were J. A. Rogers, the popular historian, Duse Mohamed, Ida B. Wells, and Mrs. Amy Jacques Garvey, who edited the Spanish edition of *Negro World.* Garvey also gained substantial moral support from Africans on the continent and in Europe. In Paris, Pan-Africanists readily combined their Garveyism with a pro-Communist philosophy as in the case of Marc Kojo Tovalou Houenou, publisher of the radical *Les Continents.*[40]

E. Franklin Frazier, a figure deeply involved in the Renaissance discovery of the masses, was fascinated by Garvey. Although he never actually supported the movement, he was impressed by its vigor and by the fact that it seemed to be drawing upon the power of the folk, rather than imposing order from above. Frazier tended to overlook the authoritarian and elitist elements in Garveyism, which openly asserted its goal of creating a new African aristocracy. He did not comment upon the orthodoxy of Garvey's movement—its philosophical ties to Blyden, Crummell, and Casely-Hayford, nor its practical similarities to the movements of Turner, Fadumah, and Sam. Nor did Frazier pay much attention to the fact that the UNIA included a number of educated and prosperous persons in its ranks. On the other hand, some of Frazier's observations were perceptive. He saw clearly that Garvey's movement appealed more to the emotions than to reason, that for many it was more of a religious than a political experience. Frazier noted that "the average Negro, like other mediocre people, must be fed upon empty and silly fictions in order that life may be more bearable." In addition to the psychological basis of the movement, Frazier noted the historical and sociological factors that contributed to its success:

> Doubtless the World War with its shibboleths and stirrings of subject minorities offered a volume of suggestion that facilitated the Garvey movement. Another factor that helped the Movement was the urbanization of the Negro that took place about that time. It is in the cities that the mass movements are initiated. When the Negro lived in a rural environment he was not subject to mass suggestion except at the camp meeting and revival.[41]

Garveyism was orthodox black nationalism modified by an urban environment, an industrial rhetoric, and a military spirit that was the heritage of the Great War. The evangelical movement that Garvey headed embodied elements of both the new and the old black nationalism. Garvey, like the old black nationalists before World War I, focused on the civilization and Christianization of Africa as the first steps toward universal emancipation of the African race.[52] Like the old black nationalists, Garvey insisted upon such ideas as "Divine Apportionment of Earth," "Purity of Race," and "God as a War Lord." William H. Ferris, a UNIA assistant president, once wrote "Our God is a man of War," and Garvey in a similar vein said:

> I believe with Napoleon. When some one asked him "On what side is God?" he replied. "God is on the side of the strongest battalion." Napoleon was right. He had a true concept of God. God is really on the side of the strongest peoples because God made all men equal and He never gave superior power to any one class or group of people over another, and any one who can get the advantage over another is pleasing God, because that is the servant who has taken care of God's command in exercising authority over the world.[43]

If Garvey intended this as a straightforward expression of belief on race and religion, then we can understand his appallingly sportsmanlike respect for the Ku Klux Klan. Garvey believed that races were doomed to conflict, and that interracial terrorists were only carrying out the divine plan of a warrior god.

Like most black nationalists of the nineteenth century, Garvey betrayed unwittingly an admiration for various elements of occidental civilization, but this is not the most important thing that can be said of him. Like his contemporaries, Du Bois and Casely-Hayford, Garvey was critical of the West, while selectively admiring and enjoying some of the benefits of European and American life. Garvey was aware of the crimes committed in Africa in the name of Christianity and civilization. As examples of "White Christian Control of Africa" he listed: "the outrages of Leopold of Belgium," and the "brutality of the English" in Kenya where black workers "were hewn down by machine guns, because they did not supply the demands of the invaders." At the same time, he exhorted his followers to profit from every opportunity to benefit from exposure to Western life and culture, with a rhetoric not unlike that of Booker T. Washington or Alexander Crummell:

> It strikes me that with all the civilization this Western Hemisphere affords, Negroes ought to take better advantage of the cause of higher education. We could make of ourselves better mechanics and scientists, and in cases where we can help our brothers in Africa by making use of the knowledge we possess, it would be but our duty. If Africa is to be redeemed the Western Negro will have to make a valuable contribution along technical and scientific lines.[44]

And Garvey, like his nineteenth century antecedents, associated himself with that variety of self-deprecation that Sterling Stuckey considers the peculiar province of black nationalists. "The Negro is dying out," he warned. "Unforunately we are the most careless and indifferent people in the world! We are shiftless and irresponsible...."[45] But such statements, whether or not they are typical of black nationalists, can hardly be described as a radical departure from mainstream racialism in the colonizationist tradition of Jefferson, Clay, Lincoln, and Bilbo.

Garveyism was somewhat radical, as Tony Martin, Robert

Hill, Theodore Vincent, and Mark Matthews have persuasively argued.[46] But the reactionary elements in Garveyism cannot be denied. Garvey's attitude towards miscegenation was worse than an accomodation to racism; it was an invitation to participate in racism, and it was a direct endorsement of laws that were written to dehumanize black people.[47] Garvey proclaimed himself spokesman for the "New Negro," using the term at least two years before Locke, but a quarter of a century after Sutton Griggs.[48] Garvey was an Ethiopian millenialist, like his nineteenth century antecedents. "Africa has still its lesson to teach the world," he once wrote, "We as a people, have a great future before us. Ethiopia shall once more see the day of her glory. . . ." Garvey was the fulfillment of the nineteenth century tradition, rather than its negation.

The Golden Age of black nationalism extended from the 1850s, when Anglo-African nationalism was dominated by Delany, Blyden, and Crummell, to the 1920s, when it was dominated by Du Bois, Garvey, and the ghost of Booker T. Washington. In the rhetoric of the classical black nationalists before the American Civil War, there is a manifest commitment to Christianity and civilization. Such tendencies were hardly obliterated during the 1920s, though there is in the rhetoric of most black writers of the post World War I era, a characteristic ambivalence or outright hostility toward the Victorian conceptions of Christianity and civilization to which classical black nationalism was sympathetic. The tendency toward hostility accelerates in the writings of cultural nationalists: McKay, Wright, Ellison, Baldwin, and Baraka, during the period from 1925 to 1975. But in the years immediately following the First Great War the attitudes of black nationalists towards the older values were ambivalent rather than hostile.

Black nationalists like Garvey and Du Bois hoped for a dramatic shift in the balance of world power, a rise in the status of the colored peoples that would correspond to the decline of the West. They were not dismayed by the rebirth of the Ku Klux Klan in the South nor by the suppression of radicals in the urban North. They viewed the rise of repressionist sentiment as the desperation of a society that realized it was in its death throes. Taking the long view, they believed that the major thrust of history was on their side and that the dominant trends were leading to the rise of Africa and Asia as the new centers of world power. But while they perceived themselves as riding the ground swell of a rising tide of color, they were nonetheless full of admiration for the values of the declining West. They betrayed consciously and unconsciously a sympathy for traditional values and for many of the ideals of Victorian bourgeois culture. Du Bois pretended to feel nothing but contempt for Anglo-Saxon values, but time and again he betrayed a commitment to bourgeois morality, and he condemned the new generation of writers represented by Van Vechten and McKay of "licentiousness." Although he would later profess a half-century's contempt for Chistian religion, Du Bois's writings of the postwar era were filled with biblical quotations and appeals to traditional religious values.

Marcus Garvey openly admitted his commitment to the old nineteenth century goal of Christianizing Africa, despite his emphasis upon bringing the black man into the twentieth century and developing a civilization that would be distinctly African. Garvey's attitudes concerning European civilization were as ambivalent as those of Du Bois. Garvey's published philosophy and opinions reveal how closely the New Negro Movement of the twenties was related to the old nineteenth century spirit of uplift and civilization. There was no Great Rift dividing the spokesmen and leaders of the Harlem Renaissance from their antecedents of the decades between the 1850 Compromise and the Great War.

While it is important to recognize elements of continuity in the Harlem Renaissance as represented in the Garvey movement, it is also important to see themes of innovation in the period. The Harlem Renaissance was more a revitalization of coninuous themes than a rebirth of traditions that had died out. Garvey's Pan-Africanism was a modification of an existing movement, rather than a new creation. Garveyism recreated in a metropolitan environment ideas that earlier leaders like Alfred C. Sam and Bishop Turner had tried to nourish in small towns and rural areas. He popularized among the urban masses ideas that had earlier been confined for the most part to urban elites. Garvey hewed out a strong, rough-edged and honest expression of black nationalist consciousness in which the formerly isolated elitist black nationalism was mingled with the exuberance of the less articulate masses of newly urbanized Negroes.

Alain Locke, Emmet Scott, and Robert S. Abbott had all noted that the urbanization of black Americans was leading to a new mentality. Photographic impressions of the period convey visual evidence of this new mentality. Columns of black men in the uniform of the United States Army march through the city of New York and home to Harlem. Masses of black folk, stylishly attired but grim and determined, take to the streets to protest lynchings. Stern ranks of black cross nurses stride the avenues, militant auxiliaries to knights of the order of the Nile. How different these visual images are from those of the old rural Negro, bent beneath the weight of a cotton sack or shuffling with lowered gaze through the dust of a small southern town.

Certain characteristics of black political consciousness since the Harlem Renaissance distinguish it from the black nationalism of the preceding age. As the 1930s commenced there was truly a New Negro, as represented by Langston Hughes, whose writings tended to emphasize differences between the white and the black world—usually perceived as healthy differences. Hughes idealized the lives of the urban poor in much the same way that Du Bois had once idealized the rural black masses as a repository of human values in an industrial wilderness. Richard Wright, another new voice of the thirties, emphasized the bleak side of the black experience, the cynicism and hardness resulting from economic exploitation and cultural isolation. Hughes and Wright were both committed to integration, but each in his own way stridently asserted a counterculturalism that would have been unthinkable for the generation of Crummell and Douglass.

Since the 1920s, literary spokespersons for black America have not been concerned with trying to accomodate their values to European Christian ideals, since European and American Christians have begun to question these ideals themselves. The decline of Victorian morality, the loss of faith in moral progress resulting from both world wars, the rise in the respectability of social science with its relativistic theories, all tended to erode the confidence of Western civilization in the rightness of its ways, and to encourage black American society to search for its values within. Crummell's old approach to civilization had assumed that Anglo-Christian values were universal. The black civilization that he hoped to found was to be little more than a mirror image of European civilization, perceived through a glass darkly. It was not until the twenties that black intellectuals envisioned and rejoiced at the possibility of creating a counterculture. Regardless of whether or not it was possible to retain a distinctive culture in an integrated and egalitarian society, the idea of doing so had its adherents.

As America entered the post World War II era, there was an increased demand for sharing in the full benefits of American civil rights, but an increasing skepticism concerning the old drive towards cultural assimilation. This was noteworthy in such works as E. Franklin Frazier's *Black Bourgeoisie,* militantly intergrationistic, but hostile to the imitation of white bourgeois values. It was visible in Martin Luther King's program for intergration, which was nonetheless critical of the society into which black Americans were to be integrated. It was audible in the vehemently integrationist pronouncements of Ralph Ellison, who insisted that he was not exclusively a black writer, but an American writer, the product of American literary traditions, but who produced a masterpiece that was very clearly a product of black cultural and intellectual history. In Elijah Muhammad alone among the important spokesmen of the fifties did we see anything resembling the old separatist African civilizationism of the nineteenth century. Black leadership of the fifties continued in the Harlem Renaissance tradition—to which even Garvey had at times adhered—of insisting on their right to become a part of the American system, while at the same time criticizing the cultural values of American society. The basic difference between Afro-American thought of the Golden Age and that which has occurred since 1960 is that nineteenth century leaders, unlike their recent counterparts, seldom saw acculturation to Western norms and values as undesirable. This was true even of extreme separatists like Crummell and Delany. Twentieth-century leaders have tended to be suspicious of cultural assimilation, regardless of whether or not they have believed in social integration, and have been equally cool to the prospects of genetic and cultural absorption.

Because of continuing ambivalence toward American folkways and toward the American people themselves (which is only partly a reaction to white racism), we may anticipate the continued existence of black separatist movements in the United States. There is little likelihood that the trend of the past fifty years will reverse itself in the next twenty-five. As existing black nationalist groups die out or abandon their separatist policies, new ones will spring up to take their places.

Notes

Chapter One

1. Roland Oliver and J.D. Fage argue in *A Short History of Africa*, pp. 112-124, that it was the demand for "new goods, of which firearms were by far the most influential," that led to the development of slavetrading economies in West Africa. Professors Fage and Oliver have suggested that African kings were forced to engage in the slave trade in order to obtain the firearms without which their nations would certainly have fallen victims to its ravages. Walter Rodney, a Marxist influenced Pan-Africanist, argues in *How Europe Underdeveloped Africa*, (London, 1972) p. 90, that African kingdoms were forced into the slave trade. The King of the Kongo, for example, "had conceived of possibilities of mutually beneficial interchange between his people and the European state of Portugal, but the latter forced him to specialize in the export of human cargo." But Archibald Dalzel, in his *The History of Dahomey: An Inland Kingdom of Africa* (London, 1793), p. 218, prints a speech said to have been made by Adahounzoo II, King of Dahomey, a justification of the slave trade delivered by an African. "In the name of my ancestors and myself I aver, that no Dahoman man ever embarked in war merely for the sake of procuring wherewithal to purchase your commodities." The prudent scholar will probably wish to postpone judgment on the issue of whether the African kings felt coerced. Phillip Curtin expresses the need for further research on this question in *African History* (New York, 1964).

2. John Hope Franklin has coined the phrase "quasi-free Negroes" in recognition of the doubtful status of antebellum free blacks. See *The Free Negro in North Carolina* (New York, 1971), p. 223; Ira Berlin utilizes the term in *Slaves Without Masters: The Free Negro in the Antebellum South* (New York, 1974), pp. 143-9; The status of free black people in the North is

described in Leon F. Litwack, *North of Slavery: The Negro in the Free States, 1790-1860* (Chicago, 1961) and V. Jacque Voegeli, *Free but Not Equal: The Midwest and the Negro during the Civil War* (Chicago, 1967).

3. While it is common for some students of Africa to emphasize the continent's ethnic diversity, others like Basil Davidson have been struck by its amazing cultural continuity. See *The African Genius* (Boston, 1969). Black writers of the nineteenth century often made the comparison between primitive Europe and primitive Africa.

4. The held view of the distinction between culture and civilization as expressed in the writing of most modern authors (Arnold Toynbee, Robert E. Park, Charles and Mary Beard) is that civilization always implies "progress" while culture does not. To Oswald Spengler, civilization implied progress, to be sure, but also decadence, sterility, and death.

5. J.A. Hobson, *Imperialism: A Study* (Ann Arbor, 1965), pp. 3-4, distinguishes these varieties of nationalism as the "disruptive form" and the "unifying or centralizing" form.

6. Black nationalism is often defined broadly enough to include persons of Egyptian nationality. Duse Mohamed Ali was an Egyptian nationalist prominently involved in American and West African black nationalism during the first half of the twentieth century. The government of Gamal Abdul Nasser was supportive of the Organization of African Unity. See Shirley Graham Du Bois, "Egypt is Africa," *The Black Scholar* (May, 1970), pp. 20-27 and concluded in the same journal (September, 1970), pp. 28-34.

7. K.R. Minogue, *Nationalism* (Baltimore, 1970), pp. 12-19.

8. C.L.R. James, *A History of Pan-African Revolt;* (Washington, 1969); George Padmore, *Pan Africanism or Communism* (New York, 1971).

9. *Constitution of the African Civilization Society* (New Haven, 1861).

10. A good recent attempt to define Pan-Africanism is Imanuel Geiss, *The Pan-African Movement* (New York, 1974); also see J. Ayodele Langley, *Pan-Africanism and Nationalism in West Africa, 1900-1945* (Oxford, 1973); George Shepperson, "Pan-Africanism and 'Pan-Africanism': Some Historical Notes," *Phylon* (Winter, 1962), pp. 346-58.

11. See Charles A. Beard and Mary R. Beard, *The American Spirit: A Study of the Idea of Civilization in the United States* (New York, 1942) which traces the history of the concept of civilization. Samuel Johnson's rejection of the term is mentioned by the Beards on p. 62.

12. I follow Arnold Toynbee's distinction between "civilizations" and "primitive societies," which he made in *A Study of History,* Vol. I (Oxford, 1933). In primitive societies, says Toynbee, mimesis is directed toward the older generation and the ancestors. Societies engaged in the civilization process tend to direct mimesis towards creative personalities. Basil Davidson in *The African Genius* notes the importance of ancestor veneration and tradition in the ordering of African societies.

13. Jose Ortega y Gasset, *History as a System* (New York, 1962), p. 63. Needless to say, the idea of organic collectivism did not erupt full-blown on New Year's Day, 1800. Such ideals can obviously be traced as far back as

the Republic of Plato, but Ortega y Gasset is perceptive in his observation as to the renewed fashionability of such ideals at the end of the 18th century. Collectivist ideals began to achieve fashionability in the wake of the French Revolution and are prominent in the writings of Herder, and Burke during the 1790's, as is noted below.

14. Blyden, *The African Problem and the Method of its Solution* (Washington, 1890), reprinted in Howard Brotz, *Negro Social and Political Thought, 1850-1920* (New York, 1966), p. 138; Crummell, *Africa and America, (Springfield, Mass., 1891),* p. 46; Young, *Ethiopian Manifesto* in Sterling Stuckey, *Ideological Origins of Black Nationalism,* (Boston, 1972), p. 37; Walker, *Walker's Appeal in Four Articles,* (Troy, N.Y., 1848), p. 30.

15. E. Franklin Frazier, *The Negro Church in America,*(New York, 1964), p. 43.

16. For example, Anthony Benezet. See George S. Brookes, *Friend Anthony Benezet* (Philadelphia, 1937), p. 83.

17. Prince Hall, *A Charge Delivered to the African Lodge, June 24, 1797, at Menotomy, Mass.,* (Boston, 1797).

18. Miles Mark Fisher, *Negro Slave Songs in the United States,* (Secaucus, N.J., 1969).

19. Joseph Arthur de Gobineau, *The Inequality of Human Races* translated by Adrian Collins (London, 1935), chapter XVI.

20. Imanuel Geiss, *The Pan-African Movement,* (London, 1974), pp. 30-40, uses the term "proto-Pan-Africanism." The theme is well treated in Robert July, *The Origins of Modern African Thought,* (New York, 1967), pp. 15-66.

21. Frazier expressed Black Nationalist and Pan-African sentiments of his own in "The Failure of the Negro Intellectual," *Negro Digest* (February, 1962), pp. 26-36.

Chapter Two

1. Among the notable instances are Thomas Hamilton's use of the term for his *Anglo-African Magazine* in 1859; William Still used it in *The Underground Rail Road: A Record . . .* (Philadelphia, 1872), p. 153; Alexander Crummell used the term in *The Future of Africa,* (New York, 1862), pp. 21 and 259. Also see J. Dennis Harris, *A Summer on the Borders of the Caribbean Sea* in Howard H. Bell, ed. *Black Separatism and the Caribbean, 1860* (Ann Arbor, 1970), p. 178. A newspaper by that name was operated by Robert Campbell in Lagos, West Africa, circa 1863; see Howard H. Bell, ed., *Search for a Place:Black Nationalism and Africa, 1860* (Ann Arbor, 1969), p. 19. Frederick Douglass used "Anglo-African" as late as 1879; see Philip S. Foner, ed., *The Life and Writings of Frederick Douglass* (New York, 1955), Vol. IV, p. 331.

2. Howard Brotz, *Negro Social and Political Thought, 1850-1920:*

Representative Texts (New York, 1966), pp. 1-33, implies such an equation in his introduction. In a similar vein, see Harold Cruse, *The Crisis of the Negro Intellectual*, (New York, 1967), pp. 5-6, and Theodore Draper, *The Rediscovery of Black Nationalism*, (New York, 1970), pp. 3-47.

3. John H. Bracey, August Meier, and Elliott Rudwick, *Black Nationalism in America* (Indianapolis, 1970), p. 114 and pp. 299-302.

4. The best work describing the formation and early years of the American Colonization Society is P.J. Staudenraus, *The African Colonization Movement, 1816-1865* (New York, 1961). This should be supplemented by Floyd J. Miller, *The Search for a Black Nationality: Black Colonization and Emigration, 1787-1863* (Urbana, 1975).

5. An introduction to the life of Paul Cuffe and a collection of his correspondence with Forten and other supporters of emigration is Sheldon H. Harris, *Paul Cuffe Black America and the African Return* (New York, 1972). The quotation from Forten's letter is on page 244.

6. Letter by C.D.T., a Philadelphian, from the *Liberator*, April 30, 1831. Reprinted in Carter G. Woodson, ed., *The Mind of the Negro as Reflected in Letters Written During the Crisis, 1800-1860* (Washington, D.C., 1926), pp. 162-63. For additional observations on the response to colonization see Louis Mehlinger, "Attitude of the Free Negro Toward African Colonization," *Journal of Negro History*, I (July, 1916), pp. 271-301.

7. Martin R. Delany, *The Condition, Elevation, Emigration, and Destiny of the Colored People of the United States Politically Considered,*(Philadelphia, 1852), pp. 169-70.

8. M.R. Delany, *Official Report of the Niger Valley Exploring Party* in Bell, *Search for a Place* (Ann Arbor, 1969).

9. For a recent treatment of Delany's African interest see Cyril E. Griffith, *The African Dream: Martin R. Delany and the Emergence of Pan-African Thought* (University Park, Pa., 1975). Delany mentions his dissatisfaction with white philanthropists and the unauthorized fund-raising activities of Campbell in *Report of the Niger Valley Exploring Party* in Bell, *Search for a Place,* pp. 42-45. White support for the African Civilization Society and Delany is discussed in Miller *The Search for a Black Nationality,* pp. 197-98.

10. Delany, *Report of the Niger Valley Exploring Party,* in Bell, *Search,* pp. 133-34.

11. The Constitution of the African Civilization Society is reprinted in Brotz, *Negro Social and Political Thought,* pp. 191-96. Some discussion of the Society is included in Earl Ofari, *Let Your Motto Be Resistance: The Life and Thought of Henry Highland Garnet* (Boston, 1972) pp. 79-98.

12. Colonization as a philanthropic movement is discussed in Staudenraus, *The African Colonization Movement,* pp. 12-22. Also see John R. Bodo, *The Protestant Clergy and Public Issues* (Princeton, 1954), pp. 128-29. An interesting illustration of what is at least an apparent

sympathy for black nationalist aspirations by a white colonization supporter is "Speech of Robert J. Breckinridge before the Maryland State Colonization Society, 2 February, 1838," reprinted in Henry S. Wilson, ed., *Origins of West African Nationalism* (London, 1969), p. 47. Originally printed in *African Repository*, XIV, 141.

13. Henry Highland Garnet, "The Past and Present Condition and the Destiny of the Colored Race," reprinted in Earl Ofari, *Let Your Motto Be Resistance*, pp. 182-83.

14. Ibid., p. 72.

15. For the rhetoric of "Blacker than thou" see George Napper, *Blacker Than Thou: The Struggle for Campus Unity*, (Grand Rapids, 1973). The Douglass/Garnet debate is chronicled in *Douglass' Monthly*, (February, 1859), pp. 19-20.

16. The white colonizationist quoted is Benjamin Coates, in Victor Ullman, *Martin Delany: The Beginnings of Black Nationalism*, (Boston, 1971), p. 214.

17. David Walker, *Walker's Appeal in Four Articles*, p. 51.

18. Too casual a reading of Brotz would certainly leave such an impression. See the introduction to his *Negro Social and Political Thought*.

19. Douglass spoke of Afro-Americans as an "oppressed nation" in *Frederick Douglass' Paper* (April 13, 1855), reprinted in Philip S. Foner, *The Life and Writings of Frederick Douglass* (New York, 1950) II, 360. Also see *North Star*, (December 14, 1849). Jane and William Pease make much of this issue of the *North Star* and its debate between Douglass and William Whipper as an indication of Douglass's nationalistic sympathies in *They Who Would Be Free: Blacks' Search for Freedom, 1830-1861*,(New York, 1974), pp. 251-52. See also Miller, p. 270 and Foner II, p. 246.

20. *Report of the Proceedings of the Colored National Convention Held at Cleveland, Ohio on Wednesday, September 6, 1848* (Rochester: North Star, 1848), p. 18.

21. Alexander Crummell's epistles to the Domestic and Foreign Missionary Society are the best source for the study of his attitudes concerning the religion of the uneducated blacks. For Payne's observations on the religion of the masses, see his *Recollection of Seventy Years* (Nashville, 1888), pp. 248-57.

22. Africanus Horton, "African Nationality," in Davidson Nicol, ed., *Black Nationalism in Africa* (New York, 1969), p. 32.

23. Edward Wilmot Blyden to John Pope-Hennesy, 4 March, 1872; "Report of the Expedition to Falaba," quoted in Hollis R. Lynch, *Edward Wilmot Blyden: Pan Negro Patriot, 1832-1912* (Oxford, 1970), p. 92. Lynch observed Blyden's westernizing and civilizationistic predilections, pp. 85-92.

24. Edward Wilmot Blyden, "Mohammedanism in Western Africa," reprinted in Blyden's *Christianity, Islam, and the Negro Race* (London, 1887). Reprint with introduction by Christopher Fyfe (Edinburgh, 1969), pp. 187-88.

25. Blyden to Hennesy, loc. cit.
26. Jas. Theo. Holly, *A Vindication of the Capacity of the Negro Race for Self-Government and Civilized Progress*. . . , reprinted in Bell, *Black Separatism and the Caribbean, 1860*, p. 65.
27. J. Dennis Harris, *A Summer on the Borders of the Caribbean Sea*, reprinted in Bell, *Black Separatism and the Caribbean*, pp. 177-79.
28. Martin R. Delany, "The Political Destiny of the Colored Race on the American Continent," in *Report of the Select Committee on House Resolution No. 576*, printed in July, 1862 by the House of Representatives, also in Sterling Stuckey, ed., *The Ideological Origins of Black Nationalism*, (Boston, 1972), p. 203.
29. Martin R. Delany, *The Condition, Elevation, Emigration, and Destiny of the Colored People of the United States*, (Philadelphia, 1852), pp. 42-43.
30. Frederick Douglass, *The Nation's Problem*, (Washington, D.C., 1889), reprinted in Brotz, *Negro Social and Political Thought*, see p. 318.
31. George Frederickson, *The Black Image in the White Mind*, (New York, 1965), see the chapter on "Romantic Racialism," p. 97-129.
32. Jacques Barzun, *Race: A Study in Superstition*, (New York, 1965), pp. 54-55.
33. Crummell, *The Future of Africa*, (New York, 1862), pp. 30-31.
34. David Walker and Henry Highland Garnet, *Walker's Appeal*, Article III is dedicated to "Our Wretchedness in Consequence of the Preachers of Jesus Christ," while all hypocritical churchmen are taken to task, particular odium is heaped upon the heads of the Catholics and the Catholic nations, as for example, on pp. 5, 13, 47.
35. Martin R. Delany, *Official Report of the Niger Valley Exploring Party*, Bell, pp. 103-104.
36. Martin R. Delany, *Blake: or The Huts of America* was originally printed in *The Anglo-African Magazine* from January to July, 1859 and *The Weekly Anglo-African*, November, 1861-May 1862. Floyd J. Miller has edited the novel and established the text which was published by Beacon Press (Boston, 1970). See pp. 257-258, for the incident of the Catholic woman, Madame Cordova. Blake himself, as well as his wife, are both converts from Catholicism to the Baptist faith.
37. *The Liberator*, Vol. 2, No. 4 (January 28, 1832), p. 14, contains a letter from "A Colored Female of Philadelphia," reprinted in Dorothy Porter, *Early Negro Writing, 1760-1837* (Boston, 1971), pp. 292-293. The letter's author, a supporter of migration to Mexico sees not only a chance to secure the fortunes of black people, but also envisions prospects for the regeneration of Mexico: ". . . the religion of that nation being Papist, . . . we can take with us the Holy Bible, which is able to make us wise unto salvation; and perhaps we may be made the honored instruments, in the hands of an all-wise God, in establishing the holy religion of the Protestant Church in that country; and that alone might be a sufficient inducement for the truly pious."

38. I use the term "romantic racialism" as George Frederickson has used it in op. cit. pp. 101-102: "Although romantic racialists acknowledged that blacks were different from whites and probably always would be, they projected an image of the Negro that could be construed as flattering or laudatory in the context of some currently accepted ideals of human behavior and sensibility." Usually the black people were endowed with certain stereotypical traits associated with childhood and/or feminity.

39. Louis L. Snyder, ed., *The Dynamics of Nationalism: Readings in its Meaning and Development* (Princeton, 1964), p. 137.

40. Ibid, p. 138.

41. Edward Wilmot Blyden, *The African Problem and the Method of Its Solution*, reprinted in Brotz, op. cit., p. 138.

42. Lynch, *Blyden*, p. 27.

43. Alexander Crummell, "The Race Problem in America," a paper read at the Church Congress of the Protestant Episcopal Church, Buffalo, N.Y., Nov. 20th, 1888, reprinted in *Africa and America*, p.46.

44. Ibid.

45. Benjamin Quarles, *The Negro in the Civil War* (Boston, 1969), pp. 24, 26.

46. Samuel Cornish, *The Sable Arm* (New York, 1956), pp. 65-66.

47. William Wells Brown, *The Negro in the American Rebellion* (Boston, 1880), pp. 56-60.

48. *The Liberator* (February 4, 1862).

49. For several issues the *Monthly* had editorialized that the dissolution of the Union was no cause for comfort, disagreeing with those who, like Wendell Philips, felt that this would bring about the abolition of slavery. See *Douglass', Monthly* (April, 1861), p. 436. His recognition that the struggle for union would become a struggle against slavery was expressed in *Douglass', Monthly* (May, 1861), pp. 452-453.

50. Ibid., p. 452.

51. Ibid., (April, 1863), p. 818.

52. Ibid., (August, 1863), p. 852.

53. Frank A. Rollin, *Life and Public Services of Martin R. Delany* (Boston, 1868), p. 169.

54. Victor Ullman, *Martin R. Delany: The Beginnings of Black Nationalism*(Boston, 1971), pp. 500-506.

Chapter Three

1. Searching for the ideological origins of black nationalism has become a common pursuit. Theodore Draper asserts that Martin R. Delany rightly owns the title, "The Father of Black Nationalism". See his article by that title in *The New York Review of Books* (March 12, 1970), pp. 33-41; also see his exchanges with more studious scholars in subsequent issues of that same journal, e.g., May 21, 1970. Draper seems to

have been unaware of the existence of Crummell, whom he mentioned neither in his article on Delany, nor in his later book, *The Rediscovery of Black Nationalism*, which is a pseudoscholarly diatribe. Floyd Miller, in "The Father of Black Nationalism: Another Contender." *Civil War History* (December, 1971), pp 310-19, presents the relatively obscure Lewis Woodson as his candidate. Rodney Carlisle in "Black Nationalism: An Integral Tradition," *Black World* (February, 1973), assigns a place of distinction to Crummell.

2. Crummell shows a recurrent interest in the subject of racial extermination. An expression of this concern is found in his essay, "The Duty of a Rising Christian State to Contribute to the World's Well-Being and Civilization," in Crummell, *The Future of Africa: Being Addresses, Sermons, etc., etc., Delivered in the Republic of Liberia* (New York, 1862), p. 70. "It is said that no enlightenment, no cultivation, not even Christianity, can save the Sandwich Islanders; the degeneracy of heathenism, their long isolation from the human family for so many centuries, have so lessened their vitality and vitiated their blood, that there is no hope for them, and they must die out." Similar remarks, and dire commentary on the American Indians as doomed peoples, are in his "The Destined Superiority of the Negro", in *The Greatness of Christ and Other Sermons*, (New York, 1882), p. 343. Crummell's response to theories of Indian decadence and inferiority, singularly lacking in moral outrage, should be compared to those of Edward Wilmot Blyden in his *Christianity, Islam, and the Negro Race*, (Edinburgh, 1967), p. 247. Blyden was steadfastly opposed to such theories.

3. Crummell quotes at length from Guizot's *General History of Civilization* in *The Future of Africa*, p. 104, but does not identify the edition from which he quotes. The *General History* was popular as a textbook in England and America throughout the nineteenth century, having gone through eight American editions by 1842.

4. *General History of Civilization*, (New York, 1842), p. 28.

5. Douglass Johnson, *Guizot, Aspects of French History*, (London, 1963) pays some attention to Guizot's development as historian.

6. Guizot, *General History*, (New York, 1842), p. 18.

7. Alexander Crummell, "The Attitude of the American Mind Toward the Negro Intellect" in *The American Negro Academy, Occasional Papers*, No. 3, (Washington, D.C., 1898), p. 15.

8. Crummell, "Civilization as a Collateral and Indispensable Instrumentality in Planting the Christian Church in Africa" in J.W.E. Bowen, ed., *Africa and the American Negro*, (Atlanta, 1896), p. 121. Information on the Stewart Missionary Foundation, can be found in Ibid., p. 9.

9. In "A Defence of the Negro Race in America," Crummell praised the native character of the Africans, arguing that their tribal cultures were innately noble and moral, but such sentiments are hardly typical.

10. Samuel T. Pickard, *Life and Letters of Johh Greenleaf Whittier* (Boston, 1894), Vol. II, 473.

11. William Wells Brown, *The Black Man, His Antecedents, His*

Genuis, and His Achievements (New York, 1863), p. 165 and *The Rising Son: or the Antecedents And Advancement of the Colored Race* (Boston, 1874), p. 456.

12. W. E. Burghardt Du Bois, *The Souls of Black Folk*, (Chicago, 1903), p. 216.

13. See the sketch of the life of Crummell in the George W. Forbes Papers, Rare Book Department, Boston Public Library. William H. Ferris identifies the senior Crummell as an African prince, kidnapped while playing on the beach. See his "Alexander Crummell, Apostle of Negro Culture," *American Negro Academy Occasional Papers*, No. 22.

14. For details on Crummell's youth see his "Eulogium on Henry Highland Garnet, D.D." which is one of the best firsthand descriptions of the experience of black bourgeois youth in Jacksonian America. Crummell and Garnet shared many adventures as boyhood friends. The Eulogium is in *Africa and America* (Springfield, Mass., 1891), pp. 269-305.

15. There were a total of 14 black boys enrolled at the time, according to Crummell, Ibid., p. 280.

16. Observe, for example, the antagonism with which the efforts of Prudence Crandall were met in Eleanor Flexner, *Century of Struggle* (New York, 1970). pp. 38-40.

17. Details on Crummell's personal life during the Liberia years were obtained from the file of his correspondence in the Church Historical Society, Austin, Texas. The letters cover the years 1853-1873 and are, for the most part, requests for money from friends of the missions in the United States. I am indebted to Professor Otey M. Scruggs of Syracuse University, who first brought these letters to my attention.

18. Crummell's tendency to use the term "civilization" in the way that twentieth century writers use the word "culture" was no personal idiosyncracy, but a common nineteenth-century practice. Guizot, for example, spoke of French civilization marching "at the head of European civilization," *General History* p. 16. The term civilization could be applied to a national culture or to the civilization of the entire Western World. More recent authorities, Robert E. Park, for example, saw culture as distinctively national, and civilization as cosmopolitan. See Park, *Race and Culture*, especially chapter 2. Also see "Kultur versus Civilization", in Peter Viereck, *Meta Politics: The Roots of the Nazi Mind* (New York, 1965), pp. 3-9.

19. *Africa and America*, p. 9. Also see similar sentiments expressed by Booker T. Washington in his *Black Belt Diamonds* (New York, 1898), p. 9. "We went into slavery without a language: we came out speaking the proud Anglo-Saxon tongue." Crummell's remarks were delivered in speeches on July 26, 1860 and again in February, 1861, at Monrovia.

20. *Africa and America*, pp. 22-31.

21. Crummell, "Hope for Africa" (1852) in *The Future of Africa*, p. 289-93.

22. Crummell, "God and the Nation" (1854) in *The Future of Africa*, p. 153, attacked what he assumed to be the materialism of indigenous

African religious practices. Crummell's rhapsodies on the sweetness of Platonic discourse are described in Forbes, op. cit.

23. Crummell, "The Relations and Duty of Free Colored Men in America to Africa" (1860) in *The Future of Africa*, p. 220.

24. One wonders what this indecent act may have been, and what Crummell's reaction to it was. See "The Race Problem in America," in Crummell's *African and America*. In this same essay, he compared black Americans to the ancient Germans, saying: "The very words in which Cicero and Tacitus describe the homes and families of the Germanic tribes can as truly be ascribed to the people of the West Coast of Africa. Their maidenly virtue, the instinct to chastity, is a marvel." Cf. Blyden's references to same in *Christianity, Islam and the Negro Race*, p. 59. Blyden argues that polygamy, slavery, and human sacrifice are in no way peculiarly African. "Take *Human Sacrifices*. Tacitus tells us that the old Teutons, generally sparing in offerings, presented on certain days human victims to Wodan."

25. Crummell, "The Duty of a Rising Christian State to Contribute to the World's Well-Being and Civilization, and the Means by Which it May Perform the Same" (1885), in *The Future of Africa* (New York, 1862), p. 84.

26. Ibid., p. 62.

27. See Crummell's "Our National Mistakes and the Remedy for Them" (1870), in *Africa and America*, pp. 165-198.

28. Ibid., p. 185.

29. August Meier, *Negro Thought in America 1880-1915*, (Ann Arbor, 1963), p. 43.

30. *Africa and America*, see the preface.

31. Crummell, "The Need of New Ideas and New Motives for a New Era" (1885), in *Africa and America*, p. 24.

32. Ibid., p. 25.

33. Ibid., pp. 29-30.

34. Ibid., pp. 35-6.

35. Crummell, "Civilization, The Primal Need of the Race" (1898), *The American Negro Academy Occasional Papers*, No. 3, p. 3.

36. Ibid., p. 4.

37. Ibid., p. 5.

38. Ibid., p. 13.

39. "Right-Mindedness," in Crummell, *Africa and America*, pp. 375-6.

40. Sutton E. Griggs, "Life's Demands, or According to Law" (Memphis, 1916), p. 29.

41. Ibid., p. 100.

42. Henry M. Turner quoted in Edwin S. Redkey, ed., *Respect Black: The Writings and Speeches of Henry M. Turner*, (New York, 1971), p. 161.

43. Ibid., pp. 143-4.

44. John E. Bruce in Peter Gilbert, ed., *The Selected Writings of John E. Bruce, Militant Black Journalist*, (New York, 1971), p. 132.

45. William Hooper Councill in Bracey et. al., *Black Nationalism in America*, p. 224.

46. Crummell, "The Destined Superiority of the Negro" (1887), in *The Greatness of Christ and Other Sermons* (New York, 1882), pp. 336-7.
47. Ibid., p. 346.
48. Carter G. Woodson, ed., *The Works of Francis J. Grimke, Vol. I, p. 31;* William H. Ferris, *"Alexander Crummell, Apostle of Negro Culture",* p. 5.
49. *Africa and America,* pp. 139-40.
50. For the reference to Grimke as a "black puritan", see Grimke, *Works,* I, xiii. See Crummell's "The Assassination of President Garfield," in *The Greatness of Christ,* pp. 325-6, 328.
51. Ibid.
52. Crummell had great respect for British social science and its use of statistics, *Africa and America,* p. 236.
53. *Africa and America,* p. 65. It is hardly possible Frazier could have been unaware of Crummell's essay, "The Black Woman of the South." It is quoted extensively in Chapter 7 of W.E.B. Du Bois's *Darkwater,* with which Frazier claimed familiarity. It appeared in such notable bibliographies as Alain Locke's in *The New Negro* (New York, 1925).
54. Frazier was aware of the work of Crummell, mentioning him in *The Negro in the United States* (New York, 1957), p. 498. But the influence of Crummell on Frazier was probably indirect, through Du Bois. Daniel P. Moynihan makes no secret of having been influenced by Frazier. See Moynihan, *The Negro Family: The Case For National Action* (Washington, D. C., 1965).

Chapter Four

1. Benjamin Quarles, *Frederick Douglass* (New York, 1968), pp. 104-7, and Philip Foner, ed., *The Life and Writings of Frederick Douglass,* vol. I, pp. 384-7. The two ladies were Eliza and Julia Griffiths. Their father had been a friend of Wilberforce, the British abolitionist. Julia Griffiths established a close relationship with the Douglass family, living for serveral years in their home. She became Douglass's English teacher, copy editor, and business manager during the early days of *The North Star,* from 1848-53. She later returned to England, where she was married, and as Julia Griffiths Crofts contributed a column to *Douglass' Monthly.*
2. Douglass, "The Nation's Problem," a speech delivered at the Bethel Literary and Historical Society in Washington, D.C., April 16, 1889, was originally published as a pamphlet (Washington D.C., 1889), and is reprinted in Brotz, *Negro Social and Political Thought,* pp. 311-28. Douglass refers to race pride as "ridiculous" on p. 317.
3. Although the fact of marriage to a white woman has never invalidated the credentials of any black nationalist. See C.L.R. James, *History of Pan-African Revolt,* pp. 75-6. The list of black nationalists married to white women includes Frantz Fanon and Kwame Nkrumah;

scholars have included Father Divine and Richard Wright, although some would not accept the latter two as nationalists.

4. Douglass's writings appear in two recent anthologies on black nationalism, John H. Bracey, August Meier, and Elliott M. Rudwick, eds., *Black Nationalism in America,* and Floyd Barbour, ed., *The Black Power Revolt.*The passage quoted is from *The North Star,* (December 3, 1847), reprinted in Foner, ed., *Life and Writings,* Vol. I, p. 281.

5. *Douglass' Monthly,* (Jan., 1859), p. 2

6. Ibid.

7. *The North Star,* (December 3, 1847), reprinted in Foner, ed., *Life and Writings,* Vol. I, p. 283.

8. Additional observations on Douglass's attitudes toward colonization can be found in Quarles, *Frederick Douglass,* pp. 124-5.

9. Foner, ed., *Life and Writings,* vol. I, p. 394.

10. *Douglass' Monthly,* (Jan., 1859), p. 4.

11. *Douglass' Monthly,* (Feb., 1859), p. 19.

12. *Douglass' Monthly,* (Feb., 1859), p. 19.

13. James Redpath and his efforts on behalf of the Haitian Bureau of Emigration are discussed in James McPherson, *The Negro's Civil War,* pp. 78-89. Also see Redpath's articles in *Douglass's Monthly,* appearing on May, 1859, p. 78; Nov., 1860, pp. 358-360.

14. *Douglass' Monthly,* (May, 1861), pp. 449-50.

15. William Wells Brown, *The Black Man,* p. 209.

16. Reactions to Lincoln's colonization plans are described in McPherson, loc. cit., and in Herbert Aptheker, *A Documentary History of the Negro People in the United States,* (New York, 1971), pp. 471-475.

17. Henry Highland Garnet, "A Memorial Discourse Delivered in the Hall of the House of Representatives, Washington, D.C., on Sabbath, February 12, 1865" (Philadelphia, 1865), reprinted in Earl Ofari, *Let Your Motto be Resistance: The Life and Thought of Henry Highland Garnet,* p. 203.

18. Frank A. Rollin, *Life and Public Services of Martin R. Delany,* pp. 168-9.

19. Victor Ullman, *Martin R. Delany: The Beginnings of Black Nationalism,* chapters 20-25.

20. Ibid., pp. 484-5.

21. See Okon Edet Uya, *From Slavery to Public Service: Robert Smalls, 1839-1915* (London, 1971), pp. 165-6. Also see Peggy Lamson, *The Glorious Failure* (New York, 1973).

22. Walter L. Fleming, "'Pap' Singleton, the Moses of the Colored Exodus," *American Journal of Sociology,* Vol. 15, No. 1 (July, 1909). Also see Nell Painter, *Exodusters* (New York, 1977).

23. Herbert Aptheker, *Documentary History of the Negro People,* pp. 713-21, calls Henry Adams "the single most influential person behind the 1879 exodus." He attacks Fleming's treatment of the exodus as a spontaneous messianic movement and sees the exodus as the culmination of a grass roots political process of some sophistication.

24. Mozell C. Hill, "The All Negro Communities of Oklahoma: The Natural History of a Social Movement," *Journal of Negro History*, Vol. XXXI, No. 3 (July, 1946).

25. Edwin S. Redkey, *Black Exodus: Black Nationalist and Back to Africa Movements, 1890-1910* (New Haven, 1969). Further information on proletarian black nationalism in the late nineteenth century is contained in George B. Tindall, "The Liberian Exodus of 1878," in *South Carolina Historical Magazine*, Vol. LIII, No. 3 (July, 1952), and William Bittle and Gilbert Geis, *The Longest Way Home*.

26. Earl Ofari, *Let Your Motto Be Resistance*, p. 123.

27. See section VI, "Delusive Colonization Schemes," in Frederick Douglass's pamphlet, *The Lesson of the Hour* (Baltimore, 1894), reprinted in Foner, ed., *Life and Writings*, Vol. IV, pp. 512-515.

28. Frederick Douglass to W.J. Wilson, reprinted in Foner, ed., *Life and Writings*, Vol. IV, p. 173.

29. I. Garland Penn, *The Afro-American Press and its Editors* (Springfield, Mass. 1891), p. 449.

30. W.E.B. Du Bois, *The Souls of Black Folk*, p. 49.

31. The position that emphasizes the differences, mainly in public style, between Frederick Douglass and Booker T. Washington has been articulated by the following scholars: Philip Foner, *The Life and Writings of Frederick Douglass*, Vol. IV, p. 148. Saunders Redding, *They Came in Chains* (New York, 1969), p. 196. Richard Bardolph, *The Negro Vanguard*, p. 113. Louis Harlan, *Booker T. Washington: The Making of a Black Leader, 1865-1910*, p. 204. Emphasizing continuity in the political thought of Frederick Douglass and Booker T. Washington, have been Samuel R. Spencer, Jr., *Booker T. Washington and the Negro's Place in American Life* (Boston, 1955), p. 108, and Howard Brotz, *Negro Social and Political Thought, 1850-1920*, p. 12. Spencer is concerned primarily with justifying Washington's accommodationism by referring to points of agreement between the two men's philosophies, such as counseling the Negro "to stay in the South, develop industrial schools, and acquire property." Brotz, in spite of overlooking the elements of nationalism in the philosophies of Washington and Douglass, correctly recognized patterns of cultural and economic assimilationism present in the writings of both.

32. Charles Cist, *Cincinnati in 1841: Its Early Annals and Future Prospects* (Cincinnati, 1841), pp. 128-32, reprinted in Caroll W. Pursell, ed., *Readings in Technology and American Life* (New York, Oxford University Press, 1969), pp. 174-177.

33. Frederick Douglass, *The Life and Times of Frederick Douglass*, chapter 20, especially pp. 178-185.

34. Frederick Douglass, *Life and Times*, p. 287.

35. Foner, ed., *Life and Writings*, Vol. II, p. 274. Douglass's advice to the freedmen in this same article was "learn trades or starve," an injunction he had already given in an editorial of March 4, 1853.

36. *Report of the Proceedings of the Colored National Convention*

Held at Cleveland Ohio, On Wednesday, September 6, 1848 (Rochester, 1848), p. 19

37. Booker T. Washington, *My Larger Education* pp. 103-110.

38. Booker T. Washington, *Frederick Douglass* p. 333.

39. Booker T. Washington, *Frederick Douglass*, p. 312.

40. Sections of Douglass's remarks at the Social Science Congress at Saratoga are reprinted in *Life and Times*, pp. 429-439. The paper was delivered in 1879, at a meeting of the American Social Science Association.

41. *Report of the . . . Colored Nation Convention . . . , 1848*, p. 6.

42. Booker T. Washington, *My Larger Education*, p. 110.

43. Booker T. Washington, *The Story of My Life and Work*, in Louis Harlan and John Blassingame, eds., *The Booker T. Washington Papers*, Vol. I, p. 56.

44. Frederick Douglass, *Life and Times*, p. 283.

45. Foner, *Life and Writings*, Vol. IV, p. 334.

46. Douglass, "The Future of the Negro," 1884 in Brotz, *Negro . . . Thought . . .* , p. 308.

47. Howard Brotz, *The Black Jews of Harlem*, (New York, 1970), p. 8.

48. Brotz, *Negro . . . Thought . . .* , p. 379.

49. Booker T. Washington, *Black Belt Diamonds* (New York, 1898), p. 41.

50. Brotz, *Negro . . . Thought . . .* , p. 318.

51. Frederick Douglass said, "Our people should not be required to buy an inferior article offered by a colored man, when for the same money they can purchase a superior article from a white man." Brotz, *Negro . . . Thought...*, p. 320. Booker T. Washington spoke in the same voice when he said, "Harmony between the two races will come in proportion as the black man gets something the white man wants." *Black Belt Diamonds*, p. 114.

52. Brotz, *Negro . . . Thought . . .* ,p. 319.

53. Booker T. Washington was the political collectivist par excellence. He minimized the importance of individual blacks becoming involved in matters of agitation and protest, believing that the interests of the race on the whole could best be represented by a single articulate spokesman— himself. Recent research has shown that while he was not an eminent publicist of the Negro's political oppression, he was an active early supporter of progressive legislation. Washington was a benevolent ward boss, not a revolutionary rhetorician.

54. Booker T. Washington, *Black Belt Diamonds* p. 5.

55. The author of the phrase, "New Negro," is unknown. I found it used in Sutton Griggs, *Imperium in Imperio* (Cincinnati, 1899), p. 244. Cf. Booker T. Washington, *A New Negro For a New Century* (Chicago 1900), pp. 3-5; also Washington's speech delivered at the Hamilton Club in Chicago on January 31, 1896, "Our New Citizen," reprinted in Brotz, *Negro Thought*, pp. 359-362. Also see p. 305, note 48.

56. Du Bois, *Souls of Black Folk*, p. 43.

57. Rayford Logan, *The Betrayal of the Negro* (New York, 1965), p. 312;

Saunders Redding, *They Came in Chains* (Philadelphia, 1950), p. 196. C. Vann Woodward, *Origins of the New South* (Baton Rouge, La., 1951), p. 323.

58. Quoted from the text of the "Atlanta Exposition Address" in John Hope Franklin, *Three Negro Classics* (New York, 1965), pp. 146-150.

59. Du Bois suggested in his *Autobiography* (New York, 1967) p. 239, that the "Tuskegee Machine was not solely the idea and activity of black folk at Tuskegee. It was largely encouraged and given financial aid through certain white groups and individuals in the North . . . " These groups saw blacks as "a strong labor force [who] properly guided . . . would restrain the unbridled demands of white labor, born of the Northern labor unions and now spreading to the South and encouraged by European socialism."

60. D.W. Culp, *Twentieth Century Negro Literature* (Toronto, 1902), note facing p. 227. Alexander Crummell described Fortune to John E. Bruce as "poet, fiddler, ruffian and buffoon." Alexander Crummell to John E. Bruce, letter of Sept. 27, 1897, Alexander Crummell Papers, Schomburg Collection, New York Public Library.

61. Fortune faced the hostility of white printers when he worked in a printer's office as a young man. The printers went on strike rather than work with a Negro, but the courageous stand of the employer resulted in Fortunes's being kept on the job. See Culp, op. cit.

62. T. Thomas Fortune, *Black and White: Land, Labor, and Politics in the South* (New York, 1884), p. 6.

63. Ibid., p. 72.

64. Fortune's tenure as editor of *Negro World* lasted from 1923 until his death on June 2, 1928. His last editorial appeared in *Negro World* posthumously on June 9, of that same year.

65. See Emma Lou Thornbrough, *T. Thomas Fortune: Militant Journalist* (Chicago, 1972), for Fortune's attacks on Theodore Roosevelt and Woodrow Wilson.

66. Culp, loc cit.

67. Archibald Grimke, "Modern Industrialism and the Negroes of the United States", *American Negro Academy Occasional Papers*, No. 12, p. 16.

68. W.E.B. Du Bois, "The Conservation of Races", *American Negro Academy Occasional Papers*, No. 2, p. 15.

69. Earl E. Thorpe, *The Negro Historians in the United States* (Baton Rouge, La., 1958), pp. 14-15. Cf. second ed. of op. cit. (New York, 1971), p. 28.

70. Du Bois, *The Souls of Black Folk*, p. 49.

71. August Meier's article "Booker T. Washington and the Talented Tenth," in his *Negro Thought in America, 1880-1915*, (Ann Arbor, 1963). Among the Latin-trained Tuskegee supporters were Mary Church Terrell and W. H. Crogman.

72. Booker T. Washington to Edna Dow Cheney, Oct. 15, 1895, letter in

the Edna D. Cheney Papers, Rare Books Department, Boston Public Library.

73. Kelly Miller, *Race Adjustment* (Washington, D.C., 1908), reprinted as *Radicals and Conservatives,* (New York, 1968), p. 34.

Chapter Five

1. The most prominent woman in the Garvey movement was Mrs. Amy Jacques Garvey, who was Garvey's second wife. She was born, like Garvey himself, in Jamaica, and did not arrive in the United States until 1919. See Elton C. Fax, *Garvey: The Story of a Pioneer Black Nationalist* (New York, 1972), pp. 108-110; Amy Jacques-Garvey, *Garvey and Garveyism* (New York, 1963), contains much valuable material throughout. Ida Wells, who held an elective office in the UNIA, says of her own relationship to Garvey that he "sent me an invitation to come to New York to deliver an address. I accepted the invitiation and was met by him at the train . . . and I talked to an audience of nearly three thousand persons that evening." See *The Autobiography of Ida B. Wells* (Chicago, 1970), pp. 380-82.

2. See Alexander Crummell's, "The Black Woman of the South: Her Neglects and Her Needs," in *Africa and America,* W.E.B. Du Bois, *The Negro American Family* (Atlanta, 1909); and "The Damnation of Women," in *Darkwater* (New York, 1920); and E. Franklin Frazier, *The Negro Family in the United States* (Chicago, 1939). Issues related to Afro-American family structure and sexual morality are currently being debated with energy, warmth and emotion. The main trend of early scholarship including that of Crummell, Du Bois, Frazier, Charles S. Johnson, Hortense Powdermaker and others tended to emphasize the catastrophic effects of slavery upon black familial and sexual standards. Recent scholars, among them Daniel Patrick Moynihan and John Blassingame, have accepted the conclusions of the earlier generation. Herbert G. Gutman's recent work, *The Black Family in Slavery and Freedom, 1750-1925* (New York, 1976) is concerned more with family structure than with sexual ethics. Gutman does seem to be in agreement with Charles S. Johnson in *Shadow of the Plantation* (1934) and T. J. Woofter in *Black Yeomanry: Life on St. Helena's Island* (1930), that "slave patterns of courtship, sexual behavior, and mating continued into the early decades of the twentieth century."[1] But Gutman, follows Johnson in associating prenuptial intercourse with "premodern" lifestyles rather than with the catastrophic effects of the slavery experience.

3. National Association for the Advancement of Colored People, *Thirty Years of Lynching in the United States, 1889-1918* (New York, 1919), pp. 29-30.

4. Frederick Douglass, *The Reason Why the Colored Man is Not Represented at the World's Columbian Exposition* (Chicago, 1892),

reprinted in Philip S. Foner, ed., *Life and Writings of Frederick Douglass*, Vol. IV, p. 474.

5. Fannie Barrier Williams says in W.H. Crogman, *Progress of a Race* (Naperville, Ill., 1902) that the clubs originated in towns and cities where the black population of literate and politically aware women was large enough to sustain them. For early women's club work see Dorothy Porter, "The Organized Educational Activities of Negro Literary Societies, 1828-1846," *Journal of Negro Education*, V (October, 1936), pp. 556-76.

6. I sometimes refer to the short-lived National Federation of Afro-American Women as if it were the National Association of Colored Women for the sake of economy. This seems reasonable, since at its first annual meeting its members voted to change the name to National Association of Colored Women. There is no history, as such, of the club movement among black women. Elizabeth Lindsay Davis, *Lifting as They Climb* is not a history, though a useful collection of documents. It contains no index and the Contents does not give page numbers. Proceedings of the national conventions are not always given in their entirety, and sometimes are not given at all. *A History of the Club Movement Among the Colored Women of the United States*, cited hereafter as *History*, bears a misleading title; it is really the proceedings of the Boston Convention of 1895 and the NFAAW convention of 1896. The most complete record of the Atlanta Congress that I have been able to locate is contained in the January, 1896 issue of *The Woman's Era*.

7. See Mary Church Terrell, *A Colored Woman in A White World* (Washington, D.C., 1940), p. 149.

8. A sketch of Mrs. Ruffin's life is to be found in Davis, *Lifting*, p. 236.

9. *The Autobiography of W.E.B. Du Bois* (New York, 1968), p. 137.

10. Davis, *Lifting*, p. 18.

11. *TWE*, March 24, 1894, contains details of the open meeting in the spring of 1893.

12. Fannie B. Williams in *Progress of a Race*, pp. 218-225, gives details of the "Ruffin incident" and excerpts from the "Official Statement of the Woman's Era Club."

13. *Crusade for Justice; The Autobiography of Ida B. Wells* (Chicago, 1970), comments on the second Mrs. Douglass, pp. 72-75; comments on Jane Addams, pp. 259-260, 276-78.

14. *Progress of a Race*, pp. 216-218.

15. See her discussion of Tuskegee in Terrell, op. cit.

16. Letter of Mrs. Booker T. Washington to Edna Dow Cheney in the Edna D. Cheney papers, Rare Books Room, Boston Public Library.

17. *"The Atlanta Exposition Address"* is quoted in John Hope Franklin, ed., *Three Negro Classics*, pp. 146-150. It may be found in any edition of Washington's *Up From Slavery*.

18. *TWE*, March 24, 1894, p. 9.

19. *TWE*, March 24, 1894, p. 3.

20. Josephine Silone Yates, in D.W. Culp., *Twentieth Century Negro Literature* (J.L. Nichols & Co., 1902), pp. 27-28.

21. *TWE*, I: 2: 8.

22. *History*, p. 3.

23. Objects of the Anti-Lynching Society and a letter from Miss Balgarnie are included in *History*, p. 28.

24. *History*, p. 3. In an Editorial in *TWE*, II: 4: 12, Mrs. Ruffin says that the Jacks letter will not be printed or discussed in the magazine. It was to be discussed in secret session at the Conference.

25. The Jacks letter was never given general publication. It was, however, reprinted and circulated. A copy of it was found in the Rare Books Room of the Boston Public Library.

26. *TWE*, II: 9: 12.

27. *History*, pp. 30-33.

28. *History*, pp. 11-12.

29. *History*, p. 9.

30. *History*, p. 9.

31. *History*, pp. 34-35.

32. *History*, p. 10

33. Davis, *Lifting*, p. 23. This statement is unexplained and contradicts other statements in the book.

34. A good discussion of the Atlanta Compromise viewing Washington as an accomodationist is to be found in Rayford W. Logan, *The Betrayal of the Negro* (New York, 1965), chapter 14.

35. Alice M. Bacon, *The Negro and the Atlanta Exposition*, John F. Slater Fund, Occasional Papers, No. 7. (Baltimore, 1896), p. 9.

36. Wells, *Crusade for Justice* (Chicago, 1970), p. 119.

37. *TWE*, II: 3: 8.

38. Ibid.

39. Editorial, *TWE*, II: 3.

40. *TWE*, II: 9: 12.

41. Bacon, 13.

42. Mrs. Wells-Barnett's opposition to Washington seems to have been both doctrinal and personal. She objected in particular to his chicken stories, as did Mrs. Terrell. But like Mrs. Terrell, she supported some elements of his program for racial uplift.

43. *TWE*, II: 10: 3.

44. Resolutions of the Congress, *TWE*, II: 9: 2-5.

45. Ibid.

46. Ibid.

47. Statement by Victoria Earle in *TWE*, II: 10: 9.

48. Ibid.

49. *TWE*, II: 9: 2-5.

50. E.C. Hobson and C.E. Hopkins, *A Report Concerning the Colored Woman of the South*, John F. Slater Fund Occasional Papers, No. 9 (Baltimore, 1896).

51. Alexander Crummell, *Africa and America: Addresses and Discourses*, pp. 68-69.

52. See, for example, Mary Church Terrell, op. cit., pp. 192-93.

53. *TWE*, II: 9: 2-5.

54. Mrs. Ruffin was apparently expected to serve on the Committee on Resolutions, but as she did not attend the Congress, she did not serve. *TWE*, II: 9: 12.

55. Letter of Mrs. Booker T. Washington to Edna Dow Cheney in the Edna D. Cheney papers, Rare Books Room, Boston Public Library, dated Nov. 23, 1896.

56. Mrs. Booker T. Washington to the women's clubs printed in *TWE*, II: 10: 9. Victoria Earle Matthews, also a Bookerite, had opposed the resolution condemning the crime that provokes lynching.

57. Charles W. Chesnutt, *The Marrow of Tradition* (Boston and New York, 1901), p. 58.

58. Booker T. Washington to Edna D. Cheney, Cheney Papers.

59. W.E.B. Du Bois, *The Conservation of Races, American Negro Academy Occasional Papers*, No. 2, p. 15.

60. Davis, *Lifting*, p. 21.

61. Mrs. Ruffin found the term cumbersome.

62. *History*, p. 45.

63. Daniels, *In Freedom's Birthplace*, pp. 163-64.

64. Since the Boston Conference was not considered a meeting of the NFA-AW, the only actual meeting of the NFA-AW was the meeting at which the NACW was organized.

65. *History*, pp. 48-49.

66 Wells, *Crusade for Justice*, pp. 111-113, 201-210.

Chapter Six

1. Du Bois's oration on Douglass was published by Herbert Aptheker in *Journal of Negro History*, Vol. 49 (October, 1964), 264-8.

2. Du Bois, *The Conservation of Races* in *The American Negro Academy Occasional Papers*, No. 2, p. 7.

3. A. Norman Klein, Introduction to the Schocken edition of W.E.B. Du Bois, *The Suppression of the African Slave Trade* (New York, 1969), xiv.

4. Du Bois, *The Autobiography of W.E.B. Du Bois* (New York, 1968), p. 126.

5. Ibid., pp. 162-5.

6. Ibid., pp. 65-73 contains all that is known of Du Bois's paternity.

7. *The Conservation of Races*, p. 7.

8. Ibid., pp. 7-8.

9. See Du Bois, *Darkwater: Voices From Within the Veil* (New York, 1920), reprinted by Schocken, (New York, 1969), p. 9. "So with some circumstance having finally gotten myself born with a flood of Negro blood, a strain of French, a bit of Dutch, but thank God! no 'Anglo-Saxon,' I come to the days of my childhood."

10. Ibid., pp. 8-9.

11. Ibid., p. 15.

12. Du Bois, *The Souls of Black Folk* (Chicago, 1903), p. 3.

13. Ibid., p. 43.

14. Ibid., p. 49.

15. Ibid., p. 80. The passage cited is taken from chapter ii, "Of the Wings of Atlanta," which is an attack on the "Gospel of Pay," p. 77, and the "Panacea of Wealth," p. 79.

16. The term, "ottantottist," defined by Peter Viereck in *Conservatism: From John Adams to Churchill* (New York, 1956), p. 11. "A reactionary king of Piedmont-Sardinia became almost a figure of fun by wandering about mumbling pathetically the word 'ottantott,' the Italian word for '88. Thereby he meant to say: all problems would vanish if only the world turned its clock back to 1788, the year before the Revolution." Viereck coined the word to signify reactionary, elitist, authoritarian conservatism. The term is generally applicable to anyone showing a nostalgia for a passing aristocratic order.

17. Du Bois, *The Autobiography of W.E.B. Du Bois*, p. 57.

18. *Horizon*, I, 2, (February, 1907), p. 7.

19. *Darkwater*, p. 208.

20. *The Crisis*, Vol. I, No. 1 (Nov., 1910), p. 7.

21. Du Bois, *Autobiography*, p. 289.

22. Ibid., p. 263.

23. *Crisis*, Vol. V, No. 1 (Nov., 1912), p. 29.

24. Du Bois, *Darkwater*, p. 147.

25. Crummell, *The Future of Africa*. p. 87.

26. *Freedomways* (Winter, 1962), p. 100.

27. Alexander Walters, *My Life and Work* (New York, 1917), pp. 257-60.

28. This five line extract was published in *The Crisis*, Vol. II No. 5 (Sept., 1911), p. 209. The entire poem is printed in *Darkwater*, pp. 275-6. The races' congress was the scene of Du Bois's encounter with the Ranee of Sarawak who gave a reception for him to which numerous dignitaries were invited, loc. cit., p. 155. It is sometimes speculated that the Ranee may have been the model for Princess Kautilya, in Du Bois's novel of 1928, *Dark Princess*.

29. Du Bois, *Autobiography*, p. 289.

30. Du Bois, *The Philadelphia Negro* (Philadelphia, 1899), p. 391.

31. Du Bois, *The Negro American Family*, (Atlanta University, 1909), pp. 18-21.

32. William H. Ferris in *Alexander Crummell, American Negro Academy Papers*, No. 20, p. 9.

33. Ibid.

34. "What is Civilization? Africa's Answer," *Forum*, (February, 1925), reprinted in Meyer Weinberg, ed., *W.E.B. Du Bois: A Reader* (New York, 1970), p. 377.

35. Du Bois, *Autobiography*, pp. 402-403.

Chapter Seven

1. While the two categories overlap, one may find it useful to distinguish between slave narratives published as abolitionist propaganda, and slave interviews collected for social studies purposes—during the 1930s for the most part. Both sets of materials have been subjected to scholarly analysis. For the slave narratives see Charles H. Nichols, *Many Thousand Gone* (Bloomington, 1969); Stanley Feldstein, *Once a Slave* (New York, 1971); *Julius Lester, To Be a Slave* (New York, 1968); Gilbert Osofsky, *Puttin' On Ole Massa* (New York, 1969); Arna Bontemps, *Great Slave Narratives* (Boston, 1969). Fine work has been done with materials based on interviews in Zora Neale Hurston, *Mules and Men* (Lippincott, 1935); B.A. Botkin, ed., *Lay My Burden Down* (Chicago, 1945); George Rawick, *From Sundown to Sunup* (Westport, Conn., 1972).

2. Cyril E. Griffith feels that *Blake* was a direct result of Delany's Southern tour in *The African Dream* (University Park, Pa., 1975), p. 4. Floyd Miller in his edition of *Blake* (Boston, 1970), p. xi, shows that some of *Blake's* themes were outlined by Delany for a series of articles in *The North Star*, April 27, 1849, p. 2; July 20, 1849, p. 3.

3. *Blake's* publication history is outlined in Miller's introduction to his edition of same.

4. Darwin Turner argues: "I would even suggest the possibility of a distinctive kind of novel which follow(s) the pattern of slave narratives. . . ." Charles H. Nichols has argued along similar lines in his lectures at Brown University. See Darwin T. Turner, "A Black-American Literary Tradition"; George E. Carter and James R. Parker, eds., *Selected Proceedings of the 3rd Annual Conference on Minority Studies* (La Crosse, Wisc., 1975), p. 17.

5. See Robert S. Starobin, ed., *Denmark Vesey* (Englewood Cliffs, 1970). The index under Saint Domingue is a good place to start. Gayraud S. Wilmore feels that the Haitian Revolution was an inspiration to Gabriel, *Black Religion and Black Radicalism* (New York, 1972), p. 77. Such a position is implicit in Herbert Aptheker, *American Negro Slave Revolts* (New York, 1943).

6. Miller, ed., *Blake*, pp. 112-13.

7. Delany, in Howard H. Bell, ed., *Search for a Place* (Ann Arbor, 1969), p. 121.

8. Miller, ed., *Blake*, p. 45.

9. *Condition of the Colored People* (Philadelphia, 1852), pp. 39-40; cf. his opinion in *Official Report of the Niger Valley Exploring Party* in Bell, *Search for a Place*, pp. 107-111.

10. Delany, "The Political Destiny of the Colored Race" in Sterling Stuckey, ed., *Ideological Origins of Black Nationalism* (Boston, 1972), p. 203.

11. Benjamin Brawley, "The Negro Genius", *Southern Workman*, XLIV (May, 1915), pp. 305-308. A book by the same title was published by Brawley (New York, 1937).

Chapter Eight

1. W.E.B. Du Bois, *The Souls of Black Folk* (Chicago, 1903), p. 3. I am indebted to a number of social and political historians for the term "Ethiopianism," notably George Shepperson; see his "Ethiopianism and African Nationalism," *Phylon*, No. I, 1953. Also see St. Clair Drake, *The Redemption of Africa and Black Religion* (Chicago, 1970), Jomo Kenyatta, *Facing Mt. Kenya* (London, 1938), and Daniel Thwaite, *The Seething African Pot* (London, 1936). Unfortunately none of these authors has been concerned with the implications of Ethiopianism for literary traditions in either Africa or the New World. F. Nnabuenzi Ugonna makes some brief but incisive observations on the tradition in his introduction to the 1969 reprint edition of J.E. Casely-Hayford's *Ethiopia Unbound* (London, 1911), and this novel is the outstanding example of Ethiopianism by a West African author in the early twentieth century. I prefer to distinguish between English-speaking Ethiopianism and Francophonic "Negritude," although Leopold Senghor ridicules the substitution of "Ethiopianism" for that term. Ethiopianism is not, as Senghor supposes, a recent development, but a centuries-old tradition.

3. For a description of the conspiratorial tradition see Vincent Harding, "Religion and Resistance Among Antebellum Negroes, 1800-1860," in August Meier and Elliott Rudwick, *The Making of Black America*, Volume I, pp. 179-197 (New York, 1971), and for more subtle forms of resistance with more clear-cut implications for literary traditionalism see Miles Mark Fisher, *Negro Slave Songs in the United States* (Ithaca, N.Y., 1953).

4. *Constitution of the African Civilization Society* (New Haven, Conn., 1861), reprinted in Brotz, *Negro Social and Political Thought, 1850-1920* (New York, 1966).

5. For some of the more famous examples see: Richard Allen and Absolom Jones, *A Narrative of the Proceedings of the Black People during the Late Awful Calamity in Philadelphia, in the Year 1793 and a Refutation of Some Censures Thrown upon Them in Some Late Publications* (Philadelphia, 1794), p. 23. Also see Peter Williams in Carter G. Woodson, *Negro Orators and Their Orations* (Washington, D.C., 1925), p. 41. Examples from the writings or Martin R. Delany, Henry Highland Garnet, Edward Wilmot Blyden, James T. Holly, and Alexander Crummell can be found in Howard Brotz, *Negro Social and Political Thought*.

6. W.E.B. Du Bois, *The Souls of Black Folk*, p. 216, viz, "Instinctively I bowed before this man, as one bows before the prophets of the world."

7. Alexander Crummell, *Africa and America: Addresses and Discourses* (Springfield, Mass., 1891), p. 265.

8. In William Wells Brown, *The Black Man, His Antecedents, His Genius, and His Achievements* (New York, 1863), pp. 209-210.

9. Reprinted in Benjamin Brawley, *Early American Negro Writers* (Chapel Hill, N.C., 1935).

10. *The Complete Poems of Paul Laurence Dunbar* (New York, 1913), p. 16.

11. David Walker, *Walker's Appeal in Four Articles*. . . . and Henry Highland Garnet, *An Address to the Slaves of the United States of America* (Troy, N.Y., 1848), especially pp. 13, 15. For the importance of Walker's *Appeal* to U.S. legal history see Clement Eaton, *The Freedom-of-Thought Struggle in the Old South* (New York, 1964), pp. 121-126.

12. Walker, p. 51.

13. The poem appears on the inside back cover of the original edition.

14. This poem appeared under at least three titles during Du Bois's lifetime. The text here is that of "The Riddle of the Sphinx" in *Darkwater: Voices from Within the Veil.* There are no substantial textual variations except that the "Hebrew Children of Morning" in the 1914 *Crisis* version become "Arabian Children of Morning" in the *Darkwater* version and the change is retained in the 1963 edition, "The White Man's Burden," which appears in *An ABC of Color* (Berlin, 1964).

15. *The Survival of the Pagan Gods* (New York, 1961).

16. Bush, *Mythology and the Romantic Tradition in English Poetry* (New York, 1963).

17. Du Bois, *The Souls of Black Folk*, pp. 135-136.

18. Du Bois, *The Quest of the Silver Fleece* (Chicago, 1911).

19. *Quest of the Silver Fleece*, p. 46.

20. Ibid., p. 100, "They heard the whispering 'swish-swish' of falling seed: they felt the heavy tread of a great coming body."

21. Ibid., pp. 337-339.

22. Ibid., p. 326.

23. Schuyler, *Black No More* (New York, 1931), p. 91.

24. Printed in *Darkwater*, pp. 187-192.

25. E. A. Wallis Budge, *The Gods of the Egyptians, or Studies in Egyptian Mythology* (London, 1904), Vol. I, 360-363.

26. *Darkwater*, p. 166; Du Bois, *The World and Africa*, p. 103.

27. *Darkwater*, p. 166.

28. *The Souls of Black Folk*, p. 4.

29. Quoted from the excerpt in *An ABC of Color*, p. 90.

30. See "The Story of Africa," *Crisis*, Sept., 1914.

31. *An ABC of Color*, p. 93.

32. The winged solar disk is a fairly common symbol in Egyptian art and architecture. It appears on the stela erected before the Great Sphinx by Thothmes IV. For some illustrations see *The Larousee Encyclopedia of Mythology* (London, 1966), pp. 19, 34, 46. Also see Budge, p. 471. The *Crisis* cover adaptation of 1911 appeared with the November issue.

33. Isaiah 25:6-8. Du Bois quoted the passage in *The World and Africa*, p. 132, using the translation of Smith and Goodspeed, *The Complete Bible* (Chicago, 1944).

34. William Rose Benet, *The Reader's Encyclopedia*, 2nd ed. (New York, 1965), p. 506.

35. *An ABC of Color*, p. 94.

36. Du Bois, *Darkwater*, p. 161. Also, *Crisis* (May, 1911), p. 19, under the title "The Woman."

37. For other black gods in Du Bois see the following sketches in *Darkwater:* "The Second Coming," "A Litany of Atlanta," and "Jesus Christ in Texas," which appeared in the *Crisis*, December, 1911, under the title "Jesus Christ in Georgia." Another *Darkwater* poem in which a black god appears is "The Prayers of God," in which a white racist is unaware that the god he addresses is a personification of Black Folk, an exceptionally ironic poem, even for Du Bois.

38. Ralph Ellison, *Invisible Man* (New York, 1952), pp. 12-13.

39. Du Bois was aware, no doubt, of the folk belief that a child born with a veil (or caul) has preternatural powers. See *The Souls of Black Folk*, p. 3, in which he speaks of the Negro as "a seventh son, born with a veil, and gifted with second-sight in this American world." For Jefferson's complaint see his *Notes on the State of Virginia*, 2nd ed. (London, 1787), pp. 228-240. Du Bois was familiar with this work as early as 1897, and refers to it in a paper read that year before the American Academy of Political and Social Science. See his *The Study of the Negro Problems* in Julius Lester, ed., *The Seventh Son: The Thought and Writings of W.E.B. Du Bois* (New York, 1971), Vol. I, 235.

40. See Kelly Miller, *Race Adjustment*, reprinted under the title *Radicals and Conservatives* (New York, 1968), pp. 28-31. For the birthday celebration, see *Autobiography*, p. 170.

41. The Garveyites, officially called the Universal Negro Improvement Association, were a stridently militaristic organization of black fascists flourishing in Harlem and Chicago during the 1920s and drawing upon the dissatisfaction of returning black soldiers from the fields of France. Garvey and Du Bois were bitter enemies. The author refers the reader to his interpretation of Garveyism in *The Black Scholar* (Nov.-Dec., 1971). The selections from Wesley's *History of Alpha Phi Alpha*, 9th ed. (Chicago, 1959), are on pages 92 and 143. Martin Kilson and Adelaide Cromwell Hill have provided a documentary history of middle-class black nationalism in *Apropos of Africa* (New York, 1971). Du Bois was a member of Alpha Phi Alpha, having become its first honorary member in 1909. One of the fraternity's founders, Henry Arthur Callis, says the founders were inspired by Du Bois's "Talented Tenth" philosophy. For Du Bois's participation in fraternity activities, see Wesley. Along with Eugene Kinckle Jones, a spokesman for the Urban League, and a number of other members he proposed establishing an alumni chapter in New York (p. 114). Du Bois was principal banquet speaker at the convention of 1944, speaking on Haiti and "the necessity of taking time to live." The distinguished historian and pioneer Pan-Africanist, Rayford W. Logan, presided over the convention that year (p. 393).

42. "The Story of Africa," appeared in the *Crisis* (Sept., 1914). The river imagery of this sketch should be compared with that in "Star of Ethiopia" as reprinted in *An ABC of Color*, p. 93.

43. Quoted from Edmund David Cronon, *Black Moses: The Story of*

Marcus Garvey and The Universal Negro Improvement Association (Madison, Wisc., 1966), p. 176.

44. Two pioneering works of the 1930s should aid the reader in pursuing the question of a black literary tradition: Benjamin Mays, *The Negro's God, as Reflected in His Literature* (Boston, 1938), and Benjamin Brawley, *The Negro Genius* (New York, 1937).

45. For discussions of Germanic influences on Du Bois see Vincent Harding, "W.E.B. Du Bois and the Black Massianic Vision," *Freedomways*, IX (First Quarter, 1969), 44-58. Francis L. Broderick, "German Influence on the Scholarship of W.E.B. Du Bois," XIX *Phylon* (Fourth Quarter, 1958), pp. 367-371, and Wilson J. Moses, "The Evolution of Black National Socialistic Thought: A Study of W.E.B. Du Bois," in Henry J. Richards, ed., *Topics in Black Studies* (Buffalo, 1971).

Chapter Nine

1. Sutton Griggs, *Life's Demands, or According to Law* (Memphis, 1916), p. 26. This is a short book on the laws of collective action for racial success and on the need for "men of exceptional strength" to provide leadership, p. 99.

2. *Life's Demands*, pp. 51-52.

3. Ibid., p. 98.

4. The source for details on the life of Griggs is his autobiography, *The Story of My Struggles* (Memphis, 1914). I am indebted to Professor David M. Tucker of Memphis State University for allowing me to read his unpublished MS, *The Black Clergy of Memphis, 1819-1969*, which includes a chapter on Griggs, and substantial biographical detail.

5. All of Griggs's novels have been reprinted by AMS Press. Editions are also available from Mnemosyne and Xerox.

6. Ralph Ellison, *Shadow and Act* (New York, 1966), p. 95.

7. Griggs, *Imperium in Imperio* (Cincinnati, 1899), p. 246.

8. Ibid., p. 263.

9. *The Hindered Hand, or The Reign of the Repressions* (Nashville, Tenn., 1905), pp. 202-204.

10. Griggs, *Unfettered* (Nashville, Tenn., 1902), p. 34.

11. Ibid., pp. 35-36.

12. Griggs, *Pointing the Way* (Nashville, Tenn., 1908), p. 24.

13. Griggs, *Overshadowed* (Nashville, Tenn., 1901), p. 169.

14. Griggs, *Life's Demands*, p. 29.

15. Griggs, *The Story of My Struggles*, p. 14.

16. Rayford W. Logan, *The Betrayal of the Negro* (New York, 1965), p. 170.

17. Ferris, *The African Abroad* (New Haven, 1913), p. 402.

18. Griggs, *Imperium in Imperio*, p. 3.

19. Griggs, *Pointing the Way*, p. 59.

20. Ibid., p. 150.
21. Ibid., p. 218.
22. Griggs, *Overshadowed*, p. 67.
23. Ibid., p. 30.
24. Sutton Griggs, although a participant in the Niagara movement, was critical of the approaches of both Washington and Du Bois. He revealed great admiration for Washington in his *Life's Demands*, p. 100-4.
25. Griggs, *Imperium in Imperio*, p. 124.
26. Rayford W. Logan, *The Betrayal of the Negro* (New York, 1965), p. 170.
27. Griggs, *The Hindered Hand*, p. 15.
28. *The Detroit Plaindealer*, September 20, 1889, p. 1.
29. *Pointing the Way*, p. 51. T.G. Stewart, "The Army as a Trained Force," in Alice Moore Dunbar, *Masterpieces of Negro Eloquence*, (New York, 1914), p. 278.
30. Griggs, *Imperium in Imperio*, pp. 80-2.
31. Griggs, *Unfettered*, pp. 210-11.
32. Griggs, *Pointing the Way*, pp. 84-5.
33. Chesnutt, *The Marrow of Tradition* (Ann Arbor, 1969), Chapter IX.
34. Griggs, *Imperium in Imperio*, p. 209.
35. Griggs, *The Hindered Hand, pp. 242-3*
36. Griggs, *Overshadowed*, pp. 101-2.
37. Griggs, *Unfettered*, p. 32.
38. Griggs, *The Hindered Hand*, p. 147; cf. *Unfettered*, p. 167, "Mr. Benjamin Kidd seems to think that the tropics can never develop the highest type of civilization."
39. Booker T. Washington, *Up From Slavery*, in John Hope Franklin, ed., *Three Negro Classics* (New York, 1965), p. 38.
40. W.E.B. Du Bois, *The Quest of the Silver Fleece* (Chicago, 1911).
41. Griggs, *The Hindered Hand*, p. 242.
42. Ibid., p. 37.
43. Booker T. Washington, *Black Belt Diamonds*, pp. 8, 9.
44. Griggs, *Imperium in Imperio, p. 245-252*.
45. Griggs, *Unfettered*, pp. 160-1.
46. Ibid., pp. 161-2.
47. Ibid., pp. 162-3.
48. W.E.B. Du Bois, "The Negro in Literature and Art." *Annals of the American Academy of Political and Social Science*, XLIX (Sept., 1913), pp. 253-7.
49. Griggs, *Pointing the Way*, p. 218.
50. William H. Ferris, *The African Abroad*, p. 405.

Chapter Ten

1. Dorothy Porter, "The Organized Educational Activities of Negro Literary Societies, 1828-1846," *Journal of Negro Education*, V (October, 1936), pp. 556-76.

2. John W. Cromwell, "History of the Bethel Literary and Historical Association" (Washington, D.C., 1896), pp. 3, 4, 5.

3. Carter G. Woodson, ed., *The Works of Francis James Grimke*, Vol. IV, Letters, especially Blyden to Grimke, Sept. 11, 1889, in op. cit., pp. 11-12.

4. *Missionary Review of the World*, June 1904, pp. 434-45.

5. J.W.E. Bowen, ed., *Africa and the American Negro* (Atlanta, 1896). For Blyden's greetings, see p. 16.

6. A description of the principal secular black literary magazines is Charles S. Johnson, "The Rise of the Negro Magazine," *Journal of Negro History*, Vol. 13 (Jan., 1928), pp. 7-21.

7. Pauline Hopkins, "Of One Blood, or The Hidden Self", *Colored American Mag.* Vol. 6, No. 7 (July, 1903), p. 492.

8. For the African return of 1878, see George B. Tindall, "The Liberian Exodus of 1878," *The South Carolina Historical Magazine*, Vol. 53, No. 3 (July, 1952), pp. 133-145. A recent study of Henry McNeal Turner is Edwin S. Redkey, *Black Exodus* (New Haven, 1969).

9. See his remarks on "Race Mixture and Emigration," in Edwin S. Redkey, ed., *Respect Black: The Writings and Speeches of Henry McNeal Turner*, pp. 143-5.

10. William J. Simmons, *Men of Mark* (Cleveland, 1887), p. 806.

11. Redkey, *Respect Black*, pp. viii-ix, and *Crisis* (July, 1915).

12. Ibid., p. 83.

13. Ibid., pp. 73-4.

14. Ibid., pp. 146, 160, 168.

15. An attempt to associate Henry M. Turner with emergent revolutionary activity in English-speaking Africa at the turn of the century has been made by George Shepperson in "Ethiopianism and African Nationalism," *Phylon*, No. 1, 1953.

16. William H. Heard, *From Slavery to the Bishopric in the AME Church* (Philadelphia, 1924), pp. 52-4.

17. D.W. Culp, *Twentieth Century Negro Literature* (Toronto, 1902), p. 444.

18. William Bittle and Gilbert Geis, *The Longest Way Home* (Detroit, 1964), pp. 69-70.

19. Ibid.

20. Ibid., p. 186.

21. Orishatukeh Fadumah, "In Memoriam, The Centenary of Sierra Leone," in *AME Church Review*, Vol. 6 (October, 1889), pp. 239-40.

22. Orishatukeh Fadumah, "Thoughts for the Times," *AME Church Review*, Vol. 5, No. 1 (July, 1888), p. 125.

23. Orishatukeh Fadumah, "The Defects of the Negro Church," *American Negro Academy Occasional Papers*, No. 10 (Washington, D.C., 1904), pp. 15-16.

24. *The Woman's Era* (March 24, 1894), p. 9.

25. August Meier, *Negro Thought in America, 1880-1915*, seems less than certain about the degree of direct control exercised by Tuskegee over

black periodicals. See pp. 225-6. If Washington did control editorial policies of these journals, he was a man of catholic taste and exceptional tolerance.

26. Alexander printed John Daniels's review of Du Bois's *Souls of Black Folk*. "It is a poem," said Daniels, "in nature, method, substance and effect it is a poem. Even the treatment of bare facts is poetical." Daniels found the book sad and bitter, but not pessimistic, "nor ultimately cynical. . . . Judge the book not as an argument, as an anti-Washington protest, but as a poem . . . " Alexander also did much, within his limited means, to support Sutton Griggs and gave *The Hindered Hand* publicity that was more than generous. See *Alexander's* (Oct., 1905), p. 8; (May, 1906), p. 27; and (Aug., 1906), p. 8.

27. Samuel Coleridge-Taylor was born in London in 1873. His mother was an English woman and his father a West African whose failure to establish a practice in London led him to abandon his wife and child and return to Africa. Colerdige died in 1912 and Frank Grimke, who happened to be traveling in England at the time attended the funeral.

28. Charles Alexander, "As to the Congo Free State," *Alexander's Magazine*, Vol. 1, No. 12 (Apr., 1906), pp. 7-21.

29. See *Alexander's Magazine* (July, 1905), p. 7.

30. "Scientific Redemption of Africa," in *Alexander's Magazine*, Vol. 1, No. 4 (Aug., 1905), p. 3.

31. "Echoes from Africa," *Alexander's Magazine*, Vol. 4, No. 4 (Aug., 1907), p. 198.

32. Information on the Liberian Development Association is contained in Redkey, *Black Exodus*, pp. 283-6, cf, *Alexander's Magazine*, Vol. 4, No. 5 (Sep., 1907), p. 254.

33. Ibid., pp. 254-5.

34. Ibid., pp. 256-7.

35. "Revolt Among Congo Natives," Vol. 4, No. 6 (Oct., 1907), p. 326. Also see "Some Conclusions Drawn from the Present Trouble in Morocco," in Ibid., pp. 326-7.

36. *Alexander's Magazine*, Vol. 5, No. 4 (Feb., 1908), p. 78. Cf. Henry McNeal Turner's similar effort from which Du Bois probably derived the idea in Redkey, ed. *Respect Black*, p. 164.

37. Walter F. Walker, "Liberia and Emigration," Vol. 6, No. 4 (Aug., 1908), pp. 162-5.

38. William H. Ferris, *The African Abroad*, Vol. 1, p. 131.

39. Ibid., p. 416.

40. Ibid., p. 419.

41. Ibid., p. 404.

42. Ibid., p. 423.

43. Ibid., pp. 430, 439.

44. William Ashby, "Alphas at Yale University in 1915," *The Sphinx*, Vol. 56, No. 2 (May-June, 1970), p. 14.

45. Ferris, *African Abroad, p. 302*.

46. Ibid., p. 304.

47. *Ibid., p. 309.*
48. *Ibid., p. 403.*
49. *Ibid., p. 403.*
50. *Ibid., p. 308.*
51. Marcus Garvey, *Philosophy and Opinions*, Vol. II, pp. 56-9.
52. William Cooper Nell, *The Colored Patriots of the American Revolution* (Boston, 1855), p. 252.
53. "Anglo-African" was used by Robert Hamilton in the magazine by that name from 1859 to 1865. William Still used it in *The Underground Railroad* (Philadelphia, 1871), p. 153; Douglass uses it in Foner, ed., *Works*, IV, 331; Crummell uses it in *Future of Africa, p. 21.*
54. The poem appeared in the issues of Oct., 1905, Dec., 1905; Jan., 1906; and April, 1907. Its author may have been white, for he was identified on Dec., 15 1905, p. 58. as having white ancestry on both sides, but, of course, such a description would have fit any number of Alexander's "black" associates as well.
55. John Daniels, *In Freedom's Birthplace: A Study of the Boston Negroes* (Boston, 1914), pp. 163-4, and 181-3.
56. *Alexander's Magazine*, Vol. 2, No. 2 (June, 1906), pp. 17-18.
57. James M. Boddy, "The Ethnic Unity of the Colored Race," *Colored American Magazine* (March, 1905), pp. 124-28.
58. T.N. Carter, "Make the Name 'Nigger' Honorable," *Alexander's Magazine*, Vol. 1, No. 2 (June, 1905), pp. 7-8.
59. T. Thomas Fortune, "Who Are We? Afro-Americans, Colored People or Negroes?" *Voice of the Negro*, Vol. 3, No. 3 (March, 1906), pp. 194-8.
60. J.W.E. Bowen, "Who Are We? Africans, Afro-Americans, Colored People, Negroes or American Negroes." *Voice of the Negro*, Vol. 3, No. 1 (January, 1906), pp. 30-6.
61. See William H. Grimshaw's *Official History of Freemasonry Among the Colored People in North America. Alexander's Magazine* also carried Masonic news as a regular feature.
62. "The First Mason, A Black Man," *Colored American Magazine* (Feb., 1903), p. 285.
63. E. Franklin Frazier, *The Negro in the United States* (New York, 1957), p. 382.
64. Charles H. Wesley, *The History of Alpha Phi Alpha, A Development in College Life,* Ninth edition (Chicago, 1959). Prominent members of AΦA are Thurgood Marshall, Edward Brooke, and John Hope Franklin. Deceased members include W.E.B. Du Bois, Martin Luther King, Adam Clayton Powell, "Duke" Ellington, and Paul Robeson.
65. See Henry Arthur Callis's tribute to Du Bois in *Freedomways*, Vol., 5, No. 1 (Winter, 1965), pp. 17-18.
66. Bittle and Geis, *Longest Way Home*, p. 21.
67. Louis R. Harlan, *Booker T. Washington*, (Oxford, 1972), p. 266.
68. Charles T. Alexander, "As to the Big Negro," *Alexander's Magazine*, Vol. 1, No. 5 (September, 1905), p. 44.

69. Ibid., p. 28.
70. *Alexander's Magazine,* Vol. 4, No. 2 (June, 1907), p. 144.
71. Paul Laurence Dunbar, a member of the American Negro Academy, was an elevator operator. This sort of fact becomes significant when we attempt to discuss the question of class stratification in the black community at the turn of the century. *The Colored American Magazine,* in describing its salespersons, tells us a lot about its readers inadvertently. See op. cit. Vol. 3, No. 1, (May, 1901), pp. 43-7. *The Colored American* had a circulation of 15,000.

Chapter Eleven

1. *Crisis* (February 1914), p. 190. Commentaries on British opposition to Chief Sam's project are in *Gold Coast Leader,* January 9, 1915, p. 4. His ship was detained for some five weeks in Sierra Leone by British authorities and one may opine that the voyagers were forced to consume much of the provision that might otherwise have been used for establishing the proposed colony.
2. For a discussion of the problems surrounding Bismark's colonial policies see William O. Aydelotte, *Bismarck and British Colonial Policy* (New York, 1970), Appendix V. Belgian policy in Africa is treated in Edmund D. Morel, *King Leopold's Rule in Africa* (London, 1904), pp. 1-28.
3. Quoted in Mark Twain, *King Leopold's Soliloquoy* (Berlin, 1971), p. 44.
4. *Crisis* (December, 1914), p. 68. Granger's poem is in Alice Moore Dunbar-Nelson, *The Dunbar Speaker and Entertainer* (Naperville, Ill., 1920), pp. 163-4.
5. The war in the German colonies is described in Mary Evelyn Townsend, *The Rise and Fall of Germany's Colonial Empire, 1884-1918* (New York, 1930), pp. 364-87.
6. Casement's African interests, his subsequent treason and trial are covered in Peter Singleton-Gates and Maurice Girodias, eds., *The Black Diaries* (New York, 1959). Also see *Gold Coast Leader,* May 20, 1916, p. 4.
7. For example see *Gold Coast Leader,* May 1, 1915, p. 8, for a letter to the editor and same newspaper, September 18, 1915, p. 4, for a rumor that Morel was a German agent. Similar insinuations appeared in *Lagos Standard,* January 27, 1915.
8. Johnston's pamphlet is quoted in *Gold Coast Leader,* May 22, 1915, p. 2. For the Chilembwe Revolt, see George Shepperson, and Thomas Price, *Independent African* (Edinburgh, 1958).
9. *Crisis* (August, 1916), pp. 166-7. For the response of one reader to this editorial and Du Bois's rejoinder see *Crisis,* (December, 1916), p. 63. Also see Du Bois's essay, "Roger Casement—Patriot, Martyr" in his *An A.B.C. of Color* (Berlin: Seven Seas Books, 1963), pp. 85-86.

10. See, for example, Christopher Lasch, *The New Radicalism in America, 1889-1963* (New York, 1965), pp. 181-224.

11. *Crisis*, November, 1914, pp. 15-16, contains a summary of the debate in the U.S. press on the question of using colored troops, and drifts onto the matter of attrocities in the South which are then compared to those perpetrated in the Congo Free State.

12. *Crisis*, September, 1917, contains a special report on the East St. Louis rioting and the casualty statistics quoted above.

13. Townsend, *Rise and Fall of Germany's Colonial Empire*, pp. 32-5, describes the growth of a German colonial cult. Fichte quoted from Justus Buchler et al., eds., *Introduction to Contemporary Civilization in the West* (New York, 1963), p. 157. Von Luschan's statement and Du Bois's reaction are contained in *Crisis*, May, 1924.

14. For a somewhat ambivalent view, see Elliot M. Rudwick, *W.E.B. Du Bois* (New York, 1968), pp. 197-207. For Hubert Harrison's accusations see his *When Africa Awakes*, pp. 66-73.

15. For Douglass's attitudes on the Civil War, see his essay, "Men of Color, To Arms!" in Philip S. Foner, ed., *The Life and Writings of Frederick Douglass*, Vol. III (New York, 1952), p. 317. On the Spanish American War see George P. Marks, *The Black Press Views American Imperialism*, (New York, 1971); Willard B. Gatewood, *Smoked Yankees and the Struggle for Empire: Letters from Negro Soldiers, 1898-1902* (Urbana, Ill., 1971).

16. *Crisis*, June, 1917, p. 62.

17. Ibid.

18. *Crisis*, September, 1918.

19. *Gold Coast Leader*, January 24, 1914, p. 5.

20. *Gold Coast Leader*, November 21, 1914, p. 3.

21. Ibid.

22. Ibid.

23. *Gold Coast Leader*, August 28, 1915, p. 4.

24. *Gold Coast Leader*, May 13, 1916, p. 5.

25. *Gold Coast Leader*, December 12, 1914, p. 5.

26. *Lagos Standard*, February 3, 1915.

27. *Lagos Standard*, January 27, 1915.

28. G. Wesley Johnson, Jr., *The Emergence of Black Politics in Senegal* (Stanford, 1971), p. 184.

29. The words of the French official are quoted from Addie W. Hunton and Kathryn M. Johnson, *Two Colored Women with the American Expeditionary Forces*, (New York, n.d.), p. 173. Randolph's statement is in the *Messenger*, January, 1918.

30. A good discussion of the army I.Q. testing program during the First World War is to be found in Ashley Montagu, *Man's Most Dangerous Myth: The Fallacy of Race* (New York, 1965), pp. 230-232. Also see Robert M. Yerkes, ed., "Psychological Examining in the United States Army," *Memoirs of the National Academy of Sciences* (1921); F.L. Marcuse and M.E. Bitterman, "Notes on the Results of Army Intelligence Testing in World War I," *Science*, CIV (1946), 231-32.

31. The excerpt, quoted from Hunton and Johnson, *Two Colored Women*, is from a report of Mr. William Stevenson to the Commanding Colonel of the Leave Area.

32. Ibid., p. 253.

33. Quoted from Louis Harlan, "Booker T. Washington and the White Man's Burden," in Okon Edet Uya, *Black Brotherhood* (Lexington, Mass., 1971), p. 135.

34. Townsend, *Rise and Fall of Germany's Colonial Empire, p. 234.*

35. Casely-Hayford's remarks on Washington and Du Bois are in his *Ethiopia Unbound: Studies in Race Emancipation* (London, 1969), p. 163.

36. Robert Russa Moton, *Finding a Way Out* (New York, 1920), pp. 236-7.

37. *Crisis*, March, 1919; Moton, *Finding a Way Out*, p. 263.

38. *Messenger*, November, 1917, p. 8.

39. *Messenger*, July, 1918, p. 13.

40. Jervis Anderson, *A. Philip Randolph: A Biographical Portrait* (New York: Harcourt Brace Jovanovich, 1973), p. 108.

41. Stephen R. Fox, *The Guardian of Boston* (New York, 1970).

42. William Monroe Trotter, "How I Managed to Reach the Peace Conference," reprinted in Philip S. Foner, *The Voice of Black America* (New York, 1972), pp. 740-2.

43. Kelly Miller, *The Everlasting Stain* (Washington, 1924), pp. 31-2.

44. Washington's first use of the term was in the title of a book, *A New Negro For A New Century* (Chicago, 1900).

45. Hubert Harrison, *When Africa Awakes* (New York, 1920), p. 76.

46. For Fortune's appreciation of George, see his *Black and White* (New York, 1969), p. 153. Henry Adams's testimony appears in Herbert Aptheker, *A Documentary History of The Negro People* (New York, 1970), pp. 715-23. Jack Turner and his activities are described in William Warren Rogers and Robert David Ward, *August Reckoning* (Baton Rouge, 1973).

47. See Richard B. Moore, "The Critics and Opponents of Marcus Garvey," in John Henrik Clarke, ed., *Marcus Garvey and the Vision of Africa*, p. 218.

48. Marcus Garvey, *Philosophy and Opinions*, II (New York, 1925), p. 120.

Chapter Twelve

1. Oswald Spengler, *The Hour of Decision*, Part One, Translated from the German by Charles Francis Atkinson (New York, 1963), p. 210.

2. Stoddard in the preface to *The Rising Tide of Color* (New York, 1920).

3. Madison Grant was chairman of the New York Zoological Society, a trustee of the American Museum of Natural History and a councillor of the American Geographical Society. He published an argument for the racial supremacy of Aryan Europe, *The Passing of the Great Race* (New York, 1918).

4. Stoddard, *Rising Tide of Color*, p. 12.

5. Ibid., p. 221.

6. Ibid., p. 99.

7. Ibid., p. 102.

8. Muret, *The Twilight of the White Races* (New York, 1926), pp. 73-74.

9. Ibid.

10. Ibid., pp. 74-75.

11. Ibid., p. 78.

12. Ibid.

13. Mathews, *The Clash of Color* (New York, 1924), pp. 20-21.

14. Ibid., p. 72.

15. Ibid., pp. 72-75.

16. Locke, *The New Negro* (New York, 1925), p. 8.

17. Ibid., p. 7.

18. Peter M. Bergman et al., *The Chronological History of the Negro in America* (New York, 1969), p. 387.

19. For remarks of Sandberg and others of like opinion see Carl Sandberg, *The Chicago Race Riots* (New York, 1919). Reprinted with a new preface by Ralph McGill (New York, 1969).

20. Park, *Race and Culture* (New York, 1950), p. vii.

21. Quoted in E. Franklin Frazier, *The Negro in the United States* (New York, 1950), p. 623.

22. Odum, *Rainbow Round My Shoulder* (Indianapolis, 1928), p. 237.

23. Pound in Nancy Cunard, *Negro* (New York, 1970), p. 393.

24. Cunard, *Negro*, Van Vechten, *Nigger Heaven* (New York, 1926); Wiener, *Africa and the Discovery of America* (Philadelphia, 1920-22); Herskovits, *The Myth of the Negro Past* (New York, 1941).

25. Cunard, *Negro*, p. xiv.

26. *Crisis*, 35, (1928), p. 202.

27. McKay, *Home to Harlem* (New York, 1928), reprinted (New York, 1965), p. 70.

28. McKay, *Banjo* (New York, 1929), p. 165.

29. Ibid., pp. 322-325.

30. Hughes, "The Negro Artist and the Racial Mountain," *The Nation* (June 23, 1926).

31. Hughes, "Jazzonia," in James Weldon Johnson, *The Book of American Negro Poetry* (New York, 1931).

32. Hughes, "Weary Blues," in Sterling Brown et al., *The Negro Caravan* (New York, 1941), p. 367.

33. *Crisis*, 33 (1926), p. 81.

34. *The New Negro*, p. 254.

35. J.A. Rogers, *World's Great Men of Color* (New York, 1972), p. 420.

36. Garvey's ties to the African Orthodox Church and the Falasha Jews are discussed in Theodore Vincent, *Black Power and the Garvey Movement* (Berkeley, 1971), pp. 134-135. Ties between Garvey and Muslim leaders Noble Drew Ali and Elijah Muhammed are discussed in Vincent, *Black Power,* pp. 222-223 and E.U. Essien-Udom, *Black Nationalism* (Chicago, 1962), pp. 62-63.

37. Details on the early life of Garvey may be obtained from Amy Jacques Garvey, "The Early Years of Marcus Garvey" in John Henrik Clarke, ed., *Marcus Garvey and the Vision of Africa* (New York, 1974), pp. 29-38.

38. Garvey, *Philosophy and Opinions* (New York, 1925), II, p. 126.

39. Robert A. Hill, "The First England Years and After, 1912-1916", in Clarke, *Marcus Garvey,* pp. 49-53, attributes Garvey's concern with "consensus" to influence of J.E. Casely-Hayford, the famed Gold Coast barrister, journalist and Pan-Africanist. Casely-Hayford, in his turn, may have been aware of Du Bois's pamphlet, *The Conservation of Races, American Negro Academy Occasional Papers* (Washington, 1897).

40. Garveyist influences in post-war Paris are discussed in J. Ayodele Langley, *Pan-Africanism and Nationalism in West Africa, 1900-1945* (Oxford, 1973).

41. E. Franklin Frazier's best known observations on Garvey are in "Garvey: A Mass Leader," *Nation* 123 (August 18, 1926), 147-148, and "The Garvey Movement," *Opportunity,* IV (November, 1926), pp. 346-348.

42. Garvey, *Philosophy and Opinions,* II, p. 42.

43. Ibid., p. 43.

44. Ibid., p. 59.

45. Ibid., p. 101.

46. Robert Hill, *First England Years;* Theodore Vincent, *Black Power;* Mark D. Matthews, "His Philosophy and Opinions:" *Black World* (February, 1976), pp. 36-48. Tony Martin, *Race First* (Westport, 1976).

47. Garvey, *Philosophy and Opinions,* I, pp. 17-18, 37.

48. Sutton Griggs, *Imperium in Imperio* (Cincinnati, 1899), p. 244. Also see "The New Negro" an address delivered by John M. Henderson at the Bethel Literary mentioned in John W. Cromwell's *History of the Bethel Literary and Historical Association* (Washington D.C., 1896), p. 30, and William Pickens, *The New Negro: His Political, Civil and Mental Status* (New York: The Neal Publishing Company, 1916).

Bibliography

A Short List
of Sources Consulted

Primary Sources

I. MANUSCRIPT COLLECTIONS

Edna Dow Cheney Papers, Rare Book Department, Boston Public
    Library.
Alexander Crummell Papers, Schomburg Collection, New York
    Public Library.
Alexander Crummell Correspondence. The Church Historical
    Society, Austin, Texas.
George W. Forbes Papers, Rare Book Department, Boston Public
    Library.
Mary Church Terrell Papers, Manuscript Division, Library of
    Congress.

II. BLACK NEWSPAPERS AND MAGAZINES

A.M.E. Church Review
Alexander's Magazine
The Anglo-African Magazine
Boston Guardian
Colored American Magazine
The Crisis
Detroit Plaindealer

Douglass' Monthly
Indianapolis Freeman
Negro World
New York Age
The Woman's Era
Voice of the Negro
Washington Colored American
Washington Bee

III. PUBLISHED MATERIALS, BOOKS AND PAMPHLETS

Alexander, William T. *History of the Colored Race in America....* Kansas City, Missouri: Palmetto Publishing Co. 1887.

Baker, Ray Stannard. *Following the Color Line: An Account of Negro Citizenship in the American Democracy.* New York: Doubleday, Page, 1908. Reprint. New York: Harper and Row, Torchbook, 1964.

Blair, Lewis H. *The Prosperity of the South Dependent Upon the Elevation of the Negro.* Richmond: E. Waddey, 1889. Reprint. Boston: Little, Brown, 1964.

Blyden, Edward W. *Christianity, Islam and the Negro Race.* With an Introduction by Samuel Lewis. London: W.B. Whittingham, Charleston, 1887. Reprint. Edinburgh: Edinburgh University Press, 1967.

Bowen, T.J. *Central Africa: Adventures and Missionary Labors in Several Countries in the Interior of Africa from 1849-1856.* Charleston: The Southern Baptist Publication Society, 1857.

Bragg, George F. *History of the Afro-American Group of the Episcopal Church.* Baltimore: Church Advocate Press, 1922. Reprint. New York: Johnson Reprint Corp. 1968.

Braithwaite, William Stanley. *The House of Falling Leaves With Other Poems.* Boston: John W. Luce, 1908.

————. *Lyrics of Life and Love.* Boston: Herbert B. Turner, 1904.

Brown, William Wells. *The American Fugitive in Europe: Sketches of Places and People Abroad....* Boston: John P. Jewett, 1855. Reprint. New York: Negro Universities Press, 1969.

————. *The Black Man, His Antecedents, His Genius, and His Achievements.* New York: Thomas Hamilton, 1863. Reprint. Johnson Reprint Corporation, 1968.

—————. *Clotel; or, The President's Daughter: A Narrative of Slave Life in the United States.* . . . London: Partridge and Oakey, 1853. Reprint. New York: Arno Press, 1969.

—————. *Clotelle; or, The Colored Heroine: A Tale of the Southern States.* Boston: Lee and Shepard, 1867. Reprint. Miami: Mnemosyne Publishing Incorporated, 1969.

—————. *The Negro in the American Rebellion: His Heroism and His Fidelity.* Boston: A. G. Brown, 1880. Reprint. Miami: Mnemosyne Publishing Incorporated, 1969.

—————. *The Rising Son: or, The Antecedents and Advancement of the Colored Race.* Boston: A.G. Brown, 1874. Reprint. New York: Negro Universities Press, 1970.

—————. *My Southern Home: or, The South and Its People.* Boston: A. G. Brown, 1880. Reprint. New York: Negro Universities Press, 1969.

Chesnutt, Charles Waddell. *The House Behind the Cedars.* Boston: Houghton Mifflin Company, 1900. Reprint. New York: Macmillan, 1969.

—————. *The Marrow of Tradition.* Boston: Houghton Mifflin Company, 1901. Reprint. Ann Arbor: The University of Michigan Press, Ann Arbor Paperbacks, 1969.

—————. *The Wife of His Youth and Other Stories of the Color Line.* New York: Houghton Mifflin Company, 1899. Reprint. Ann Arbor: The University of Michigan Press, Ann Arbor Paperbacks, 1969.

Cromwell, John W. *History of the Bethel Literary and Historical Association.* . . . Washington: R.L. Pendleton, 1896.

—————. *The Negro in American History: Men and Women Eminent in the Evolution of the American of African Descent.* Washington, D.C.: The American Negro Academy, 1914. Reprint. New York: Johnson Reprint Corporation, 1968.

Crummell, Alexander. *Africa and America: Addresses and Discourses, by Rev. Alex. Crummell.* Springfield, Massachusetts: Wiley & Company, 1891. Reprint. New York: Negro Universities Press, 1969.

—————. *The Future of Africa: Being Addresses, Sermons, Etc., Etc., Delivered in the Republic of Liberia.* New York: Charles Scribner, 1862. Reprint. Detroit: Negro History Press, 1969.

————. *The Greatness of Christ, and Other Sermons, by Rev. Alex. Crummell.* New York: T. Whittaker, 1882.

Daniels, John. *In Freedom's Birthplace: A Study of the Boston Negroes.* New York: Houghton Mifflin Company, 1914. Reprint. New York: Johnson Reprint Corporation, 1969.

Davis, Elizabeth Lindsay. *Lifting as They Climb.* Washington, D.C.: The National Association of Colored Women, 1933.

Delany, Martin R. *Blake; or the Huts of America.* Edited by Floyd J. Miller from the original serialized version in *The Anglo-African Magazine* and *The Weekly Anglo-African* from 1859-1862. Boston: Beacon Press, 1970. ————. *The Condition, Elevation, Emigration and Destiny of the Colored People of the United States Politically Considered.* Philadelphia: The Author, 1852.

————, *Official Report of the Niger Valley Exploring Party.* New York: T. Hamilton, 1861. Reprinted in *Search for a Place; Black Separatism and Africa,* ed. by Howard H. Bell. Ann Arbor: The University of Michigan Press, 1969.

Douglass, Frederick. *The Life and Times of Frederick Douglass.* . . . New Revised Edition, Boston: DeWolfe, Fiske & Company, 1892. Reprinted with a new Introduction by Rayford W. Logan. New York: Collier Books, 1962.

————. *My Bondage and My Freedom With an Introduction* by James McCune Smith, New York: Miller, Orton, & Mulligan, 1855. Reprint: New York: Arno Press, 1969.

————. *Narrative of the Life of Frederick Douglass, an American Slave.* Boston: The Anti-Slavery Office, 1845. Reprint. Garden City, New York: Doubleday & Company, Dolphin Books, 1963.

Du Bois, W.E. Burghardt. *The Autobiography of W.E.B. Du Bois: A Soliloquy on Viewing My Life from the Last Decade of Its First Century.* New York: International, 1968.

————. *The Black Flame: A Trilogy.* New York: Mainstream Publishers. 1957-1961, including three volumes: Volume I, *The Ordeal of Mansart,* 1957. Volume II, *Mansart Builds a School,* 1959. Volume III, *Worlds of Color,* 1961.

————. *Black Folk Then and Now: An Essay in the History and Sociology of the Negro Race.* New York: Henry Holt, 1939.

———. *Dark Princess: A Romance.* New York: Harcourt Brace, 1928.

———. *Darkwater: Voices from Within the Veil.* New York: Harcourt Brace and Howe, 1920. Reprint. New York: Schocken Books, 1969.

———. *Dusk of Dawn: An Essay Toward an Autobiography of A Race Concept.* New York: Harcourt Brace, 1940. Reprint. New York: Schocken Books, 1968.

———. *The Gift of Black Folk: The Negroes in the Making of America.* Introduction by Edward F. McSweeny. Boston: The Stratford Company, 1924. Reprint. New York: Washington Square Press, 1970.

———. *The Negro.* Home University of Library of Modern Knowledge, Number 91. New York: Henry Holt, 1915. Reprint. Oxford University Press, London, 1970.

———, ed., *The Negro American Family. Report of a Racial Study.* . . . Atlanta: The Atlanta University Press, and The Atlanta University Publications Number XIII, 1908.

———. *The Philadelphia Negro: A Social Study Together with a Special Report on Domestic Service,* by Isabel Eaton, Publications of the Unversity of Pennsylvania. Series in Political Economy and Public Law, Number XIV, Philadelphia: Published for the University of Pennsylvania, 1899.

———. *The Quest of the Silver Fleece:* A Novel. Chicago: A.C. McClurg, 1911. Reprint. Miami: Mnemosyne Publishing Inc., 1969.

———. *The Souls of Black Folk: Essays and Sketches.* Chicago: A.C. McClurg, 1903. Reprint. New York: Johnson Reprint Corp., 1968.

———, and Booker T. Washington. *The Negro in the South.* New York: Citadel, 1970.

Dunbar, Paul Laurence. *The Sport of the Gods.* New York: Dodd, Mead, 1902. Reprint. Miami: Mnemosyne Publishing Inc., 1969.

Ferris, William H. *The African Abroad: or, His Evolution in Western Civilization, Tracing his Development Under Caucasian Milieu.* Two Volumes. New Haven: Tuttle, Morehouse & Taylor, 1913. Reprint. New York: Johnson Reprint Corp., 1968.

Forten, Charlotte [Mrs. Charlotte Forten Grimke]. *The Journal of Charlotte Forten: A Free Negro in the Slave Era With an Introduction and Notes by Ray Allen Billington.* New York: Collier-Macmillan, Collier Books, 1961.

Fortune, Timothy Thomas. *Black and White: Land, Labor, and Politics in the South.* New York: Fords, Howard & Hulbert, 1884. Reprint. New York: Arno Press, 1969.

Fowler, Charles H. *Historical Romance of the American Negro.* Baltimore: Thomas & Evans, 1902. Reprint. New York: Johnson Reprint Corp., 1970.

Garrison, William Lloyd. *Thoughts on African Colonization....* Boston: Garrison and Knapp, 1832. Reprint. New York: Arno Press, 1969.

Garvey, Marcus. *The Philosophy and Opinions of Marcus Garvey.* Edited by Amy Jacques-Garvey. New York: Universal, 1923-1925 Two volumes. Reprint. Atheneum, New York, 1969.

Griggs, Sutton E. *Guide to Racial Greatness: or, The Science of Collective Efficiency.* Memphis, Tennessee: National Public Welfare League, 1923.

――――. *Kingdom Builders' Manual. Companion Book to Guide to Racial Greatness.* Memphis, Tennessee: National Public Welfare League, 1924.

――――. *The Hindered Hand: or, The Reign of the Repressionist.* Nashville: Orion, 1905. Reprint. Miami: Mnemosyne Publishing Inc., 1969.

――――. *Imperium in Imperio.* Cincinnati: The Editor Publishing Co., 1899. Reprint. Miami: Mnemosyne Publishing Inc., 1968.

――――. *Life's Demands: or, According to Law.* Memphis, Tennessee: National Public Welfare League, 1916.

――――. *Overshadowed. A Novel.* Nashville: Orion, 1901. Reprint. New York: AMS Press, 1973.

――――. *Pointing the Way.* Nashville: Orion, 1908. Reprint. New York: AMS Press, 1974.

――――. *The Story of My Struggles.* Memphis, Tennessee: National Public Welfare League, 1914.

――――. *Unfettered. A Novel.* Nashville: Orion, 1902. Reprint. New York: AMS Press, 1971.

_____. *Wisdom's Call.* Nashville: Orion, 1911. Reprint. Miami: Mnemosyne Publishing Inc., 1969.

Grimke, Archibald H. *William Lloyd Garrison: The Abolitionist.* New York: Funk & Wagnalls, 1891. Reprint. New York: Negro Universities Press, 1969.

Grimshaw, William H. *Official History of Freemasonry Among the Colored People in North America. . . .* New York: Broadway Publishing Co., 1903. Reprint. New York: Negro Universities Press, 1969.

Heard, William H. *From Slavery to the Bishopric of the A.M.E. Church: An Autobiography.* Philadelphia: The A.M.E. Book Concern, 1924.

Higginson, Thomas Wentworth. *Army Life in A Black Regiment.* Boston: Fields, Osgood, 1870. Reprint. New York: Collier Macmillan, Collier Books, 1962.

History of the Club Movement Among the Colored Women of the United States of America, The. 1902.

Holly, James T. *A Vindication of the Capacity of the Negro Race for Self-Government and Civilized Progress, as Demonstrated by Historical Events of the Haytian Revolution and the Subsequent Acts of that People Since Their National Independence.* New Haven, Connecticut: Afric-American Printing Company, 1857. Reprinted in *Black Separatism and the Caribbean,* 1860. Edited, with an Introduction, by Howard H. Bell. Ann Arbor: The University of Michigan Press, 1970.

Holtzclaw, William H. *The Black Man's Burden.* New York: Neale Publishing Co., 1915.

Johnson, James Weldon. *Along This Way: The Autobiography of James Weldon Johnson.* New York: Viking Press, 1933. Reprint. 1961.

_____. *The Autobiography of An Ex-Colored Man.* With an Introduction by Carl Van Vechten. New York: Alfred A. Knopf, 1927.

Kenyatta, Jomo. *Facing Mt. Kenya: The Tribal Life of the Gikuyu.* With an Introduction by B. Malinowski. London: Secker and Warburg, 1938. Reprint. New York: Random House, 1962.

Kletzing, H.F., and Crogman, W.H. *Progress of a Race; or, The Remarkable Advancement of the Afro-American Negro From the Bondage of Slavery, Ignorance and Poverty, to the Freedom of Citizenship, Intelligence, Affluence, Honor and Trust.* With an Introduction by Booker T. Washington. Atlanta: J.L. Nichols & Co., 1897. Reprint. New York: Negro Universities Press, 1969.

Lynch, John R. *Reminiscences of an Active Life. The Autobiography of John R. Lynch.* Edited, with an Introduction, by John Hope Franklin. Chicago: University of Chicago Press, 1970.

Matthews, Victoria Earle, ed., *Black-Belt Diamonds: Gems from the Speeches, Addresses, and Talks to Students of Booker T. Washington, Principal of Tuskegee Institute, Tuskegee, Alabama.* Introduction by T. Thomas Fortune. New York: Fortune and Scott, 1898. Reprint. Miami: Mnemosyne Publishing Inc., 1969.

Miller, Kelly. *An Appeal to Conscience: America's Code of Caste, a Disgrace to Democracy.* With an Introduction by Albert Bushnell Hart. New York: Macmillan, 1918.

_____. *Out of the House of Bondage.* New York: The Neale Publishing Co., 1914. Reprint. New York: Schocken Books, 1971.

_____. *Race Adjustment: Essays on the Negro in America.* New York: The Neale Publishing Co., 1908. Reprint. New York: Schocken Books, 1968.

Mossell, Mrs. N.F. [Mrs. Gertrude Mossell]. *The Work of the Afro-American Woman.* Philadelphia: G.S. Ferguson, 1894. Reprint. Freeport, New York: Books For Libraries Press, 1971.

Moton, Robert Russa. *Finding a Way Out: An Autobiography.* New York: Doubleday, Page & Co., 1920. Reprint. New York: Negro Universities Press, 1969.

Parks, Willis B., ed., *The Possibilities of the Negro in Symposium: A Solution of the Negro Problem Psychologically Considered. The Negro Not "A Beast."* The Franklin Printing and Publishing Co., 1904.

Payne, Daniel A. *A History of the African Methodist Episcopal Church.* Edited by Rev. C.S. Smith. Nashville: Publishing House of the A.M.E. Sunday-School Union. 1891. Reprint. New York: Arno Press, 1969.

————. *Recollections of Seventy Years.* With an Introduction by Rev. F.J. Grimke. . . . Nashville, 1888. Reprint. New York: Arno Press, 1969.

Pipkin, J.J. *The Story of a Rising Race.* Edited by Rev. C.S. Smith. 1902.

Ponton, M.M. *Life and Times of Henry M. Turner.* . . . Atlanta: A.B. Caldwell, 1917.

Reuter, Edward Byron. *The Mulatto in the United States: Including A Story of the Role of Mixed Blood Races throughout the World.* Boston: R.G. Badger, 1918.

Richings, G.F. *Evidences of Progress among Colored People.* Philadelphia: George S. Ferguson, 1900. Reprint. Chicago: Afro-American Press, 1969.

Rollin, Frank A. *Life and Public Services of Martin R. Delany.* . . . Boston: Lee and Shepard, 1868.

Scott, Emmett J. *Negro Migration during the War.* New York: Oxford University Press, 1920. Reprint. New York: Arno Press, 1969.

Shannon, A.H. *Racial Integrity and Other Features of the Negro Problem.* Nashville: Publishing House of the A.M.E. Church, South, 1907.

Stephenson, Gilbert Thomas. *Race Distinctions in American Law.* London: D. Appleton, 1910. Reprint. New York: Negro Universities Press, 1969.

Suksdorf, Henry F. *Our Race Problems.* New York: The Shakespeare Press, 1911.

Twain, Mark [Samuel Langhorne Clemens]. *King Leopold's Soliloquy: A Defense of His Congo Rule.* Boston: R.P. Warren, 1906. Reprint. New York: International Publishers, New York, 1970.

Walker, David, and Garnet, Henry Highland. *Walker's Appeal in Four Articles.* . . . *And also, Garnet's Address to the Slaves of the United States of America.* New York: Printed by J.H. Tobbitt, 1848. Reprint. New York: Arno Press, 1969.

Ward, Samuel Ringgold. *Autobiography of a Fugitive Negro: His Anti-Slavery Labours in the United States, Canada, & England.* London: John Snow, 1855. Reprint. New York: Arno Press, 1969.

Washington, Booker T. *Frederick Douglass*. Philadelphia: George W. Jacobs & Co., 1907.

————. *My Larger Education: Being Chapters from My Experience*. Garden City, New York: Doubleday, Page & Co., 1911

————, Du Bois, W.E.B.; Chesnutt, Charles W.; Smith, Wilford H.; Kealing, H.T.; Dunbar, Paul L.; and Fortune T. Thomas. *The Negro Problem: A Series of Articles by Representative American Negroes of Today*. New York: J. Potts, 1903. Reprint. New York: Arno Press, 1969.

————. *A New Negro For A New Century: An Accurate and Up-to-Date Record of the Upward Struggles of the Negro Race*. Chicago: The American Publishing House, 1900. Reprint. Miami: Mnemosyne Publishing Inc., 1969.

————. *Up From Slavery. An Autobiography*. New York: Doubleday, Page & Co., 1902.

Wells, Ida B. *Crusade for Justice*. Chicago: University of Chicago Press, 1970.

————. *Mob Rule in New Orleans*. Chicago, [1900]. Reprinted in *Ida B. Wells On Lynchings*. Edited by August Meier. New York: Arno Press, 1969.

————. *A Red Record: Tabulated Statistics. . . .* Chicago: Donohue & Henneberry, 1894? Reprinted in *Ida B. Wells On Lynchings*. Edited By August Meier. New York: Arno Press, 1969.

————. *Southern Horrors: Lynch Law in all its Phases*. New York: New York Age Print, 1892. Reprinted in *Ida B. Wells On Lynchings*. Edited by August Meier. New York: Arno Press, 1969.

IV. Published Primary Source Collections

The American Negro Academy. *Occasional Papers*, New York: Arno Press, 1969.

Aptheker, Herbert, ed., *And Why not Every Man? The Story of the Fight against Negro Slavery*. New York: International Publishers, 1961.

————. *A Documentary History of The Negro People in The United States*. Three volumes. New York: Citadel Press, 1971-73.

Barbour, Floyd, ed., *The Black Power Revolt.* New York: Collier Books, 1968.

Barrows, Isabel C., ed., *Mohonk Conference on the Negro Question. Held at Lake Mohonk, Ulster County, New York. First and Second, June 4, 5, 6, 1890 and June 3, 4, 5, 1891.* Boston: George H. Ellis, 1890-1891. Reprint. New York: Negro Universities Press.

Bell, Howard Holman, ed., *Minutes of the Proceedings of the National Negro Conventions, 1830-1864.* New York: Arno Press, 1969.

Betts, Raymond F., ed., *The Ideology of Blackness.* Lexington, Massachusetts: D.C. Heath & Company, 1971.

Bontemps, Arna, ed. *Great Slave Narratives.* Boston: Beacon, 1969.

Bowen, J.W.E., ed., *Addresses and Proceedings of the Congress on Africa.* Atlanta: Gammon Theological Seminary, 1896.

Bracey, John H. August Meier, and Elliott Rudwick, eds. *The Afro-Americans: Selected Documents.* Boston: Allyn and Bacon, 1972.

————. *Black Nationalism in America.* Indianapolis: Bobbs-Merrill, 1970.

Brown, Seerling A., Arthur P. Davis, and Ulysses Lee, eds. *The Negro Caravan.* New York: Arno, 1970.

Brotz, Howard, ed. *Negro Social and Political Thought, 1850-1920: Representative Texts.* New York: Basic Books, 1966.

Butcher, Philip, ed. *The William Stanley Braithwaite Reader.* Ann Arbor: University of Michigan Press, 1972.

Calverton, V.F., ed. *Anthology of American Negro Literature.* New York: Modern Library, 1929.

Clarke, John Henrik, ed. *Marcus Garvey and the Vision of Africa. New York: Random House, Vintage Books, 1974.*

Culp, D.W., ed. *Twentieth Century Negro Literature: or A Cyclopedia of Thought on the Vital Topics Relating to the American Negro.* Toronto: J.L. Nichols & Co., 1902.

Dorson, Richard M., ed. *American Negro Folktales.* Greenwich, Conn.: Fawcett, 1956.

Dunbar-Nelson, Alice More, ed. *The Dunbar Speaker and Entertainer: Containing The Best Prose and Poetic Selections* by and about The Negro Race, with Programs Arranged for Special Entertainments. Naperville, Ill.: J.L. Nichols, 1920.

Dunbar, Alice Moore, ed. Masterpieces of Negro Eloquence: The Best Speeches Delivered by The Negro From the Days of Slavery to the Present Time. New York: The Bookery Publishing Co., 1914.

Fishel, Leslie H. and Benjamin Quarles, eds. The Black American: A Documentary History. Glenview, Ill.: Scott, Foresman, 1970.

Foner, Philip S., ed. The Voice of Black America: Major Speeches by Negroes in the United States, 1797-1971. New York: Simon and Schuster, 1972.

_____. The Life and Writings of Frederick Douglass. 4 vols. New York International Publishers, 1955.

Foner, Philip S., ed. W.E.B. Du Bois Speaks: Speeches and Addresses 1890-1963. 2 vols. New York: Pathfinder Press, 1970.

Frazier, Thomas R., ed. Afro-American History: Primary Sources. New York: Harcourt, Brace and World, 1970.

Fyfe, Christopher, ed. Sierra Leone Inheritance. London: Oxford University Press, 1964.

Gatewood, Willard B. "Smoked Yankees" and the Struggle for Empire: Letters from Negro Soldiers, 1898-1902. Urbana: University of Illinois Press, 1971.

Gilbert, Peter, ed. The Selected Writings of John Edward Bruce: Militant Black Journalist. New York: Arno, 1971.

Grant, Joanne, ed. Black Protest: History, Documents, and Analyses, 1619 to the Present. New York: Fawcett, 1968.

Hill, Adelaide Cromwell, and Martin Kilson, eds. Apropos of Africa: Afro-American Leaders and the Romance of Africa. Anchor Books, Garden City, New York: Anchor Books, 1971.

Hurston, Zora Neale. Mules and Men. Philadelphia: Lippincott, 1935.

Killian, Charles, ed. Sermons and Addresses, 1853-1891: Bishop Daniel A. Payne. New York: Arno, 1972.

Lester, Julius, ed. The Seventh Son: The Thought and Writings of W.E.B. Du Bois. 2 volumes. New York: Random House, Vintage Books, 1971.

Lynch, Hollis R., ed. *Black Spokesman: Selected Published Writings of Edward Wilmot Blyden.* New York: Humanities Press, 1971.

McPherson, James M. *The Negro's Civil War: How American Negroes Felt and Acted During the War for the Union.* New York: Random House, Vintage Books, 1965.

Meier, August, Elliott Rudwick, and Francis L. Broderick, eds. *Black Protest Thought in the Twentieth Century.* 2nd. ed., Indianapolis: Bobbs-Merrill, 1971.

Nicol, Davidson, ed. *Black Nationalism in Africa, 1867: Extracts from the Political, Educational, Scientific and Medical Writings Of Africanus Horton.* New York: Africana Publishing Corporation, 1969.

Osofsky, Gilbert, ed. *Puttin' On Ole Massa: The Slave Narratives of Henry Bibb, William Wells Brown, and Solomon Northup.* New York: Harper and Row, Torchbooks, 1969.

Padmore, George, ed. *History of the Pan African Congress.* London: The Hammersmith Bookshop, 1947.

Penn, I. Garland, ed. *The United Negro: His Problems and His Progress, Containing the Addresses and Proceedings of the Negro Young People's Christian and Educational Congress, Held August 6-11, 1902.* D.E. Luther Publishing Co., 1902.

Porter, Dorothy, ed. *Early Negro Writing, 1760-1837.* Boston: Beacon, 1971.

_____. *Negro Protest Pamphlets.* New York: Arno, 1969.

Redkey, Edwin S., ed. *Respect Black: The Writings and Speeches of Henry McNeal Turner.* New York: Arno, 1971.

Renfro, G. Herbert, ed. *Life and Works of Phillis Wheatley: Containing Her Complete Poetical Works. Numerous Letters. And a Complete Biography of this Famous Poet of a Century and a Half Ago.* Washington, D.C.: Robert L. Pendleton, 1916.

Stuckey, Sterling, ed. *The Ideological Origins of Black Nationalism.* Boston: Beacon, 1972.

Vincent, Theodore G., ed. *Voices of a Black Nation: Political Journalism in the Harlem Renaissance.* San Francisco: Ramparts Press, 1973.

Wilson, Henry S., ed. *Origins of West African Nationalism*. New York: St. Martin's Press, 1969.

Woodson, Carter G., ed. *The Mind of the Negro as Reflected in Letters Written During the Crisis, 1800-1860*. Washington, D.C.: The Association for the Study of Negro Life and History, 1926.

————. *Negro Orators and Their Orations*. Washington, D.C.: Associated Publishers, 1925.

————. *The Works of Francis J. Grimke*. 4 Vols. Washington, D.C.: The Associated Publishers, 1942.

V. PRIMARY SOURCES: ARTICLES

Alexander, Charles. "Dr. Booker T. Washington's Mistake." *Alexander's Magazine*, Vol. 1, No. 5 (September, 1905), p. 39.

Archer, S.H. "Football in Our Colleges." *Voice of the Negro*, Vol. III, No. 3 (March, 1906) pp. 215-6.

Bowen, J.W.E. "Who Are We? Africans, Afro-Americans, Colored People Negroes or American Negroes?" *Voice of the Negro*, Vol. III, No. 1 (December, 1906), pp. 30-36.

Bridgman, Frederick B. "The Ethiopian Movements in South Africa." *Missionary Review of the World*, XVII (June, 1904), pp. 434-45.

Chesnutt, Charles W. "Race Prejudice; Its Causes and Its Cure." *Alexander's Magazine*, Vol. 1, No. 3 (July 15, 1905), p. 21.

Daniels, John. "The Wretchedness of the Congo Natives." *Voice of the Negro*, Vol. IV, No. 1 (Jan.-Feb., 1907), pp. 22-30.

Fortune, T. Thomas. "Who Are We? Afro-Americans, Colored People or Negroes?" *Voice of the Negro*, Vol. III, No. 3 (March, 1906), pp. 194-8.

Grimke, Archibald H. "Joseph Benson Foraker: or The Man and the Hour." *Alexander's Magazine*, Vol. 4, No. 1 (May, 1907), p. 31.

Hewin, F. Thomas. "The Separate Car Law in Virginia." *Colored American Magazine*, Vol. I, No. 1 (May, 1900), pp. 30-5.

Houston, G. David. "The Negro Graduates of Harvard University, 1905." *Alexander's Magazine*, Vol. 1, No. 3 (July, 1905), p. 1.

Hunton, Mrs. A.H. "Kindergarten Work in the South." *Alexander's Magazine,* Vol. 2, No. 3 (July, 1906), p. 29.

J.R.M. "St. Benedict's Colored Catholic Church." *Alexander's Magazine,* Vol. 5, No. 4 (February, 1908), p. 116.

Middleton, Henry Davis. "The Ebonville Woman's Club." *Voice of the Negro,* Vol. III, No. 5 (May, 1906), pp. 350-3.

Miller, Kelly. "The Anglo-Saxon and the African." *Colored American Magazine,* Vol. VI, No. 3 (January, 1903), pp. 200-5.

Pace, Harry Herbert. "The Case of the Negro Elks." *Voice of the Negro,* Vol. IV, No. 6 (June, 1907), pp. 253-5.

Pickens, William. "Jesse Max Barber." *Voice of the Negro,* Vol. III, No. 11 (November, 1906), pp. 483-8.

Poindexter, C.C. "Some Student Experiences." *Voice of the Negro,* Vol. III, No. 5 (May, 1906), p. 335.

Powell, A. Clayton, D.D. "A Band of Selected Patriots: A Sermon Delivered Before the Veterans of the Connecticut National Guard." *Alexander's Magazine,* Vol. 1, No. 3 (July, 1905), p. 35.

Ransom, Reverdy C. "How Should the Christian State Deal With the Race Problem." *Alexander's Magazine,* Vol. 1, No. 6 (October, 1905), p. 39.

_____. "Socialism and the Negro." *Alexander's Magazine,* Vol. 1, No. 1 (May, 1905), p. 15.

Scarborough, W.S. "English Principle vs. American Prejudice." *Voice of the Negro,* Vol. III, No. 5 (May, 1906), pp. 346-9.

Steward, T.G. "Something About Our Flag." *Alexander's Magazine,* Vol. 1, No. 1 (Feb., 1906), p. 53.

Villard, Oswald Garrison. "The Negro and the Domestic Problem." *Alexander's Magazine,* Vol. 1, No. 7 (November 15, 1905), p. 1.

Warren, Francis H. "The Upbuilding of Liberia, West Africa." *Alexander's Magazine,* Vol. 3, No. 4 (February, 1907), p. 183.

Walker, Walter F. "The Northeastern Federation." [of Women's Clubs] *Alexander's Magazine,* Vol. 1, No. 5 (September, 1905), p. 20.

_____. "Three Promising Young Women of New England." *Alexander's Magazine,* Vol. 1, No. 3 (July, 1905), p. 7.

Washington, Booker T. "Samuel Coleridge-Taylor, Composer: A Sketch." *Alexander's Magazine,* Vol. 1, No. 1 (May, 1905), p. 33.

Wayman, H. Harrison. "The American Negro Historical Society of Philadelphia and its Officers." *Colored American Magazine,* Vol. VI, No. 4 (February, 1903), p. 287.

Work, John W. "The Songs of the Southland." *Voice of the Negro,* Vol. IV, No. 1 (Jan.-Feb., 1907), p. 51-4.

Secondary Sources

I. BOOKS AND PAMPHLETS

Ajala, Adekunle. *Pan-Africanism: Evolution, Progress and Prospects.* New York: St. Martin's Press, 1974.

Aptheker, Herbert. *American Negro Slave Revolts.* New York: International Publishers, 1969.

Bailey, Hough C. *Liberalism in the New South: Southern Social Reformers and the Progressive Movement.* Coral Gables, Fla: University of Miami Press, 1969.

Bardolph, Richard. *The Negro Vanguard.* New York: Vintage Books, 1959. Reprint. Westport, Ct.: Negro Universities Press, 1972.

Barzun, Jacques. *Race: A Study in Superstition.* New York: Harper and Row, Torchbook, 1965.

Bell, Howard Holman. *A Survey of the Negro Convention Movement.* 1830-1861. New York: Arno Press and the New York Times, 1970.

Bennett, Lerone. *Pioneers in Protest.* Baltimore: Penguin, 1969.

Bittle, William E., and Gilbert Geis. *The Longest Way Home: Chief Alfred C. Sam's Back to Africa Movement.* Detroit: Wayne State University Press, 1964.

Bodo, John R. *The Protestant Clergy and Public Issues, 1812-1848.* Princeton, New Jersey: Princeton University Press, 1954.

Bone, Robert A. *The Negro Novel in America.* New Haven: Yale University Press, 1965.

Bontemps, Arna and Jack Conroy. *Anyplace but Here.* New York: Hill and Wang, 1966.

Botkin, B.A. *Lay My Burden Down: A Folk History of Slavery.* Chicago: University of Chicago Press, 1945.

Brawley, Benjamin. *The Negro Genius.* New York: Dodd, Mead, 1937.

Broderick, Francis L. *W.E.B. Du Bois: Negro Leader in a Time of Crisis.* Standord, California: Stanford University Press, 1959.

Brotz, Howard. *The Black Jews of Harlem: Negro Nationalism and The Dilemmas of Negro Leadership.* New York: Schocken, 1964.

Brown, Thomas N. *Irish-American Nationalism, 1870-1890.* Philadelphia and New York: J.B. Lippincott Company, 1966.

Bush, Douglas. *Mythology and the Romantic Tradition in English Poetry.* Cambridge, Mass.: Harvard University Press, 1937.

Carlisle, Rodney. *The Roots of Black Nationalism.* Port Washington, New York: Kennikat Press, 1975.

Clarke, John Henrik, ed. *Marcus Garvey and the Vision of Africa.* New York: Random House, Vintage Books, 1973.

Cleage, Albert B., Jr. *The Black Messiah.* New York: Sheed and Ward, Search Book, 1969.

Cone, James H. *Black Theology and Black Power.* New York: The Seabury Press, 1969.

Cronon, Edmund David. *Black Moses: The Story of Marcus Garvey and the Universal Negro Improvement Association.* Madison, Wisconsin: University of Wisconsin Press, 1966.

Cruse, Harold. *The Crisis of the Negro Intellectual.* New York: William Morrow & Co., 1967.

Davis, John P. ed. *The American Negro Reference Book.* Englewood Cliffs, New Jersey: Prentice-Hall, Inc., 1966.

Deutsch, Karl W. *Nationalism and Communication: An Inquiry Into Foundations of Nationality.* Cambridge, Mass.: The M.I.T. Press, 1966.

Du Bois, W.E. Burghardt. *Black Folk Then and Now.* New York: Henry Holt & Co., 1939.

Drake, St. Clair. *The Redemption of Africa and Black Religion.* Chicago: Third World Press, 1970.

Draper, Theodore. *The Rediscovery of Black Nationalism.* New York: Viking, 1970.

Ellison, Ralph. *Shadow and Act.* New York: Signet, 1966.

Essien-Udom, E.U. *Black Nationalism: A Search for an Identity in America.* Chicago: University of Chicago Press, 1962.

Farrison, William Edward. *William Wells Brown: Author and Reformer.* Chicago: University of Chicago Press, 1969.

Fauset, Arthur Huff. *Black Gods of the Metropolis: Negro Religious Cults in the Urban North.* Philadelphia: University of Pennsylvania Press, 1971.

Fax, Elton C. *Garvey: The Story of a Pioneer Black Nationalist.* New York: Dodd Mead, 1972.

Fox, Stephen R. *The Guardian of Boston: William Monroe Trotter.* New York: Atheneum, 1970.

Franklin, John Hope. *Reconstruction: After the Civil War.* Chicago: University of Chicago Press, 1961.

Frederickson, George M. *The Black Image in the White Mind: The Debate on Afro-American Character and Destiny, 1817-1914.* New York: Harper & Row, Torchbook, 1971.

Frazier, E. Franklin. *Black Bourgeoisie.* Glencoe, Illinois: Free Press, 1957

———. *The Negro Church in America.* New York: Schocken, 1964.

———. *The Negro in the United States.* New York: MacMillan, 1957.

Fullinwider, S.P. *The Mind and Mood of Black America: Twentieth Century Thought.* Homewood, Illinois: Dorsey Press, 1969.

Fyfe, Christopher. *Africanus Horton: West African Patriot.* New York: Oxford Press, 1972.

Garraty, John A. *The New Commonwealth.* New York: Harper & Row, Torchbooks, 1968.

Garvey, Amy Jacques. *Garvey and Garveyism.* London: Collier-MacMillan, Collier Books, 1970.

Geiss, Imanuel. *The Pan-African Movement.* New York: Holmes & Meier, 1974.

Gloster, Hugh M. *Negro Voices in American Fiction.* Chapel Hill: The University of North Carolina Press, 1948.

Griffith, Cyril E. *The African Dream: Martin R. Delany and the Emergence of Pan-African Thought.* University Park: Pennsylvania State University Press, 1975.

Gutman, Herbert G. *The Black Family in Slavery and Freedom, 1750-1825*. New York: Pantheon Books, 1976.

Hare, Nathan. *The Black Anglo-Saxons*. London: Collier-Mac-Millan, Collier Books, 1970.

Harlan, Louis R. *Booker T. Washington: The Making of a Black Leader, 1856-1901*. New York: Oxford University Press, 1972.

Hays, Samuel P. *The Response to Industrialism*. Chicago: University of Chicago Press, 1957.

Henri, Florette. *Bitter Victory: A History of Black Soldiers in World War I*. New York: Doubleday & Company, Zenith Books, 1970.

Hofstadter, Richard. *The Age of Reform: From Bryan to F.D.R.* New York: Random House, Vintage Books, 1955.

Hooker, James R. *Black Revolutionary: George Padmore's Path From Communism to Pan-Africanism*. New York: Praeger, 1970.

Huggins, Nathan Irvin. *Harlem Renaissance*. New York: Oxford University Press, 1971.

James. C.L.R. *A History of Pan-African Revolt*. Washington, D.C.: Drum and Spear Press, 1969.

Johnson, Charles S. *Backgrounds to Patterns of Negro Segregation*. New York: Harper and Brothers, 1943.

Johnson, G. Wesley. *The Emergence of Black Politics in Senegal: The Struggle for Power in the Four Communes, 1900-1920*. Standord, California: Stanford University Press, 1971.

Johnson, James Weldon. *Black Manhattan*. New York: Knopf, 1930.

Jordan, Winthrop D. *White Over Black: American Attitudes Toward the Negro, 1550-1812*. Baltimore: Penguin, 1969.

July, Robert W. *The Origins of Modern African Thought*. New York: Frederick A. Praeger, Inc., 1967.

Katzman, David M. *Before the Ghetto: Black Detroit in the Nineteenth Century*. Urbana: University of Illinois Press, 1973.

Kedourie, Elie. *Nationalism in Asia and Africa*. New York: World Publishing Company, Meridian Books, 1970.

Lamson, Peggy. *The Glorious Failure: Black Congressman Robert Brown Elliott and the Reconstruction in South Carolina.* New York: W.W. Norton & Company, Inc., 1973.

Langley, J. Ayodele. *Pan-Africanism and Nationalism in West Africa 1900-1945.* New York: Oxford University Press, 1973.

Lanternari, Vittorio. *The Religions of the Oppressed: A Study of Modern Messianic Cults.* New York: Alfred A. Knopf, 1963.

Lasch, Christopher. *The New Radicalism in America, 1889-1963. The Intellectual as a Social Type.* New York: Random House, Vintage Books, 1965.

Legum, Colin. *Pan Africanism: A Short Political Guide.* London: Pall Mall Press, 1962.

Lincoln, C. Eric. *The Black Muslims in America.* Boston: Beacon, 1961.

Litwack, Leon F. *North of Slavery: The Negro in the Free States, 1790-1860.* Chicago: University of Chicago Press, 1961.

Logan, Rayford W. *The Betrayal of the Negro, From Rutherford B. Hayes to Woodrow Wilson.* London: Collier-Mac-Millan, Collier Books, 1965.

Lynd, Staughton. *Intellectual Origins of American Radicalism.* New York: Random House, Vintage Books, 1969.

Lynch, Hollis R. *Edward Wilmot Blyden: Pan-Negro Patriot, 1832-1912.* London: Oxford, 1970.

Maglangbayan, Shawna. *Garvey, Lumumba and Malcolm: National-Separatists.* Chicago: Third World Press, 1972.

Martin, Tony. *Race First: The Ideological and Organizational Struggles of Marcus Garvey and the Universal Negro Improvement Association.* Westport, Connecticut: Greenwood Press 1976.

Mathurin, Owen Charles. *Henry Sylvester Williams and the Origins of the Pan-African Movement 1869-1911.* Westport, Connecticut: Greenwood Press, 1976.

Miller, Floyd J. *The Search for a Black Nationality: Black Colonization and Emigration 1787-1863.* Urbana: University of Illinois Press, 1975.

Minogue, K.R. *Nationalism.* Baltimore: Penguin, 1970.

Montagu, Ashley. *Man's Most Dangerous Myth: The Fallacy of Race.* Cleveland: Meridian Books, 1965.

Mays, Benjamin E. *The Negro's God As Reflected in His Literature.* New York: Chapman and Grimes, 1938.

Meier, August. *Negro Thought in America, 1880-1915: Racial Ideologies in the Age of Booker T. Washington.* Ann Arbor: The University of Michigan Press, 1963.

National Association for the Advancement of Colored People. *Thirty Years of Lynching in the United States, 1889-1918.* New York: The National Association for the Advancement of Colored People, 1919.

Nichols, Charles H. *Many Thousand Gone: The Ex-Slaves' Account of their Bondage and Freedom.* Bloomington, Indiana: Midland Books, 1969.

Ofari, Earl. *Let Your Motto Be Resistance: The Life and Thought of Henry Highland Garnet.* Boston: Beacon, 1972.

Oliver, Roland, and Fage, J.D. *A Short History of Africa.* Baltimore: Penguin, 1962.

Osofsky, Gilbert. *Harlem: The Making of A Ghetto.* New York: Harper & Row, Torchbook, 1968.

Padmore, George. *Pan Africanism or Communism.* Garden City, New York: Doubleday & Company, 1971.

Painter, Nell Irvin. *Exodusters: Black Migration to Kansas After Reconstruction.* New York: Knopf, 1977.

Park, Robert E. *Race and Culture.* Glencoe, Illinois: The Free Press, 1950.

Pease, Jane H., and Pease, William H. *They Who Would be Free: Blacks Search for Freedom, 1830-1861.* New York: Atheneum, 1974.

Pinkney, Algernon. *Red, Black and Green.* New York: Cambridge University Press, 1976.

Quarles, Benjamin. *Frederick Douglass.* New York: Atheneum, 1968.

Ramparsad, Arnold. *The Art and Imagination of W.E.B. Du Bois.* Cambridge. Massachusetts: Harvard University Press, 1976.

Redkey, Edwin S. *Black Exodus: Black Nationalist and Back to Africa Movements, 1890-1910.* New Haven: Yale University Press, 1969.

Rodney, Walter. *How Europe Underdeveloped Africa.* London:

Bogel-L'Overture Publications, 1972. Reprint. Howard University Press, 1974.

Rudwick, Elliott M. *W.E.B. Du Bois: Propagandist of the Negro Protest*. New York: Atheneum, 1969.

Seznec, Jean. *The Survival of the Pagan Gods: The Mythological Tradition and its Place in Ranaissance Humanism and Art*. Torchbooks, New York: Harper & Brothers, 1961.

Shafer, Boyd C. *Nationalism: Myth and Reality*. New York: Harcourt Brace and Co., 1955.

Shepperson, George, and Price, Thomas. *Independent African: John Chilembwe and the Origins, Setting and Significance of the Nyasaland Native Rising of 1915*. Edinburgh: The University of Edinburgh Press, 1958.

Simmons, William J. *Men of Mark: Eminent, Progressive and Rising*. Cleveland, Ohio: Geo. M. Rewell & Co. 1887.

Snyder, Louis L. *German Nationalism: The Tragedy of a People*. Port Washington, New York: Kennikat Press, 1969.

———. *The Dynamics of Nationalism*. New York: Van Nostrand, 1964.

Sochen, June. The Unbridgeable Gap: *Blacks and Their Quest for the American Dream, 1900-1930*. Chicago: Rand McNally, 1972.

Spear, Allan H. *Black Chicago: The Making of a Negro Ghetto, 1890-1920*. Chicago: University of Chicago Press, 1967.

Stampp, Kenneth M. *The Era of Reconstruction, 1865-1877*. New York: Random House, Vintage Books, 1965.

Staudenraus, P.J. *The African Colonization Movement, 1816-1877*. New York: Columbia University Press, 1961.

Sterling, Dorothy. *The Making of an Afro-American: Martin Robinson Delany, 1812-1885*. Garden City, New York: Doubleday & Co., 1971.

Sweet, Leonard I. *Black Images of America 1784-1870*. New York: W.W. Norton & Co., Inc., 1976.

Thornbrough, Emma Lou. *T. Thomas Fortune: Militant Journalist*. Chicago: University of Chicago Press, 1972.

Thorpe, Earl E. *Black Historians: A Critique*. New York: William Morrow & Co., 1971.

———. *The Mind of the Negro: An Intellectual History of Afro-Americans*. Westport, Connecticut: Negro Universities Press, 1970.

Thwaite, Daniel. *The Seething African Pot: A Study of Black Nationalism*, 1882-1935. London: Constable & Co., 1936.

Ullman, Victor. *Martin R. Delany: The Beginnings of Black Nationalism*. Boston: Beacon Press, 1971.

Uya, Okon Edet. *From Slavery to Public Service: Robert Smalls, 1839-1915*. New York: Oxford Press, 1971.

Viereck, Peter. *Metapolitics: The Roots of the Nazi Mind*. New York: Capricorn Books, 1971.

Vincent, Theodore G. *Black Power and the Garvey Movement*. Berkeley: Ramparts, 1971.

Walzel, Oskar. *German Romanticism*. New York: Capricorn Books, 1966.

Washington, Joseph R. *Black Sects and Cults*. Garden City, New York: Doubleday & Company, Anchor Books, 1973.

Weisbord, Robert G. *Ebony Kinship: Africa, Africans, and the Afro-American*. Westport, Connecticut: Greenwood Press, 1973.

Wesley, Charles H. *The History of Alpha Phi Alpha: A Development in College Life*. Chicago: Foundation Publishers, 1959.

———. Richard Allen: *Apostle of Freedom*. Washington, D.C., Associated Publishers, 1935.

West, Richard. *Back to Africa: A History of Sierra Leone and Liberia*. New York: Holt, Rinehart and Winston, 1971.

Wiebe, Robert H. *The Search for Order, 1877-1920*. New York: Hill and Wang, 1968.

Wilmore, Gayraud. *Black Religion and Black Radicalism: An Examination of the Black Experience in Religion*. Garden City, New York: Doubleday, Anchor Books, 1973.

Woodward, C. Vann. *The Strange Career of Jim Crow*. New York: Oxford Press, 1955.

Woodson, Carter G. *The History of the Negro Church*. Washington, D.C.: Associated Publishers, 1972.

II. ARTICLES

(The abbreviation, *JNH*, signifies *The Journal of Negro History; MHVR* signifies *The Mississippi Valley Historical Review; TBS* signifies *The Black Scholar*.)

Ahmend, Muhammed. "The Roots of the Pan-African Revolution." *TBS*, Vol. 3, No. 9 (May, 1972), pp. 48-55.

Anderson, S.E. "Revolutionary Black Nationalism is Pan-African." *TBS*, Vol. 2, No. 7 (March, 1971), pp. 16-22.

Anthony, Earl. "Pan-African Socialism." *TBS*, Vol. 3, No. 2, pp. 40-45.

Aptheker, Herbert. "Militant Abolitionism." *JNH*, Vol. XXVI, No. 4 (October, 1941), pp. 438-84.

Ashby, William. "Alphas at Yale University in 1915." *The Sphinx* Vol. 56, No. 2 (May-June, 1970), pp. 12-14.

Billingsley, Andrew. "Edward Blyden: Apostle of Blackness." *TBS* Vol. 2, No. 4 (December, 1970), pp. 3-12.

Carlisle, Rodney. "Black Explorers of Africa." *Negro History Bulletin*, Vol. 37, No. 2 (February-March, 1974), pp. 210-13.

Chase, Hal. "William C. Chase and the Washington Bee." *Negro History Bulletin*, Vol. 36, No. 8 (December, 1973), 172-4.

Cobb, W. Montague. "The Father of Negro History." *Journal of the National Medical Association*. Vol. 62, No. 5, (September, 1970), pp. 385-92, 402.

Contee, Clarence G. "Du Bois, The NAACP, and the Pan-African Congress of 1919." *JNH*, Vol. LVII, No. 1 (January, 1972), pp. 13-19.

————. "Ethiopia and the Pan-African Movement Before 1945." *Black World* (February, 1972), pp. 24-30.

————. "Henry Sylvester Williams: Pioneer Pan-Africanist." *Black World*, Vol. XXIII, No. 5 (March, 1974), pp. 32-7.

Draper, Theodore and Ofari, Earl. "A Debate." *TBS*, Vol. 2, No. 10 (June, 1971), pp. 36-44.

Fleming, Walter L. "Pap' Singleton, The Moses of the Colored Exodus." *American Journal of Sociology*, Vol. 15, No. 1 (July, 1909), pp. 61-82.

Forsythe, Dennis. "Blacks and the Dialectics." *TBS*, Vol. 3, No. 1 (September, 1971), pp. 50-66.

Hamilton, Charles V. "Pan-Africanism and the Black Struggle." *TBS* Vol. 2, No. 7 (March, 1971), pp. 10-15.

Hargreaves, John D. "African Colonization in the Nineteenth Century: Liberia and Sierra Leone." *Boston University Papers in African History*, Vol. I (1964).

Langley, Jabez Ayodele. "Marcus Garvey and African Nationalism." In S. Okechukwu Mezu and Ram Desai, eds., *Black
Leaders of the Centuries* (Buffalo: Black Academy Press,
1970), pp. 185-202.

Levstik, Frank R. "William H. Holland: Black Soldier, Politician
and Educator." *Negro History Bulletin,* Vol. 36, No. 5
(May, 1973), pp. 110-11.

Lynch, Hollis R. "Pan-Negro Nationalism in the New World,
Before 1862." In Okon Edet Uya, *Black Brotherhood:
Afro-Americans and Africa* (Lexington, Mass.: D.C.
Heath & Co., 1971), pp. 41-62.

Malveaux, Julianne. "Revolutionary Themes in Martin Delany's
Blake." *TBS,* Vol. 4, No. 10 (July-August, 1973), pp. 52-6.

Marable, W. Manning. "A Black School in South Africa." *Negro
History Bulletin.* Vol. 37, No. 4 (June/July, 1974), pp.
258-261.

McLendon, William H. "The Black Perspective of Frederick
Douglass." *TBS,* Vol. 3, No. 7-8 (March-April, 1972), pp.
7-16.

Mehlinger, Louis. "The Attitude of the Free Negro Toward
African Colonization." *JNH,* I (July, 1916), pp. 271-301.

Miller, Floyd J. "The Father of Black Nationalism: Another
Contender." *Civil War History* (December, 1971), pp.
310-19.

Moore, Richard B. "Du Bois and Pan Africa." *Freedomways,* Vol.
5, No. 1 (Winter, 1965), pp. 166-187.

Moses, Wilson J. "Marcus Garvey: A Reappraisal." *TBS,* Vol. 4,
No. 3 (November/December, 1972), pp. 38-49.

———. "The Evolution of Black National-Socialist Thought: A
Study of W.E.B. Du Bois." In Henry J. Richards, ed.,
Topics in Afro-American Studies (Buffalo: Black Acade-
my Press, 1971), pp. 77-100.

Obatala, J.K. "Liberia: The Meaning of 'Dual Citizenship,'"
TBS, Vol. 4, No. 10 (July-August, 1973), pp. 16-19.

Ofari, Earl. "The Emergence of Black National Consciousness in
America." *Black World,* Vol. XX, No. 4 (February, 1971),
pp. 75-86.

———. "A Review of Theodore Draper's *The Rediscovery of
Black Nationalism.*" *TBS,* Vol. 2, No. 2 (October, 1970),
pp. 47-52.

———. "W.E.B. Du Bois and Black Power." *Black World*, Vol. XIX, No. 10 (August, 1970), pp. 26-8.

Okoye, Felix. "The Afro-American and Africa." In Henry J. Richards, ed., *Topics in Afro-American Studies*. (Buffalo: Black Academy Press, 1971), pp. 37-58.

Pease, Jane H. and William H. "Organized Negro Communities: A North American Experiment." *JNH*, Vol. XLVII, No. 1 (Jan., 1962), pp. 19-34.

Porter, Dorothy. "The Organized Educational Activities of Negro Literary Societies, 1828-1846." In August Meier and Elliott Rudwick, eds., *The Making of Black America* (New York: Atheneum, 1971), pp. 276-89.

Reed, Adolph L., Jr. "Pan-Africanism: Ideology for Liberation?" *TBS*, Vol. 3, No. 1 (September, 1971), pp. 2-13.

Rushing, Byron. "A Note on the Origin of the African Orthodox Church." *JNH*, Vol. LVII, No. 4 (January, 1972), pp. 37-9.

Shepperson, George. "Ethiopianism and African Nationalism." *Phylon*, Vol. I, No. 1, pp. 9-18 1953.

———. "Notes on Negro American Influences on the Emergence of African Nationalism." *Journal of African History*, Vol. 1, No. 2, 1960, pp. 299-312.

———. "Pan-Africanism and 'Pan-Africanism': Some Historical Notes." *Phylon*, Vol. XXIII, No. 4 (Winter, 1962), p. 350.

Sherwood, Henry Noble. "Early Negro Deportation Projects." *MVHR*, Vol. II, No. 4 (March, 1916), pp. 484-508.

Spady, James G. "The Afro-American Historical Society." *Negro History Bulletin*, Vol. 37, No. 4 (June/July, 1974), pp. 254-7.

Sundiata, Phaon. "A Portrait of Marcus Garvey." *TBS*, Vol. 2, No. 1 (September, 1970), pp. 7-19.

Thornbrough, Emma Lou. "Booker T. Washington as Seen by his White Contemporaries." *JNH*, Vol. LII, No. 2 (April, 1968), pp. 161-82.

———. "The National Afro-American League, 1887-1908." *Journal of Southern History*, Vol. XXVII, No. 4 (November, 1961), pp. 494-512.

Tindall, George B. "The Liberian Exodus of 1878." *South Carolina Historical Magazine*, Vol. LIII, No. 3 (July, 1952), pp. 133-145.

Turner, James. "Black Nationalism." In Henry J. Richards, ed.,
    Topics in Afro-American Studies. (Buffalo: Black Acade-
    my Press, 1971), pp. 59-76.
Walters, Ronald. "African-American Nationalism." *Black World*
    Vol. XXII, No. 12 (October, 1973), pp. 9-27.
Washington, Joseph R. "Black Nationalism: Potentially Anti-
    Folk and Anti-Intellectual." *Black World* (July, 1973),
    pp. 32-9.
Weisenburger, Francis P. "William Sanders Scarborough." *Ohio
    History*, Vol. 71, No. 3 (October, 1962), pp. 203-289; and
    Vol 72, No. 1 (January, 1963), pp. 25-88.
Wesley, Charles H. "Lincoln's Plan for Colonizing the Emanci-
    pated Negroes." *JNH*, Vol. IV (January, 1919), pp. 7-21.

Index

Abbott, Robert S., 269
Abolitionism, 51, 64, 72; as
 contradiction of colonization,
 43-44; gradual and immediate,
 53
Abolitionists: romantic racialism
 in thought of, 46-47; found
 school in New Hampshire, 63;
 criticized by Douglass, 92
Accommodationism: Rudwick
 accuses Du Bois of, 227; of
 West Africans in World War I,
 235; of Washington, 189, 289
Acculturation, 10, 11, 131, 142, 174,
 268, 270; of William H. Ferris,
 214
Adams, Agnes: on social purity,
 116
Adams, Henry, 90, 248
Addams, Jane, 139
African Civilization Society:
 constitution of, 18, 275;
 relationship to American
 Colonization Society, 37, 87;
 and Garnet, 38; and Douglass,
 38, 86-88; and Ethiopian
 prophecy, 157

African Methodist Episcopal
 Biishops: and Pan-Africanism,
 200, 202
African Methodist Episcopal
 Church, 209
African Methodist Episcopal Zion
 Church 19, 206
Afro-American: as term, 32;
 favored, 127 *Woman's Era* finds
 cumbersome, 127-128; preferred
 by Fortune, 216. *See also*
 Anglo-African; Euro-African;
 Negrosaxon
Akim Trading Company, 218
Alexander, Charles, 205-219
 passim; admires and criticizes
 Washington, 205; favors term
 "Negro," 215
Alexander's Magazine. See
 Alexander, Charles
All Africa Conference, 19
Alpha Phi Alpha: Ethiopianism
 in poetry of, 167-168; founding
 of, 217-218; and "Talented
 Tenth," 295; prominent
 members, 300
AME Church. *See* African
 Methodist Episcopal Church